EATING DISORDERS MONOGRAPH SERIES NO. 4

Males with Eating Disorders

Edited by

ARNOLD E. ANDERSEN, M.D.

Associate Professor of Psychiatry and Behavioral Sciences,
Director, The Eating and Weight Disorders Clinic,
The Johns Hopkins Medical Institutions,
Baltimore, Maryland

BRUNNER/MAZEL, *Publishers* · New York

Library of Congress Cataloging-in-Publication Data

Males with eating disorders/edited by Arnold E. Andersen.
    p. cm.—(Brunner/Mazel eating disorders monograph series; 4)
    Includes bibliographical references.
    ISBN 0-87630-556-7
    1. Eating disorders. 2. Men—Mental health. I. Andersen, Arnold
E. II. Series.
    DNLM: 1. Anorexia Nervosa. 2. Bulimia. 3. Eating Disorders.
4. Men—psychology. W1 BR917D v. 4 / WM 175 M246]
RC552.E18M35 1990
616.85'26'0081—dc20
DNLM/DLC
for Library of Congress   89-23909
                                           CIP

Published by
BRUNNER/MAZEL, INC.
19 Union Square
New York, New York 10003

MANUFACTURED IN THE UNITED STATES OF AMERICA

10 9 8 7 6 5 4 3 2 1

Contents

v

Contributors

Arnold E. Andersen, M.D.
Associate Professor of Psychiatry and Behavioral Sciences; Director, The Eating and Weight Disorders Clinic, The Johns Hopkins Medical Institutions, Baltimore, Maryland.

Isabel S. Bradburn, M.Ed.
Research Coordinator, Eating Disorders Unit, Massachusetts General Hospital, Boston, Massachusetts.

Thomas Burns, M.D.
St. George's Hospital Medical School and Department of Psychiatry, Jenner Wing, Cranmer Terrace, Tooting, London SW17, England.

Arthur H. Crisp, M.D.
Professor of Psychiatry, St. George's Hospital Medical School, Tooting, London SW17, England.

David H. Edwin, Ph.D.
Assistant Professor, Medical Psychology and Psychiatry, The Johns Hopkins Medical Institutions, Baltimore, Maryland.

Paul E. Garfinkel, M.D.
Professor and Vice-Chairman, Department of Psychiatry, University of Toronto, Psychiatrist-in-Chief; Toronto General Hospital, Toronto, Ontario, Canada.

David M. Garner, Ph.D.
Professor of Psychiatry, Michigan State University, West Fee Hall, East Lansing, Michigan.

Jerome Gotthardt, Ph.D.
Center for the Treatment of Eating Disorders, Columbus, Ohio.

David B. Herzog, M.D.
Director, Eating Disorders Unit, Associate Professor of Psychiatry, Massachusetts
General Hospital, Boston, Massachusetts.

Ann Kearney-Cooke, Ph.D.
Private Practice, Cincinnati, Ohio.

Michael P. Levine, Ph.D.
Department of Psychology, Kenyon College, Gambier, Ohio.

Angela D. Mickalide, Ph.D.
The Johns Hopkins University, School of Hygiene and Public Health, Department
of Health Policy and Management and School of Medicine, Department of
Psychiatry and Behavioral Sciences, Baltimore, Maryland.

Kerry Newman, B.A.
Research Assistant, Eating Disorders Unit, Massachusetts General Hospital, Boston,
Massachusetts.

Trent A. Petrie, M.A.
Department of Counseling Psychology, Ohio State University, Columbus, Ohio.

Wendi Rockert, BSc
Psychometrist, Psychiatry Research, Toronto General Hospital, Toronto, Ontario,
Canada.

Todd D. Sevig, M.A.
Department of Counseling Psychology, Ohio State University, Columbus, Ohio.

Joseph A. Silverman, M.D.
Clinical Professor of Pediatrics, Columbia University, College of Physicians
& Surgeons, New York, New York.

Paule Steichen-Asch, Ph.D.
Adjunct Assistant Professor of Psychology, Department of Psychiatry, University
of Cincinnati, Cincinnati, Ohio.

Ralph F. Wilps, Jr., Ph.D.
Clinical Psychologist, Pittsburgh, Pennsylvania.

D. Blake Woodside, M.D.
Lecturer, Department of Psychiatry, Research Fellow, Eating Disorders Centre,
Toronto General Hospital, Toronto, Ontario, Canada.

Preface

The subject of anorexia nervosa and, more recently, bulimia nervosa in males has been a source of interest and controversy in the fields of psychiatry and medicine for more than 300 years. At times the very existence of this topic has been imperiled by theoretical dogma, despite the fact that one of the first two case reports on anorexia nervosa was a male. The subject has periodically been neglected and rediscovered. Recent trends in industrialized countries sharing an emphasis on the value of thinness suggest that these disorders may be increasing in males, perhaps altered in form from the typical presentation in women.

These disorders, sometimes called eating disorders, raise basic questions concerning the nature of abnormalities of the motivated behaviors: Are they subsets of more widely recognized illnesses such as mood disorders? Are they understandable by reference to underlying abnormalities of biochemistry or brain function? In what ways are they similar to and in what ways do they differ from anorexia nervosa and bulimia nervosa in females? Joseph Silverman, a distinguished student of the history of medicine, uncovered the following quote from Hippocrates: "It is more difficult for boys to withstand fasting."

Whether Hippocrates discovered millennia ago that boys have a lower percentage of stored energy in the form of body fat than girls, or suggested something more complex, it is intriguing to think that the ancient physician may have observed something that at least partially explains the gender related difference in the incidence of anorexia nervosa and bulimia nervosa. Incidentally, the terms "males" and "females" are generally used in this book, despite the clinical sound of these terms, rather than "boys and men" or "girls and women," which would be too cumbersome. Where appropriate, only one of these terms may be used when the age range suggests such a designation.

Initially, this book was conceptualized as a single-author work growing out of our experience at the Johns Hopkins Hospital, Department of Psychiatry. It quickly became apparent that the work would be strengthened by our devoting the majority of the book to up-to-date contributions from clinicians and researchers around the world with special interest and experience in this area.

We hope the book will be of interest to a wide variety of people—physicians, psychologists, nurses, social workers, occupational therapists, nutritionists, educators, and all others who may be interested for personal or professional reasons. Although some of the material is moderately technical in nature, most of it is accessible to families and others without a medical background. One of our goals has been to encourage the development of further research in this area of suffering from an illness unique to human beings. Anorexia nervosa and bulimia nervosa touch on the search for self-esteem, for personal identity, and for meaning, as well as on the quest for relief from painful mood states, from conflicts in personal development, and from struggles in family functioning. We believe that these disorders represent, at least partially, a specific solution within this particular era and stage of human development of issues within the individual, the family, and society in general that are, in fact, ageless and universal.

We teach our students and residents that if they really understand the nature, course, and treatment of the "eating disorders," they understand most of the field of psychiatry (except perhaps dementia), much of human psychology, physiology, and internal medicine, as well as something about the issues of the individual in cultural and transcultural perspective. Every organ system is affected by the eating disorders. Every facet of personal and interpersonal life is affected.

We hope this work will stimulate interest in the area of anorexia nervosa and bulimia nervosa in all its aspects. Treatment has been effective in decreasing immediate mortality and morbidity. Long-term studies are needed to understand which of our efforts are helpful in the long run. The best form of medicine is prevention. Although the probability of development of effective means of preventing the emergence of disorders so intimately linked with widespread sociocultural norms and age-old issues in human experience seems remote, it is not beyond reason to devote ourselves to these efforts.

It has been a pleasure to work with and learn from the distinguished contributors to this volume, some well known, others emerging on the scene.

ARNOLD E. ANDERSEN, M.D.

SECTION I

History, Sociocultural Studies, and Psychological Functioning

1

Anorexia Nervosa in the Male: Early Historic Cases

Joseph A. Silverman

Reports of anorexia nervosa in the male are rarely found in early medical publications. A search of the literature has resulted in the discovery of three case reports which were published between the years 1689 and 1790. One may quibble about how well these descriptions satisfy the criteria of Feighner et al. (1972) or the Diagnostic and Statistical Manual of Mental Disorders, (DSM-III, 1980). Nonetheless, these accounts cause one to believe that their authors were indeed describing anorexia nervosa long before Gull (1874) and Lasègue (1873) gave the disease its cumbersome and inaccurate name.

In 1689, Richard Morton, a London physician and Fellow of the College of Physicians, published his magnum opus, *Phthisiologia, seu Exercitationes de Phthisi.* In this seminal volume, translated into English five years later, and subtitled *A Treatise of Consumptions*, he outlined in painstaking detail the many disease processes that cause wasting of body tissues. All of the material was based on his own clinical observations, with little reference to books. The text, which is richly descriptive, is best known for his comments on tuberculosis. A specialist in the treatment of this disease, he was the first physician to state that tubercles are always present in the pulmonary form.

Morton is best known today as the author of the first medical account of anorexia nervosa, a condition that he referred to as "a Nervous Consumption," caused by "Sadness and anxious Cares." In his book, he described two such

3

patients: "History 1," Mr. Duke's daughter, is known to all; "History 2" recounts the first case of anorexia nervosa in the male.

The report, printed in its entirety, is as follows:

> The Son of the Reverend Minister Steele, my very good Friend, about the Sixteenth Year of his Age, fell gradually into a total want of Appetite, occasioned by his studying too hard, and the Passions of his Mind, and upon that into an Universal Atrophy, pining away more and more for the space of two Years, without any Cough, Fever, or any other Symptom of any Distemper of his Lungs, or any other Entrail; as also without a Looseness, or Diabetes, or any other sign of a Colliquation, or Preternatural Evacuation. And therefore I judg'd this Consumption to be Nervous, and to have its seat in the whole habit of the Body, and to arise from the System of Nerves being distemper'd. I began, and first attempted his Cure with the use of Antiscorbutick, Bitter, and Chalybeate Medicines, as well Natural as Artificial, but without any benefit; and therefore when I found that the former Method did not answer our Expectations, I advis'd him to abandon his Studies, to go into the Country Air, and to use Riding, and a Milk Diet (and especially to drink Asses Milk) for a long time. By the use of which he recover'd his Health in great measure, though he is not yet perfectly freed from a Consumptive state; and what will be the event of this Method, does not yet plainly appear (Morton, 1689, 1694).

In 1764, Robert Whytt of Edinburgh published a description of "a nervous atrophy" and presented a case study. Writing 75 years after Morton's *Phthisiologia*, Whytt made the following comments:

> . . . A marasmus, or sensible wasting of the body, not attended with sweatings, any considerable increase of the excretions by urine or stool, a quick pulse, or feverish heat, may deserve the name of nervous . . . But this kind of atrophy, tho' not, perhaps owing to any fault in the spirits, or even in the brain or nervous system in general, may yet deserve the name of nervous, as it seems, frequently, to proceed from an unnatural or morbid state of the nerves, of the stomach, and intestines . . . Further, the watching or want of refreshing rest, and low spirits or melancholy, which generally accompany this disease, may contribute to prevent the proper nutrition of the body . . .

Whytt's case report is printed in its entirety:

ANOTHER lad of 14 years of age, of a thin and delicate habit, and of quick
and lively feelings, whose pulse in health used to beat beyond 70 and 80
times in a minute; about the beginning of June 1757, was observed to be
low-spirited and thoughtful, to lose his appetite, and have a bad digestion.
Altho' he lost flesh daily, yet he had no nightsweats, no extraordinary
discharge of urine and was costive. His tongue was clean, his skin cooler
than natural, and when in bed, his pulse beat only 43 times in a minute; nay
about the middle of July, when reduced almost to skin and bone, his pulse,
in a horizontal posture, did not exceed 39. About the end of August, his
distemper took a sudden turn; he then began to have such a craving for
food, with a quick digestion, that he grew faint unless he eat almost every
two hours; he had two or three stools a-day; his pulse beat from 96 to 110;
his skin was warm, and his veins, which scarce could be seen before, became
now turgid with blood. The strong apprehensions he formerly had of dying
left him, he was sure he should recover; and accordingly, by the middle of
October, he was plumper than ever he had been before. Towards the end
of November, his appetite became moderate, and his pulse gradually
returned to its natural state.

It was observable, that the pulse was slowest towards the evening, and
generally of a proper strength and fulness.

SINCE, with all my attention, I neither could discover the cause of the
patient's first complaints, nor of the sudden and contrary turn which they
took afterwards; I shall not pretend to reason on his case; but I thought it
deserved to be mentioned, as a good instance of a nervous atrophy; and of
the effect of such disorders in making the pulse much slower, than ever it
has been observed in a natural state (Whytt, 1764).

In 1790, Robert Willan, in London, published an account entitled *A
Remarkable Case of Abstinence,* in which he described the death in 1786 of
a young Englishman who had fasted for 78 days.

Willan's comments about his 15 bedside visits are most enlightening and are
excerpted here.

The propositus, "a young man of a studious and melancholic turn of mind,"
had developed symptoms of indigestion during the years 1784-5. On Jan. 21,
1786, he embarked on a severe course of abstinence allegedly in the hope of
relieving his disagreeable complaints. Willan, however, suggests that the
fasting was a result of "some mistaken notions in religion."

The patient " . . . suddenly withdrew from business, and the society of his
friends, took lodgings in an obscure street, and entered upon his plan; which
was, to abstain from all solid food, and only to moisten his mouth, from time

to time, with water slightly flavoured with juice of oranges." He drank eight to 16 ounces of water daily. He passed a stool on day 2, and again on day 40 of his fast.

Willan states, "After three days of abstinence, the craving, or desire for food, which was at first very troublesome, left him entirely."

For the first 50 days, he was able to pursue his studies, which consisted of copying the Bible in shorthand. In fact, he had progressed almost to the second book of Kings!

From the 50th to the 60th day, his strength failed rapidly, causing him great alarm. He had hitherto believed that "his support was preternatural." By day 60, Willan comments that this " . . . delusion had vanished; he found himself gradually wasting and sinking to the grave."

Physical examination on March 23, 1786, revealed the following:

> He was at that time emaciated to a most astonishing degree, the muscles of the face being entirely shrunk; his cheek-bones and processus zygomatici stood prominent and distinct, affording a most ghastly appearance: his abdomen was concave, the umbilicus seeming to be retracted, from the collapsed state of his intestines; the skin and abdominal muscles were shrunk below the brim of his pelvis, . . . His limbs were reduced to the greatest degree of tenuity . . . His whole appearance suggested the idea of a skeleton, prepared by drying the muscles upon it . . . His eyes were not deficient in lustre, and his voice remained clear and sound, notwithstanding his general weakness.

Willan visited his patient daily from March 23-28, 1786, and placed him on a diet consisting of barley-water, mutton-tea, and mutton-broth. By March 25th (day 63) the young man developed food cravings. The next day, on his own, he ate a great quantity of bread and butter (in his nurse's absence), and vomited. He also had "a figured natural stool, and presently after two or three loose motions."

The patient seemed to be doing well until March 29th (day 67), at which time he developed memory lapses and became frantic and unmanageable. He began to rave and speak incoherently. Treatment consisted of a strong purgative draught and two clysters.

For the next three days, he ate little, and became sullen and withdrawn. From April 2-5, 1786, Willan was unable to see his patient, who "was removed at this time into the country."

Willan visited him daily from April 6-8 and states that he took whatever nourishment was offered. The next day, in the morning, the young man died.

These three reports constitute the most important early descriptions of anorexia nervosa in the male.

Addendum

All three authors, Morton, Whytt, and Willan, led brilliant medical careers. Morton became physician in ordinary to William III, and censor of the College of Physicians in London (Silverman, 1983).

Whytt became Professor of the Theory of Medicine at Edinburgh, a member of the Royal Society in London, First Physician to the King (George III) in Scotland, and President of the Royal College of Physicians in Edinburgh (Silverman, 1987).

Willan went on to become known as the father of English dermatology, as a result of his magnum opus, *The Description and Treatment of Cutaneous Diseases*, which was published in parts from 1798-1808 (Silverman, 1987).

REFERENCES

American Psychiatric Association. (1980). *Diagnostic and Statistical Manual of Mental Disorders, (3rd ed.)*. Washington, D.C.: Author.

Feighner, J. P., Robins, E., Guze S. B., Woodruff, R. A., Jr., Winokur, G., and Munoz, R. (1972). Diagnostic criteria for use in psychiatric research. *Arch. Gen. Psychiatry, 26*, 57–63.

Gull, W. W. (1874), Anorexia nervosa. *Trans. Clin. Soc.* (London), 7, 22–28.

Lasègue, C. (1873). De l'anorexie hystérique. *Arch. Gen. de Med., 2*, 367.

Morton, R. (1689). *Phthisiologia, seu Exercitationes de Phthisi*. London: S. Smith.

Morton, R. (1694). *Phthisiologia: Or a Treatise of Consumptions*. London: S. Smith and B. Walford.

Silverman, J. A. (1983). Richard Morton, 1637–1698, Limner of anorexia nervosa: His life and times. *JAMA, 250*, 2830–2832.

Silverman, J. A. (1987) An eighteenth century account of self-starvation in a male. *Int. J. Eating Disorders, 6*, 431-433.

Silverman, J. A. (1987). Robert Whytt, 1714–1766, Eighteenth century limner of anorexia nervosa and bulimia. *Int. J. Eating Disorders, 6*, 143–146.

Silverman, J. A. (1988). Richard Morton's second case of anorexia nervosa: Reverend Minister Steele and his son—An historical vignette. *Int. J. Eating Disorders, 7*, 439–441.

Whytt, R. (1764). *Observations on the Nature, Causes, and Cure of Those Disorders Which Have Been Commonly Called Nervous, Hypochondriac or Hysteric to*

Which Are Prefixed Some Remarks on the Sympathy of the Nerves. Edinburgh: Becket, DeHondt, and Balfour.

Willan, R. (1790). A remarkable case of abstinence. *Medical Communications, 2,* 113–122.

2

Male Bulimia Nervosa: An Autobiographical Case Study

Ralph F. Wilps, Jr.

The existence of eating disorders in male populations, especially if one considers some forms of obesity to be eating disorders, has been recognized for many years (Andersen, 1984; Crisp & Burns, 1983; Herzog et al., 1984; Scott, 1986; Sterling & Segal, 1985). However, the predominance of female sufferers of anorexia nervosa and bulimia has been repeatedly documented (Garner & Garfinkel, 1985). This fact has spurred the analysis of modern Western sociocultural pressures on young women and their contribution to the development of eating disorders. It has also meant that clinicians in eating disorders have focused almost exclusively on the assessment and treatment of women.

Similarly, research findings related to men with eating disorders have been sparse, and often reported as "by-products" in demographic studies (Pyle et al., 1986) or as "special cases" in descriptions of treatment programs for anorexia. What findings there are typically relate to anorexia in males, reporting it to be approximately one-tenth as common as it is in females (Scott, 1986), as showing similar patterns of onset age, diagnostic criteria, and specific psychopathology, and as demonstrating a treatment course either similar to or more difficult than anorexia in females.

Specific study of bulimia in men is in its infancy, with only one report (Pope, Hudson, & Jonas, 1986) finding patterns of demography, associated psychopathology, family history, and treatment response similar to those in 15 male bulimics to 102 female bulimic controls. Studies of the prevalence of bulimic behavior in college students indicate a prevalence of 0-5% in males as compared with 5-10% in females. Additionally, the number of college men reporting the termination of binge-eating by self-induced vomiting doubled from 1980 to 1983 (Pyle et al., 1986). If the frequently quoted ratio of a 15-to-1 predominance of bulimia to anorexia in college-age women (Lucas et al., 1983) also holds true for men, then the possibility exists that the number of bulimic men may well exceed that of anorexic women in the United States.

In any clinical area in which research is in its infancy, case studies are likely to be found as the initial anecdotal vehicles for information and speculation about the entity studied. This has been the case in anorexia (Gull, 1874; Morton, 1694) and, although the syndrome was often not recognized as such in the reports, in bulimia (Lindner, 1955; Binswanger, 1957). Along with case studies, another feature of the beginning stages of examination of anorexia and bulimia has been the publishing of autobiographical accounts of anorexic and bulimic women. These accounts, often written by celebrities, have provided some phenomenological understanding of the disorders to professionals in the field, but are often marred by efforts to cater to a public avid for dramatic and intimate details of a "popular" illness in a popular person. Additionally, these accounts have not been written by knowledgeable clinicians, and focus, understandably, on the sometimes idiosyncratic course of onset and recovery experienced by these sufferers. Analyses of predisposing factors are usually limited, and comparisons of various treatment of self-help efforts are not typically found.

To my knowledge, there have been no detailed case studies of male bulimia published to date. I believe that I am in a special position to begin to remedy this lack in the literature, since I engaged in bulimic behavior (binge-eating followed by prolonged fasting and compulsive exercising) for approximately 15 years. Those years involved several years of graduate study in clinical psychology, the dissolution of my marriage, and my work as a mental health clinic psychologist, as an administrator in the field of mental retardation, and as a clinical psychologist in private practice. They span two separate courses of individual psychotherapy (in neither of which was my eating disorder specifically addressed), and a trial-and-error approach to my own recovery.

For the past four years, I have been actively engaged in the treatment of patients with eating disorders in my private practice, and have focused on the needs of "atypical" eating disorder patient populations such as males, the handicapped, and older onset sufferers. I have also been involved in the Pittsburgh Educational Network for Eating Disorders, and have worked with other professionals in the Pittsburgh area to begin a support group for men with eating disorders. These demands have made it critical for me to keep current on research and treatment literature on eating disorders, and I hope that currency can add relevance to my assessment of my own course of illness and recovery.

Clearly, in a case such as mine, the dangers of subjectivity are massive. I face them daily in the management of countertransference issues with my patients—patients who need my support and commitment, but who may not be helped by the same techniques and insights which helped me. I certainly expect that the following description will be subjective—that is, after all, an important part of its purpose—but I hope that the effort to make sense of my own eating disorder, using the tools of an objective clinician, can provide a basis for testable hypotheses.

HISTORY AND PREDISPOSING FACTORS

I was born the oldest of two children in a middle-class Roman Catholic family. My parents were relatively old when I was born (my father was 42 and my mother 39). My father, of Lithuanian extraction, was the oldest of seven children born in an impoverished coal mining family in a small town in Southwestern Pennsylvania. He went to work in the mines at nine years of age, and took on major responsibility for supporting the family when his father died in the influenza epidemic of 1917. He became the surrogate father for his brothers and sisters, and, ever since, has demonstrated a strong work ethic, with value placed on caring for those in need, but with subtle disparagement of those who are weak enough to need such caring.

My father, like his brothers, inherited a powerful physique from his mother's side, and soon worked his way out of the deep mines by engaging in semiprofessional baseball and football—both of which were extremely popular in the small mining towns of the region. His prowess on the football field led ultimately to a scholarship to the University of Pittsburgh, and he was the first in his family to experience such an escape from the mines. He studied civil engineering and began work for a local corporation after college.

My mother was the only daughter in a large Northern Italian family. The family was better off financially than my father's. As in my father's family, my maternal grandmother was a matriarchal head. My mother's early life was, reportedly, a near-idyllic one. As the only sister in the band of siblings, she was protected and nurtured, and she recalls frequently being carried on her brothers' shoulders so she would not have to walk. She had a deep connection to her family roots. The role of women in the family was clear-cut, and pride was taken in the ability to feed and care for the big, expansive men in their lives.

My mother's life changed significantly after she finished high school. She was pressed into service to provide extra money so that her two younger brothers could go to college. When she met my father through one of her brothers, she was immediately attracted to him, but, after they married, she resented being taken away from her family to a somewhat unstable newlywed existence. This resentment, possibly fueled by her original shift from favored daughter to supporter of younger brothers, was a constant factor in my parents' relationship.

I was a wanted child, and was apparently conceived after several years of trying by my parents. I am aware of no significant medical or developmental problems in my infancy. Very few stories of sibling rivalry are told about me and my sister during our preschool years, and my impression of those years is that they were quiet and, probably, happy.

At the time I entered school, my family moved to an apartment building my father had built as a part of his effort toward independence. My mother never could get used to living in a two-bedroom apartment, and, to make matters worse, our building was in a town several miles from my mother's family. My father, perhaps in retreat, buried himself in work. Both he and my mother were emotionally distant, and could relate to others only in areas of personal interest.

It soon became apparent that I was not going to be a football player. Also, although I was "bookish," I didn't gravitate to the concrete subjects which would make sense to my parents. Instead, I read voraciously in byways of fiction, in speculative science, travel, history, and mythology. My parents were, in general, too busy to try to empathize with this peculiar, quiet son of theirs. Thus, I adapted to solitude and came to prize it. My parents' reaction to all this was to bear down rather harshly on me, decrying my escapist reading, and pointing out how frequently I would "alibi" to escape work.

I went to work on my father's land surveying crew when I was very young. I worked hard to obtain approval from my father and his men, and, because of my slightness, nearsightedness, and tension, was teased frequently. However, I remember those times as happy ones. I learned valuable skills, and was, indeed, toughened emotionally by what I went through. I was outdoors and this enhanced my sensitivity to the world of nature.

I never developed the muscular size and strength of my father and his brothers. In junior high school, my physical build was the cause of great pain to me, since I was softly built, like my mother's younger brothers. This physique may also have been affected by an injury to the testicles which I had at age 13, and which was, in future years, to cause enormous problems for my wife and me when we wanted to have a child. Parenthetically, I might add that, although there is some evidence for lowered testosterone output in males with eating disorders (Scott, 1986), no studies have yet examined the possibility that a preexisting testosterone deficiency can either directly or indirectly influence the onset of an eating disorder in males. I believe that it is certainly a possibility in my case that my low self-esteem and body image problems are related to this.

I think the roots of my eating disorder can be found in my experiences in junior high school. I was frequently bullied, and broke every knuckle in both hands in fights (all of which I lost). My parents both insisted that I not run from fights, and I still vividly recall the dizziness and anticipatory physical shock I would feel when someone would sidle up to me and say with a smile, "I'll be waiting for you after school . . . " More and more, I took refuge in my books and in snacks. Frequently, when I would get home from school, both of my parents would be working in my father's office, and it would be with great relief that I would settle down, alone, with a book and whatever food I had bought from the corner store.

My increasing investment with food was relatively easy in my family, since food had many intense meanings for both my parents. My mother saw it as the repository of a family history, and treasured handed-down recipes for traditional dishes. When she would cook such dishes, each stage of the preparation was accompanied by traditional stories about her family members. My father acted out the ritual of denial and feast which was a part of his past. He would, for example, take four strawberries (he loved them and grew them), mash them in a soup bowl, fill the bowl with chunks of bread, and pour milk over all—unwilling to simply enjoy the "richness" of strawberries undiluted. He would, however, eat a quart of ice cream with fruit in the evening, and related how his mother and brother could eat a half gallon in a sitting between them.

This pattern of withdrawal to reading and food continued through high school for me, though the physical violence I experienced in junior high school diminished. I did well, though not "up to potential," was in school band, and finally began to develop some friendships with peers. I continued to search for adult approval, but began to develop some personal interests, especially horseback riding. I continued to work on weekends and summers for my father, and gradually was put into a construction crew, which I enjoyed greatly. Physically, I was much the same, slightly overweight and with a gynoid pattern of fat distribution (Bjorntorp, 1986) which embarrassed me.

I attended the same local university as my father, even though I had offers from several schools in other parts of the country which were appealing to me.The choice of schools was one, like many others, which was made as part of "acting a role" for approval by my parents. They enjoyed the visits to campus which they made weekly, and my father seemed to like talking more with the athletes on my dormitory floor than he did to me. My own interests were not encouraged. I look back on such times, and others like them, now not as evidence that I was uncared about, but rather as evidence that my parents had difficulty showing me directly that I was important to them.

My eating habits in college were quite similar to most of my male peers, but the importance of food in my life as a marker of safety was different from their views. On my first day of college, I recall my overriding excitement that I could eat anything I wanted, any time I wanted, and no one would be there to interrupt me or to tell me to "get busy." I kept an electric skillet in my room, and would cook food from home, feeding the athletes on our dorm floor, and unconsciously duplicating the feminine pattern of food use which my mother demonstrated. Although I was overeating and slowly gaining weight, I did not think of these episodes as binges, and none of us ever purged food in any way. Otherwise, I preferred eating alone in the cafeteria, usually with a book to read, if I had time. Thus, I was showing the psychological reliance on food for non-nutritional needs (in my case, safety and affiliation) typical of patients with eating disorders long before I actually began bingeing.

My other habits during college were relatively normal for a somewhat shy young man with a poor self-image. I read, as before, voraciously, and my pleasure reading often conflicted with my studies. I joined the university marching band, and there experienced a male bonding process similar to fraternity or boot camp hazing and initiation. I exercised only sporadically, certainly not with the compulsive devotion with which I do now, and my physical condition remained stable, with very slow weight gain. I drank periodically at local bars, but did not use alcohol as a "drug of choice." I met my wife, also a shy person, during a rare fraternity get-together to which I was invited, and our relationship was a quiet one. We dated until she went away to college in another state (she had been a senior in high school when we met), and resumed dating when she transferred to a college in Pittsburgh. As in most of my younger days, our relationship seemed to be a "given," entered into without a feeling of choice—part of a role for each of us.

As my undergraduate career continued, I grew more interested in psychology because I discovered that I had an ability to listen and counsel which probably stemmed from my sensitivity to nature and its subtle nuances. Additionally, I was not interested in the quantitative subjects (especially

chemistry) which I was taking as part of my pre-med course, and was doing badly in them. Thus clinical psychology seemed a logical alternative to
medicine to me, and, with the generous support of my advisor and several
other psychology professors, I made plans for graduate work in psychology.
My parents, after initial distress, adapted to this change, and I was ultimately
accepted into Adelphi University's Institute for Advanced Psychological
Studies (now the Derner Institute), in Garden City, New York.

ONSET OF SYMPTOMS

The actual onset of eating disorder symptoms occurred during my second
year in graduate school. My first year there involved an intensification of
food-related patterns of safety and affiliation-seeking. During my first term I
was aware of the lack of kinship I felt with my classmates, most of whom were
New York City residents, relatives or friends of famous analysts, of Jewish
background (my family was deeply Catholic), and older or with other graduate
degrees. I actually did not mind this emotional isolation, and made friends with
the owners of a local sailboat yard. I related to them in a submissive fashion,
acting as an unpaid helper, and getting to sail occasionally—a pattern similar
to that of my earlier years with horseback riding.

I knew many of the local grocers—aided by my mother, who, on her first
visit to me in New York, marched me to the local butcher shop and instructed
the owner to take care of me! I became expert at preparing rich, creamy cas-
seroles and enjoyed displaying, on occasion, how well I could care for myself
by inviting classmates to dinner. I never, of course, invited married classmates—only those who seemed needier and more vulnerable than myself.

During this time I was sexually inactive except for frequent masturbation, my
fianceé finishing her undergraduate work in Pittsburgh while living with her
parents. We had never had sexual relations during our college dating, and did
not until marriage. Actually, the time before her visits was a tense, unpleasant
one for me, and the visits themselves were blurred weekends which ended
with a sigh of relief, at least for me. I felt my life to be a cozy one, and was not
looking forward to our marriage, which was to take place in the summer after
my first year of graduate school.

The life in which I had wrapped myself was rudely shattered by my
professors after my first term. Hearing the interactions of my classmates about
their lack of preparation or concern about academics, I took this as the norm,
studied little, and intermittently skipped classes to work at the boatyard. I was

put on academic probation, and instructed to seek therapy. It was a mark of my innocence that I had never before even considered the personal need for that which I was supposedly being trained to give.

I entered once-a-week therapy with a graduate of Adelphi's Institute. Clearly, it was a major force in the integration of my potentials and my subsequent success in graduate school. I developed a much stronger self-image, ceased my search for surrogate parents, and learned the social skills needed to grow professionally. My confidence increased, and I began to identify myself as a psychologist in the making, and a member of the Institute—all attitudes which were fostered and supported there. I continued to gain weight steadily and attempted desultorily to jog at night, but without significant improvement. Eating disorders were never mentioned in training at that time (the late 1960s) and my only contact with such a disorder came when I would listen to the agonized, tearful confessions of some of my female classmates about their food binges and their distress about their bodies. I do not recall ever hearing one of them confess to purging food.

I was married in August of 1968. My wife, V., and I moved into the same small apartment I had rented during my first year in Long Island, and she began teaching kindergarten in a nearby school district. The adjustment was a difficult one for both of us—for V., being away from her family and being identified as a responsible professional teacher, and for me, sharing this small space and having to divide my energies between the increasing demands of graduate school and my home. As I look back on it, my near-anorexic weight loss resulted from this stress. I weighed approximately 185 lbs. at my heaviest, and my decision to begin losing weight stemmed from a solo winter hiking trip. I was to have stayed just overnight, but a sudden blizzard paralyzed all traffic, and I was first forced to rescue a party of hikers stranded by the storm, then to stay at a mountain lodge until the plows began moving. I could not get closer than 20 miles to my home, so I abandoned the car and hiked the rest of the way through the snow. For the rest of that week, New York was at a standstill, and my wife and I hoarded food and bundled up like pioneers. It was exciting and pleasurable, but I saw the reality of how tenuously the society around me was anchored and the fragility of all the social structures with which I had identified. I then fell back to my old pattern of isolated survival, and determined that nothing would ever trap me the way those around me were. That included marital relationships, professional identities, or physical incapacities.

I then began to diet in earnest. It was easy, initially, because my schedule of internship work and classes was increasing in intensity. I gulped an instant breakfast drink before leaving in the morning, skipped lunch, and would eat a large, but light salad when I got home, often quite late. I lost weight quickly, and should have known that I was having problems when I began using my lunch hour to go to the patients' library in the VA hospital in which I was interning, carrying a bag of peanuts and a candy bar, then hiding in a corner munching while I read cookbooks about ethnic food! My behavior mirrored, of course, that of volunteers in classic starvation studies (Keys et al., 1950), and the food preoccupations of female anorexics.

Within four or five months I had lost 60 lbs. and had become thin enough to have fatigue and dizziness daily. I welcomed these sensations, however, because they seemed proof to me that I was continuing to lose weight. I became "addicted" to scales, knowing where they were throughout the university and hospital settings I frequented, and weighing myself several times each day. At first my weighings were pleasurable, as I saw the needle drop. In later years they became fraught with tension as I monitored variations of a pound up or down.

I never made the conscious decision that I was done losing weight. Instead, I began alternatively bingeing and fasting. I vividly remember my first binge. I weighed about 135 lbs. and felt fairly good about my weight. I had been reading (as was my wont) a book on traditional English cooking. I read an evocative description of "fish and chips" and a recipe for making this meal at home. I prepared everything excitedly, buying beer to go with it, and enjoyed frying about 1 1/2 lbs. of fish with french fries that day. The alcohol in the beer I had bought acted as disinhibitor, and I discovered that I was ravenously hungry. I sat drinking beer and eating the oily, salty food until I had finished it. As soon as some of the initial drowsiness wore off, I became terrified of what I had done—that I had "relaxed my guard" and would start on the unstoppable road up the scale again. The decision not to eat at all the next day was easily made. Carrying it out was not terribly difficult, either. I was uninterested in food until midafternoon, and the subsequent weakness and dizziness from the fast were familiar friends to me. They reassured me that I was burning away the unwanted weight, and I had my first nervous trips to the scale that day. The following morning I felt clear, bright, and sharply hungry, and was very relieved to find that my weight was back to pre-binge status.

Initially my food binges were rather benign, involving large "peasant gourmet" dinners with careful shopping for just the right breads, cheeses, wines, etc., and eaten with my wife present. As my work and study schedule intensified, however, I often would come home late in the evening, having "saved up" my hunger for the pleasure of letting down at dinner. My wife was often ready for bed when I was ready to eat.

My wife's stress was compounded by her distance from her family and the increasing pressure she was under from them to provide the family's first grandchild. I was nervous about the idea of having children, but we agreed to try. At that point, the combination of my marginal fertility (due to the accident as a 13-year-old) and my increasing dependence on social withdrawal and eating as a stress-reducer in the evenings all conspired to frustrate our efforts. Five years of increasingly mechanical efforts to have a child had begun.

By the time my graduate program was finished, our life as a couple had deteriorated severely. Since our apartment lease was up several months before my dissertation was due to be completed, V. decided (to my relief) to return to the Pittsburgh area to set up an apartment for us in the building which my parents owned and in which they lived. I stayed with friends for approximately three months, during which time my binges were increasingly alcohol-involved. Although I was not seriously abusing alcohol, my food binges were typically on "bar foods" (cheese, pretzels, smoked sausage, hard-boiled eggs) which were associated in my mind with the working-class taverns of my home town. As before, symbolic affiliation without real human contact and the nurtured, sleepy feeling of being very full and slightly drunk were my goals. My binges were always followed by fasts of one full day, with a typical pattern of grogginess in the morning, clarity by afternoon, and shivering exhaustion and cold by bedtime. My binge frequency at that time had increased to approximately 1/week.

PERIOD OF GREATEST SYMPTOM INTENSITY

The period of greatest symptom intensity began for me after I completed my work for the Ph.D. degree and returned home to the Pittsburgh area. It lasted from 1972 until approximately 1979, and was characterized by increasing frequency of binges and corresponding increases in the disruption of my personal and professional life. My marriage dissolved during this time, I changed professional identity from psychologist to administrator and back again, became involved in a guilt- and duty-ridden relationship with the mother of a severely retarded young man, and was, at times, very near to suicide.

Those years started quietly enough, with my bingeing usually occurring on Sunday nights. I saw them as a reward for having compulsively completed everything I had to during the week, and as a way of staving off Monday morning. I was working in a mental health clinic, and I slipped easily into a duplication of my pattern of staying late for meetings at the agency and bingeing when I got home. I recall my relief at seeing that my wife was asleep when I'd return home at night.

Clearly, with the pressure on V. from her parents to have a child and the seductiveness of my work to me, we were pushed further and further apart. When M., whose son was a former patient of mine, opened a friendly door to her family, I gladly responded. I was attracted to her intensity and to her husband's blunt masculinity. I went hunting with her husband, and experienced a resurgence of the male bonding I had longed for in high school. I urged my wife to get involved with this family also; she tried, but her subdued personality was as uninteresting to them as theirs were grating to her.

My friends' marriage was in trouble. M. had been physically abused but was afraid to move because of her extremely vulnerable son. In a surge of quixotic chivalry, I assured her that I would support her no matter what it took. To this woman, 13 years my senior, I was offering what was tantamount to a proposal of marriage and she leaped gratefully onto it. The tenuous relationship between M. and her husband fragmented completely with my involvement, and I saw with horror that I had blindly destroyed a fragile family structure with my naive impulsiveness.

This complication threw my personal life into chaos. Torn between my wife and M., I responded to the need which, to me, was the most intense, and began considering separation from V. Ironically, just as the conflict reached a crescendo internally, V. revealed that she was finally pregnant! There ensued a quiet period of several months during which I binged more frequently because the pressure to try to conceive a child was now gone. However, as the time came near for our child's birth, the questions about our marriage redoubled. We separated when he was six weeks old.

Internal darkness clouded much of the next two years for me. I lived in a tiny two-room furnished apartment over a garage and tried to cope with the changes in my life. I had custody of my infant son during weekends and one night per week. I had been asked to become the administrator of a community living arrangement system for retarded clients of my agency. Meanwhile, my friend's life with her handicapped son and other children was even more stressful than mine.

The effect of all this on my eating was to deeply cement bulimia as a part of my lifestyle. I would sigh with relief when Sunday evening came, since I had no work responsibilities until the next morning, and I would have just returned my son to his mother's custody. I would then carefully shop at convenience stores for "just right" combinations of cheese, lunch meats, snack chips, and sweets such as chocolate bars. I would also make a stop at a neighborhood newsstand to buy escapist paperback novels (an essential part of the binge) and then settle down for a three-hour session of reading and slow eating until I could barely keep my eyes open. My binges took the place of Sunday dinner, averaging approximately 6000 kilocalories in size. Following the binge, my stomach aching with distention, I would carefully clean my teeth, wash all the dishes, and fall into a drugged slumber.

I would typically schedule the following day as a heavy working day with evening meetings in order to distract myself from increasing hunger as I fasted. I began running with the same motivation I had for my original weight loss—the development of a hard, sharp, unassailable physique. I would typically run for one hour, four to five days per week, and walked to work as a further weight control measure.

I had confided to my friend, M., that I binged on food on Sunday nights, and she was supportive of my need for relaxation. She was not, however, aware of the significance of the routine I was building. Neither was my therapist. I had found an excellent psychologist and worked with him for two years, sharing issues in my work on agency cases and in my personal relationships. I never revealed to him, however, that I was bingeing heavily, and I doubt if, at that time, he would have attached any special significance to those behaviors other than their obvious relationship to stress.

In 1977, my bingeing increased in frequency and became more clearly addictive in nature. I would experience waves of an aching, almost flu-like feeling in midafternoon during the week, and realize that I wanted to have a binge evening. I would go through a ritualized phone call to M. in which I berated myself for the feeling, receive "absolution" and support for my social withdrawal, and then busy myself almost cozily for my ensconcement in my apartment that night surrounded by food and paperback novels. The actual binges themselves were unchanged, except that I had sensed for some time that mixing alcohol with my primary "drug of choice" was quite dangerous psychologically for me, and so I was drinking quarts of tea or diet soft drinks with my binge rather than beer. I drank these non-caloric beverages because I reasoned that I wanted to get the most enjoyment possible from each calorie, and I found solid food much more satisfying than sugary soft drinks.

As time went on, I increased the frequency of these binges, probably because of the decreasing structured demands for my time. They went from weekly to twice per week, then I was either bingeing or fasting with no normal days in my week at all. My sleep patterns were either near-comatose or restless, with either sweating after a binge or shivering after a fast. I became increasingly irritable and withdrawn, prompting increased demands from M. that I spend more time with her, and prompting increased guilt on my part that I resented the intrusion of my friends, my patients, and even my son into my cycle.

The nadir of my life as a bulimic occurred when I found myself calling patients whom I had scheduled for evening appointments, explaining to them that I was ill, and then using the freed evening for bingeing. I never broke my pattern of fasting to block weight gain—I was too terrified of the possibility of even slight weight gains to do that. However, my life was obviously dominated by my disorder, my judgment was impaired, I was distracted during sessions with thoughts of bingeing, and I had no therapeutic resources available to me, at least as I saw it. I was physically exhausted most of the time, and my hands, feet, and abdomen were frequently puffy and edematous, which I, of course, interpreted as gain in body fat and which contributed to my obsession with weight and food. I weighed myself several times per day in various locations, attending to half pound variations as though my life depended on them. My dreams were often nightmares of dead, rubbery flesh in strips wrapping around me and inserting itself into my mouth. As in graduate school, I alternated thoughts of food with those of suicide, and frequently stared at myself in the mirror while holding a pistol to my head.

RECOVERY PHASE

My recovery from bulimia has been a piecemeal thing, characterized by the gradual dismantling of the components of the behavior pattern in a trial-and-error fashion. It began when I developed a sore leg from running and was fearful that lack of aerobic exercise would allow me to gain weight again. M. suggested I try swimming, which I did, and found thoroughly enjoyable. I began to use an hour of lap swimming as a "positive addiction" competing with my bingeing, although I did not know at the time I was doing that. I felt better and was able at times to conceive of a life without bingeing and fasting.

A second prop removed from my bulimia involved food allergies. I had been working as a consultant to a local agency which ran preschools for retarded children and was asked to look into research on the Feingold diet for hyperactive children which was, at the time, ongoing at the University of Pittsburgh's Western Psychiatric Institute and Clinic. It included complex food allergy testing for subjects.

Out of curiosity, I had the test run on myself. To my surprise, it revealed that I was allergic to all the foods on which I typically binged, and to little else. I discussed this with the allergist on the project, who had not before considered the connection between allergies and eating disorders, and we hypothesized that allergens in foods could possibly create a non-food "rush" which could cause them to become addictive in certain psychologically vulnerable patients.

I then began to experiment with my binges, substituting for the foods to which I had indicated allergies. I was able to do this over a period of about six months, and even though I continued to binge, I did not awaken with the respiratory distress, nightmares, or deep grogginess which I had previously taken for granted. The substitution process also weakened the symbolic links which binges had to affiliation and nurturance, since I was now choosing food based on criteria other than its symbolic meaning to me.

My next step was to binge only on food which I would otherwise be eating normally, and telling myself that I was simply "feasting" on tomorrow's food rather than bingeing on "forbidden foods." In doing that, I was normalizing the nutritional composition of my binges, and also, without knowing it, applying cognitive behavioral strategies to block my self-berating for bingeing. The effect of this effort was an experience of increased physical endurance, which allowed my swimming to be harder, and concomitant changes in my muscle tone began to be apparent.

Prior to this time, my efforts had been to decrease the side effects of my disorder rather than altering the frequency of bingeing itself. My successes and general increases in well-being prompted me to seriously consider altering the basic fact of my bingeing. My first effort to do so involved Overeaters Anonymous and was a failure. I had heard about the group, but had assumed it to be focused on obesity and "compulsive overeating." With some trepidation, I attended a meeting and attempted to study the Alcoholics Anonymous "Big Book" used as a Bible by 12-step self-help groups in general. I also picked up a copy of the standard diet which, at the time, was recommended for OA members. I recall being strongly uneasy in the intimate group setting and cringed inwardly at the implicit demands to acknowledge helplessness over the disorder. The last straw, for me, was the standard diet, which involved careful measuring of food. I tried it for several days and felt heavily deprived. I did not return to the group, and evaded the calls from group members for some time thereafter.

Unlike other benchmarks in my illness, it is hard for me to remember the precise events which led to the first reduction in the frequency of my bingeing. This may be because the changes in my bingeing patterns which I had already made had begun to erode the rewarding quality of the binges, and their less frequent occurrence may not have been felt as strongly depriving. I began to use breakfast as a "mini-binge," at least psychologically, giving myself ample time to read while eating slowly from a large bin of "trail mix," stopping when I was not hungry anymore and never measuring how much I ate.

My "experiments in lifestyle" were sometimes failures. I became interested in vegetarian foods from books I had read, and in vegetarianism as a way of eating. All that happened was that I became very proficient at baking crusty loaves of whole-grain bread, would take hours doing so on weekends (while my son boredly watched TV), and then binge on them Sunday evenings! I went back to eating fish and small amounts of meat in normal dinners, and at least had more time with my son even though I still binged after I took him home each weekend.

I was more successful at reversing the pattern of midweek binges, however, after having made such lifestyle changes. I was now beginning to define myself as a physically fit endurance athlete, while my identity as a private practice psychologist was solidifying. Both of these attitudinal changes led to my decision to keep my work week "clean."

My initial efforts to endure binge urges without succumbing to them revealed to me the intensity of my addiction. I developed withdrawal symptoms of moderate intensity, involving irritability, tremors, restlessness, disturbed sleep, and muscular tension and pain. They came in waves of increasing intensity, which often could be borne only if I were working hard or asleep. The interval between these waves gradually increased until I was not experiencing discomfort with only one binge per week on Sunday nights.

The complete elimination of my binges came about by accident. My son had been complaining of flu-like symptoms, and I hoped to be able to put him to bed early enough for a reasonable start on my binge. However, he had a syncopy attack (fainting spell) after having a hot bath, which evolved into a brief grand mal seizure. We rushed him to the hospital and I stayed the night with him, leaving, of course, my binge food untouched. The following day I ate normally, reasoning that he would need me to be alert and strong. I described in wonder to M. over dinner on the following evening that I seemed to have just gone longer without bingeing than I had in years. Her response was a subtly challenging one, "Gee, I wonder how long you can keep it going?" I continued to eat normally. Very quickly, the residual edema diminished, and I felt physically much clearer and healthier than I ever had before. The waves of binge urge came less and less frequently, as did the concomitant depressions and suicidal thoughts. I experienced no relapses and have not binged since that time, over five years ago.

CURRENT FUNCTIONING

Even though I have not binged since 1983, I would not consider myself cured, but only recovered from bulimia. I recognize that I still have many of the personality features which make me at risk for bulimic behavior. I am still compulsive and can easily become nearly terrified if my daily exercise routine is interrupted in any way. I tightly schedule patients and allow only the minimum time for me to get to the swimming pool, rush through my twomilesof swimming, and rush back to the office. I am almost always late for the ensuing appointments.

As long as I get my exercise done, however, I do not usually think about food throughout the day. I continue to eat a large, unmeasured breakfast of trail mix, fruit, and herb tea with a vitamin supplement, and am not hungry until abouta half hour before dinnertime. My dinners are always eaten out, since I now live alone, and consist of large salads or a light fish, vegetable, and salad meal. I continue to work on broadening my diet and I am encouraged to find that I tolerate many of my previously "forbidden" foods if I eat them in the morning.

I continue to have allergic reactions to certain foods at other times, however. I do not think these are completely psychogenic, since I had a strong allergic reaction to a glucose intravenous solution when I was in an emergency room following a bronchitis attack. The symptoms, particularly after sugar ingestion, are predictable - red hands, feet, and facial coloration, swollen veins, general malaise and irritability, a blurry, "woozy" feeling, slurred speech, and craving for sweets. Lesser reactions still occur to dairy products.

My weight has remained constant for many years and I do not weigh myself. I continue, however, to be vulnerable to fears of weight gain and catch myself pinching at my waistline at times if I feel that I've eaten too much. However, the successful experience of having gained and then lost "that bloated feeling" time and again has been an important tool; now I can say with conviction that such discomfort is temporary and will pass.

I think that the greatest change in me in the last five years has been a psychological one. I have become more accepting of the imperfections in myself and others, and more truly patient. I react to my own resentment now as a signal that I am in need of something and I try to obtain that for myself.

I have said little about my religious faith, I realize now. That also has deepened. My Catholic upbringing and return to the faith often made the difference between life and death during suicidal episodes. I am now more honest and, in a sense, more childlike as I worship; I think I am in the process of reparenting myself with a new role model as a father—that of a loving God. I see many clients who are religiously committed—Catholic clergy, new-wave Charismatic Protestants, or Orthodox Jews—and I enjoy the affirmation of their spiritual growth that occurs in my work with them.

In the past three years, my psychological growth has also been furthered by my work with my current therapist, a former professional dancer and teacher who is eclectically trained in body therapy techniques. I have developed increasing appreciation for my own "internal gyroscopes" and for the sensitivity and complexity of my physical self (Mengato, 1986).

One final thing has happened which represents, to me, the distance I have come. For 30 years I have dreamed of flying a small aircraft. At each stress point in my adult life I tried again to actually begin to fly, joining a soaring club, taking lessons in power flying in rented airplanes, attempting to buy a fragile, ultralight aircraft. Each time the money ran out and I would force myself not to look up at the sky for years. Since my bulimia has abated, I have worked so much more efficiently that I can now realize my dream.

DISCUSSION

Perspective is a difficult thing to achieve, especially about one's own behavior, so I will keep this section brief and tentative. However, on looking at my own story as a clinician with a specialty in eating disorders, several points stand out. The first involves the similarity in the actual onset of my bulimic behaviors to those of bulimic women who have an anorexic history. My current lifestyle could easily be described as a positive adjustment by a long-term anorexic. However, the enmeshed, overprotective families typically described in relation to anorexia (Minuchin, Rosman, & Baker, 1978) are not, so far as I can tell, similar to my family. Clearly, there were elements of rigidity and demandingness in it for me, but I was certainly not seen as "the best little boy in the world." Separation and individuation in my case were probably prematurely done, with the result that my basic self-concept was not built on positive interactions with nurturing caregivers. It is significant that the reparenting process I am going through personally now is similar in content to the imagery work which I do with adults who have been either sexually or in other ways abused by family members as children.

A second point which my story highlights, I think, is the peculiar quality of physical vulnerability which I hear again and again from my male clients but almost never from my female clients. This relates, in my thinking, to the cultural pressures on boys who are deviant from societal male body-type ideals. Boys who deviate, and especially those who are physically clumsy or immature to boot, are in much greater danger of suffering physical violence than are girls. The implicit (and sometimes explicit) approval of physical violence as a problem-solving tool for males in our culture can be a particular stress on softly built, slender, or obese boys in competitive school settings. The resultant valuation of "hardness" as opposed to sheer slenderness has until now, in my opinion, been unique to male eating disorder sufferers. With increasing parity of men and women in professional, business, and athletic areas, however, and the message of women's advocacy groups that women have the right and responsibility to fight back against the various forms of rape in their lives, we may see changes in this area.

Relative to the above, I am struck by the connection between the body type which caused me so much trouble and the endocrine problems which occurred at puberty for me. Without attempting to prescribe the use of hormonal supplements to make us all wedge-shaped *Ubermenschen*, I think that endocrine and other metabolic factors can produce fragile areas in the perceived self, which can then lead, along with external attacks, to a deep belief that one is, at the heart, worthless and physically disgusting. Cognitive revaluation techniques are not terribly useful in the face of constant physical reminders that this condition exists. Thus, some medical help to these boys, along with adaptive physical education programs in noncompetitive settings, may be superficial to the dynamically oriented therapist, but a great kindness in reality.

Above all, being a man with an eating disorder and treating other men with eating disorders has shown me the heterogeneity of the problem in males. Because the intense cultural pressures regarding thinness and food use which are applied to women are not applied to men, we find a broad variation in the configuration of eating disorders in men. Food is used as the "drug of choice" for many reasons, and those reasons may change in the course of the disorder.

Because of this, I have found it useful to categorize males with eating disorders using a four-level schema based on the level of personality development accompanying the symptoms. The first level is that of the borderline personality whose anorexia or bulimia is an effort to stave off fears of engulfment, dissolving, or, conversely, abandonment. The provision of a "holding environment" is essential to these men and allows the coalescence of a basic sense of self.

The second level is that of the addictive or character-disordered personality whose bulimia or compulsive overeating is the effort to dull frustration or to obtain rapid physical gratification. These men have not learned empathy or truly cooperative behavior and impulse control is typically faulty. Their predominant affect is rage and they respond best to addiction counseling methods.

The third level is that of the neurotic personality whose anorexia, bulimia, or overeating is the result of faulty learning about emotions. Their predominant affect is guilt and they respond well to individual therapy techniques involving a mixture of insight, cognitive restructuring, behavioral rehearsal, and other traditional tools. Much of my recovery has been in this area.

The fourth area is that of the integrated personality whose bulimia or overeating is the result of extreme sensitivity without the proper training in the acceptance and use of that sensitivity. This group shades into the previous one when the sensitivities in question are emotional arousals which have been taught to be feared. These men respond best to consciousness-raising techniques designed, paradoxically, to *increase* their sensitivity while they are learning new ways to interpret and respond to their awareness in a self-validating manner.

Given the above general levels of personality development, any male eating-disordered patient may be, at the time of initial consultation, at one of a variety of points in relation to the actual changes needed for his recovery. Recent work by Prochaska and DiClemente (1984, 1986) describing a transtheoretical approach to the process of change provides, I think, an excellent structure for sorting out possible therapeutic strategies for the most timely intervention.

Recall that my history reflected, first, family factors, then physiological, interpersonal, and vocational stress patterns, with intrapersonal neurotic symptoms, addictive behaviors, and existential issues as a result. My capacity for change varied as the disorder progressed. A sensitive therapist would have needed to understand the sequence through which I was moving and to accept that bulimia was filling a changing role in my life. As I continue to work with men who suffer from eating disorders, I find myself taking an eclectic role much more frequently, selecting interventions using guidelines from the above sources, as well as those recently proposed by Beutler (1986) and Lazarus (1976, 1981, 1986). When treating disorders with the intensity and disruptive power that these have, I believe that an organizing structure for choosing interventions is critical for therapeutic success.

Finally, I would like to add a few words about the general cultural milieu in which the therapeutic endeavor is carried out. Those of us who work in the field of eating disorders in Pittsburgh are blessed with a relaxed and supportive multidisciplinary network and an organization—the Pittsburgh Educational Network for Eating Disorders—which puts us together with sufferers and their families in cooperative outreach, educational, and advocacy ventures. This is a very good thing as it destroys some of the artificial barriers we all erect to insulate ourselves from the pain which we face as sufferers or helpers. It can provide some awkward moments, however, especially when one is, like myself, both a sufferer and a helper. I have had to accept that some of the most humbling details of my behavior as a bulimic would be common knowledge. I have accepted this so that other men with eating disorders could recognize their need for help, know that help existed, and feel less trepidation about reaching out.

I have devised rules for myself which have made it possible for me to survive as an effective therapist in this setting, the most important of which is that my patients' well-being always comes first and that I never do anything which would prevent me from immediately shifting roles into the therapeutic one for them.

A second rule is related to the first, and that is that I inform all new eating-disordered patients that I am a recovered bulimic, that I am associated with eating disorders groups, and that I am often in the public view in such matters. The reaction to this statement has been predominantly positive.

My final rule involves my own eating disorder. As I said, I have not binged or fasted since 1983. If I should relapse or if (and this last has occurred several times) I find myself experiencing significant waves of longing for binge-eating, I immediately seek therapeutic help for myself and begin to double-check my work with eating disordered patients. I now have trusted therapeutic allies who are not in the eating disorders field and who are not looking to me as a role model or a leader. Their objectivity has often been essential, since I feel great pain when I think of the gap between what I have been able to do to help others and what I actually have done. If I can be honest with them, I can rest easy that I am giving my patients my best.

REFERENCES

Andersen, A.E. (1984). Anorexia nervosa and bulimia in adolescent males. *Pediatric Annals, 13*, 901-907.

Beutler, Larry E. (1986). Systematic Eclectic Psychotherapy. In J.C. Norcross (Ed.), *Handbook of Eclectic Psychotherapy*. New York: Brunner/Mazel.

Binswanger, L. (1957). The case of Ellen West. In R. May (Ed.), *Existence*. New York: Basic Books.

Bjorntorp, P. (1986). Fat cells and obesity. In K.D. Brownell & J.P. Foreyt (Eds.), *Handbook of Eating Disorders*. New York: Basic Books.

Crisp, A. H., & Burns, T. (1983). The clinical presentation of anorexia nervosa in males. *International Journal of Eating Disorders, 2*, 5-10.

Dantini, D. C., Jr. (1987). Personal communication.

Garner, D. M., & Garfinkel, P. E. (1985). *Handbook of Psychotherapy for Anorexia Nervosa and Bulimia*. New York: Guilford.

Gull, W. W. (1874). Anorexia nervosa (apepsia hysterica, anorexia hysterica). *Transactions of the Clinical Society of London, 7*, 22-28.

Herzog, D. B., et al. (1984). Sexual conflict and eating disorders in 27 males. *American Journal of Psychiatry, 141*, 989–990.

Keys, A., et al. (1950). *The Biology of Human Starvation*. Minneapolis: University of Minnesota Press.

Lazarus, A. A. (1976). *Multimodal Behavior Therapy*. New York: Springer.

Lazarus, A. A. (1981). *The Practice of Multimodal Therapy*. New York: McGraw-Hill.

Lazarus, A. A. (1986). Multimodal therapy. In J. C. Norcross (Ed.), *Handbook of Eclectic Psychotherapy*. New York: Brunner/Mazel.

Lindner, R. (1955). The case of Laura. In *The Fifty Minute Hour*. New York: Holt, Rinehart.

Lucas, A. R., et al. (1983). Epidemiology of anorexia nervosa and bulimia: Background of the Rochester Project. *International Journal of Eating Disorders, 2,* 85-90.

Mengato, M. P. (1986). Personal communication.

Minuchin, S., Rosman, B. L., & Baker, L. (1978). *Psychosomatic Families: Anorexia Nervosa in Context*. Cambridge, MA: Harvard University Press.

Morton, R. (1694). *Phthisiologica: Or a Treatise of Consumptions*. London: S. Smith & B. Walford.

Pope, H. G., Hudson, J. I., & Jonas, J. M. (1986). Bulimia in males: A series of 15 cases. *Journal of Nervous and Mental Disorders, 174,* 117-119.

Prochaska, J., & DiClemente, C. (1984). *The Transtheoretical Approach: Crossing the traditional boundaries of therapy*. Homewood, IL: Dow Jones/Irwin.

Prochaska, J., & DiClemente, C. (1986). The transtheoretical approach. In J. C. Norcross (Ed.), *Handbook of Eclectic Psychotherapy*. New York: Brunner/Mazel.

Pyle, R. L., et al. (1986). The increasing prevalence of bulimia in freshman college students. *International Journal of Eating Disorders, 5,* 631-647.

Scott, D. W. (1986). Anorexia nervosa in the male: A review of clinical, epidemiological, and biological findings. *International Journal of Eating Disorders, 5,* 799-817.

Sterling, J. W., & Segal, J. D. (1985). Anorexia nervosa in males: A critical review. *International Journal of Eating Disorders, 4,* 559-572.

3

Sociocultural Factors Influencing Weight Among Males

Angela D. Mickalide

"Nobody loves a fat man," according to silent film star Fatty Arbuckle (1907). Current data suggest that while societal pressures to be slim, svelte, and thin, are exerted more strongly and consistently on women than men, males do develop eating disorders. Vague "sociocultural factors" are often alluded to as etiologic in the development of eating disorders in the male (Schneider & Agras, 1987). The aim of this paper is to discuss specific sociological and cultural phenomena which might influence males' attitudes and behaviors concerning their weight and the probability of developing an eating disorder.

HISTORICAL PERSPECTIVES

Ideal male body form has varied in a cyclical nature over the generations. A young, perfectly formed, athletic physique characterized the ideal male in Greece in the fourth century B.C. Physical perfection was inextricably bound with intellectual and spiritual attainment. Bennett and Gurin (1982, p. 186) describe a satirical vase painting: "Two muscular boys go through their workout at the athletic field while two others, one tall and skinny, the other short and chubby, idle their time in a pointless argument. Greeks of the Classic era did not portray older or imperfect bodies as belonging to happy people."

Both underweight and overweight conditions have plagued men for centuries, but their plight has been eclipsed by societal attention to women with weight disorders. The first well-documented case of anorexia nervosa occurred in a 16-year-old male (Morton, 1694). Several reports were published in the 17th, 18th, and 19th centuries which described self-starvation in adolescent and young adult males (Silverman, 1987). Franz Kafka, author of *The Hunger Artist* (1922) and *The Metamorphosis* (1912) is viewed as having suffered from atypical anorexia nervosa (Fichter, 1987). In *Never Satisfied*, Schwartz (1986) documents in great detail the obsessive weighing rituals of men in the 1700s. Further, William Howard Taft was the only U.S. President who was excessively fat and "was dismayed by his bulk and struggled to reduce it" (Bennett & Gurin, 1982, p. 191).

According to the National Center for Health Statistics (1988), approximately one-quarter (24%) of Americans are overweight, defined as 20% or more above desirable body weight. Objectively, a larger percentage of males (25.9%) than females (22.3%) are considered overweight. Yet men appear more comfortable with their weight and perceive less pressure to be thin than women. In a study of 340 male college students, 65% reported weighing within 5 percentage points of their self-reported ideal weight (Franco, Tamburrino, Carroll, & Bernal, 1988). A national survey revealed that only 41% of men are dissatisfied with their weight as compared with 55% of women. In fact, underweight was a much greater taboo for males; only 77% of underweight men liked their appearance as opposed to 83% of underweight women (Cash, Winstead, & Janda, 1986). The Gallup Organization's national body image survey revealed that the average American woman wants to lose 11 pounds whereas the average American man is much more satisfied with his weight and wants to lose only one pound (Britton, 1988).

MEDIA

The media portray men as concerned with physical fitness and women as obsessed with their weight. This is most interesting, considering that men (43%) participate in regular exercise at only slightly higher rates than women (38%) (National Center for Health Statistics, 1988). DiDomenico and Andersen (1988) found that magazines targeted primarily to women included a greater number of articles and advertisements aimed at weight reduction (e.g., diet, calories) and those targeted at men contained more shape articles and advertisements (e.g., fitness, weight lifting, body building, or muscle toning). The magazines most read by females aged 18-24 had 10 times more diet content than those most popular among men in the same age group. This mirrors the 10-to-one ratio of female to male eating disorder patients (Andersen & Mickalide, 1983).

Men's magazines emphasize activity, movement, and physical prowess. While both men and women engage in athletics, only males were portrayed on the covers of the April and May 1988 issues of *Runner's World, Golf Digest, Tennis*, and *Bicycling*. Two new magazines have emerged on the scene, *Men's Health* and *Men's Fitness*, both of which focus on physical fitness rather than on slenderness. A *Psychology Today* poll confirms this dichotomy (Cash, Winstead, & Janda, 1986). Male respondents were more likely than female to claim that if they were fit and exercised regularly, they felt good about their bodies. Women respondents were more concerned with aspects of their appearance, particularly weight. The authors claim, "Little boys are taught to be proud of themselves because they are strong and athletic. Little girls learn to value beauty." Few would dispute that even in the 1980s women are still judged disproportionately on the basis of their appearance and men disproportionately on the basis of their wealth and power.

A distinct disadvantage of males' obsession with physical fitness is the epidemic use of anabolic steroids to build muscle mass and boost strength. Anabolic steroids can cause psychotic reactions, such as auditory hallucinations, manic symptoms and depression. Approximately 85% of all professional football players and 1 to 3% of all college seniors in the U.S. have used steroids (Slothower, 1988). Another potential pitfall is that athletic activity may become obsessive and detrimental to the physical and mental well-being of the individual (Burckes-Miller & Black, 1988; Katz, 1986; Rowley, 1987; Yates, Leehey, & Shisslak, 1983). Garner and Garfinkel (1985) report a 70% increase in diet articles in women's magazines between 1968 and 1979 compared to the previous 10 years. No comparable study tracks variations in messages aimed at males, attesting to the relative lack of concern with males, weight among sociocultural researchers.

Television portrays Americans as slim and fit. Gerbner and colleagues' (1981) analysis of a week's sample of dramatic programs revealed that fewer than 6% of all males and 2% of all females were obese, a significant underrepresentation of obesity in the general population. The threefold greater percentage of obese males to females, underrepresentative as it is of male obesity, may be a function of greater societal acceptance of corpulence among men. Further, obese males are often portrayed as powerful and authoritative; Cannon, Perry Mason, and Jake's partner, the Fat Man, are prime examples. The majority of obese women on television are black (e.g., Nell Carter, Mrs. Jefferson), perpetuating the stereotype of the black matriarch, or of low socioeconomic status (e.g. Roseanne).

DIETING PATTERNS

According to data from the National Center for Health Statistics (1988), 56% of all overweight Americans (20% above desirable weight for height) are trying to lose weight. Approximately 48% of males are attempting to lose weight by reducing caloric intake, increasing exercise, or both, as compared with approximately 64% of females. Emphasis on weight reduction and slenderness begins early in the socialization process, particularly among females. In a sample of 1,373 high school students, girls (63%) were four times more likely than boys (16%) to be attempting to reduce weight through exercise and caloric intake reduction. Boys were three times more likely than girls to be trying to gain weight (28% versus 9%), conforming to stereotypical ideals favoring slender women and athletic, muscular men (Rosen & Gross, 1987). The authors note that over the past 20 years weight reduction efforts have doubled among adolescent females but have remained constant among adolescent males.

A survey of 240 Sydney, Australia high school students indicated that sex differences in attitudes and behaviors about weight control are not solely a United States and European phenomenon. Specifically, 54.3% of the girls, compared to only 13.5% of the boys, desired a weight greater than 10 percent below appropriate body weight for height. Seventy-nine percent of the girls claimed to weigh themselves frequently compared with 41% of the boys. Of interest is that 40 subjects had to be excluded from analysis because desired weight was not specified. The majority of these were boys (36), many of whom later remarked that they never even considered themselves to have a desired weight (Huon & Brown, 1986).

Klesges and colleagues' (1987) study of 102 female and 102 male undergraduates confirmed that females were much more weight conscious than men. They engaged in more safe and dangerous food restriction practices and participated in more appropriate and inappropriate physical activities than males.

Fallon and Rosen (1985) detected profound sex differences in perceptions of desirable body shapes. A total of 248 male and 227 female undergraduates rated their current figure, their ideal figure, the figure they believed would be most attractive to the opposite sex, and the opposite sex figure they were most attracted to, using a set of figure drawings ranging from very thin to very heavy. Among male respondents, the current, ideal, and most attractive figures were virtually identical, allowing them to feel comfortable with their weights. Among female respondents, current figures were heavier than ideal figures due to cultural proscriptions of femininity and attractiveness. According to Drewnowski and Yee (1987), the chief risk factor for developing eating disorders may be dieting itself. Based on a questionnaire administered to 226 college freshman (98 males and 128 females) concerning weight, body shape, dieting, and exercise history, the authors found that 26 percent of the men and 48 percent of the women described themselves as overweight. Yet women usually dieted to lose weight, whereas men usually exercised. Drewnowski and Yee concluded that, "It may be that the key difference between the sexes with respect to the etiology of eating disorders is not dissatisfaction with body weight but rather actual behaviors related to diet and exercise."

SOCIOECONOMIC STATUS

As socioeconomic status (typically measured by income and education) varies, so too does weight. Overweight, defined as 20% or more above desirable body weight for height, is inversely related to education and income in the aggregate (National Center for Health Statistics, 1988). The inverse relationship is more marked among women than men. As Table 1 indicates,

TABLE 1

Percent of Persons 18 Years of Age and Over Who Were 20% or More Above Desirable Body Weight by Sex, Age, and Selected Characteristics: United States, 1985

Characteristic	Both Sexes	Male	Female
All persons	24.0	25.9	22.3
Education			
Less than 12 years	30.7	28.5	32.5
12 years	24.3	27.0	22.2
More than 12 years	19.3	23.5	14.8
Family Income			
Less than $10,000	26.0	20.7	29.2
$10,000–$19,999	25.9	26.2	25.6
$20,000–$34,999	23.8	27.0	20.4
$35,000–$49,999	22.3	28.2	16.1
$50,000 or more	19.6	25.9	12.7
Race			
White	23.5	26.4	20.8
Black	30.8	24.8	35.5

Source: National Center for Health Statistics, C.A. Schoenborn. 1988. Health promotion and disease prevention. United States, 1985. *Vital and Health Statistics.* Series 10, No. 163. DHHS Pub. No. (PHS) 88-1591. Public Health Service. Washington, D.C.: U.S. Government Printing Office, p. 20.

rates of overweight are two and one-half times greater for women in the lowest education and income categories as compared with the highest education and income categories. Rates of overweight among men are fairly consistent across the education and income levels.

The notion that eating disorders were more prevalent among higher SES populations went undisputed for several decades. A century ago, Fenwick (1880) noted that anorexia nervosa was most common in "the wealthier classes of society than amongst those who have to procure their bread by daily labour" (p. 107). Recent studies have demonstrated higher rates of anorexia nervosa among private school students than among public school students (Crisp, Palmer, & Kalucy, 1976; Szmukler, 1985). Conversely, several researchers have found anorexia nervosa and bulimia to be distributed equally across socio-economic classes, undermining the notion that eating disorders occur only in the middle and upper classes (Granther, Post, & Zaynor, 1985; Herzog, Norman, Gordon, & Pepose, 1984). Unexpectedly, Pope and colleagues (1987) found eating disorders more common among lower income respondents. The initial perception of eating disorders as an upper class phenomenon may have been due to better access to medical care, and hence diagnosis, among wealthier populations. It now appears that anorexia nervosa and bulimia may not discriminate on the basis of social class.

RACIAL AND ETHNIC INFLUENCES

Obesity rates are higher among blacks (30.8%) than among whites (23.5%) according to data from the National Center for Health Statistics (1988). Although the rate for white males (26.4%) is only slightly higher than that for black males (24.8%), the rate for black females of 35.5% is highest of all—almost 75% higher than the 20% rate for white females. Hence, the black/whitedifferential is attributed to variations in female weights, not male weights.

For many years, no cases of anorexia nervosa and bulimia in minorities appeared in the literature, supporting the notion that only Caucasians equate extreme thinness with beauty. Yet eating disorders are becoming more common in blacks, with 25 cases documented in the literature to date (Andersen & Hay, 1985; Hsu, 1987). Male to female ratios of eating disorders in minorities have not been established to date. Gray and colleagues (1987) found low rates of bulimia among Caucasian and Black males in their college population. Compared to Caucasian males, Black males reported a higher frequency of bingeing, fasting, and dieting. However, black males were also significantly less likely to consider themselves overweight. This unexpected finding warrants further research.

OCCUPATIONAL HAZARDS

Male jockeys, wrestlers, swimmers, models, dancers, and flight attendants are vulnerable to eating disorders because their professions necessitate weight restriction. This is not a 20th-century phenomenon. In 1747 a jockey donned six waistcoats, ran two or three miles, and immersed himself in a hot dunghill to lose weight before a race (Schwartz, 1986). Jockeys currently "waste" themselves through food intake restriction, excessive sauna use (up to four hours with a seven-pound weight loss), laxative abuse, intake of diuretics and appetite suppressants, and self-induced vomiting (King & Mezey, 1987). Exercise is performed strenuously for weight reduction rather than for physical fitness. Irritability, decreased energy, and diminished sexual drive stem from wasting.

Adolescent wrestlers who engage in repeated cycles of weight loss and regain affect their resting metabolic rates and hinder future weight control (Steen, Oppliger, & Brownell, 1988). Despite strong warnings from both the American Medical Association and the American College of Sports Medicine, food and fluid deprivation practices are engaged in by wrestlers to "make weight" for matches. Forty-one percent of wrestlers reported weight fluctuations of 5 to 9 kg every week of the season, according to data collected at a major college wrestling tournament (Steen & Brownell, 1986). In addition to metabolic aberrations, weight "cutting" has been shown to exert adverse effects on body composition, nutrient intake, nutrient absorption, renal function and electrolyte balance, thermal regulation, testosterone levels, and strength. Yet during the off-season, jockeys and wrestlers usually cease all dietary restraint, unlike eating disorder patients whose obsession with slimness persists endlessly. Functional weight loss for vocational success differs from an eating disorder when the central psychopathology is absent. Whether males with aberrant eating patterns and body image distortions seek out particular professions or whether occupational choices give rise to eating-disordered behavior remains an unanswered question.

SEXUALITY

Infertility among women due to excessive dieting and/or exercise has been well-documented by Frisch (1988). Yet the relationship between fat andreproductive ability among men has received sparse attention. Keys and colleagues' classic study of starvation in men revealed that sperm production is diminished among men weighing 25% less than ideal body weight (Frisch, 1988). Testosterone lowering occurs among male marathoners and top-ranked athletes, yet the effect on fertility is unknown. A study by Andersen and Mickalide (1983) suggests that a disproportionate number of male anorectics may have persisting or preexisting problems in testosterone production.

The prevalence of homosexuality in eating-disordered males is under debate. Herzog and colleagues (1984) reported a 26% incidence of homosexuality among anorectic and bulimic males, compared with 4% among female anorectic and bulimic patients cared for in the same unit. Fichter andDaser (1987) noted that 25% of their male patients had homosexual contacts. Conversely, Pope and colleagues (1986) found homosexual activity in only one of 14 patients (7%) and none of Burns and Crisp's (1984) male patients was involved in a homosexual relationship.

In the past, the most attractive body form in the gay community has been ectomorphic. Perhaps with the increasing incidence of AIDS and its ravaging effects on the human body, mesomorphic builds will become increasingly more desirable in the gay community. The trend toward desiring excessively slim body builds will decrease to avoid the appearance of illness with AIDS. The illness has been described in slang usage as "slims" in some countries.

The ancient Greek motto of "nothing to excess, everything in moderation" should be adhered to, as concerns eating and exercise, by males who weigh too much or too little. Shakespeare articulated well the wisdom of ideal weight maintenance when he wrote:

They are as sick that surfeit with too much as they that starve with nothing.

William Shakespeare (1564-1616)
Merchant of Venice I.ii.

An understanding of the sociocultural forces influencing body shape and size in males may help us understand not only why eating disorders are less frequent in men than in women, but also why they occur in those males who do experience them and why eating disorders may be overrepresented in certain subgroups of the male population.

REFERENCES

Andersen, A. E., & Hay, A. (1985). Racial and socioeconomic influences in anorexia-nervosa and bulimia. *International Journal of Eating Disorders*, 4, 479–487.

Andersen, A. E., & Mickalide, A. D. (1983). Anorexia nervosa in the male: An underdiagnosed disorder. *Psychosomatics*, 24, 1067–1075.

Bennett, W., & Gurin, J. (1982). *The Dieter's Dilemma*. New York: Basic Books, Inc.

Britton, A. G. (July/August 1988). Thin is out, fit is in. *American Health*, 66–71.

Burckes-Miller, M. E., & Black, D. R. (February/March 1988). Eating disorders: A problem in athletics? *Health Education*, 22–25.

Burns, T., & Crisp, A. H. (1984). Outcome of anorexia nervosa in males. *British Journal of Psychiatry, 145*, 319–328.

Cash, T. F., Winstead, B. A., & Janda, L. H. (April 1986). The great American shape-up. *Psychology Today*, 30–37.

Crisp, A. H., Palmer, R. L., & Kalucy, R. S. (1976). How common is anorexia nervosa? A prevalence study. *British Journal of Psychiatry, 128*, 549–554.

DiDomenico, L., & Andersen, A. E. (1988). Sociocultural considerations and sex differences in anorexia nervosa. Unpublished manuscript.

Drewnowski, A., & Yee, D. K. (1987). Men and body image: Are males satisfied with their body weight? *Psychosomatic Medicine, 49*, 626-634.

Fallon, A. E., & Rosen, P. (1985). Sex differences in perceptions of desirable body shape. *Journal of Abnormal Psychology, 94*, 102–105.

Fenwick, S. (1880). *On Atrophy of the Stomach and on the Nervous Affections of the Digestive Organs*. London: Churchill., p. 107.

Fichter, M. M. (1987). The anorexia nervosa of Franz Kafka. *International Journal of Eating Disorders, 6*, 367–377.

Fichter, M. M., & Daser, C. (1987). Symptomatology, psychosexual development and gender identity in 42 anorexic males. *Psychological Medicine, 17*, 409–418.

Franco, K. S. N., Tamburrino, M. B., Carroll, B. T., & Bernal, G. A. A. (1988). Eating attitudes in college males. *International Journal of Eating Disorders, 7*, 285–288.

Frisch, R. E. (March, 1988). Fatness and fertility. *Scientific American*, 88–95.

Garner, D. M. & Garfinkel, P. E. (1982). *Anorexia Nervosa: A Multidimensional Perspective*. New York: Brunner/Mazel.

Garner, D. M. & Garfinkel, P. E. (1985). *Handbook of Psychotherapy for Anorexia Nervosa and Bulimia*. New York: The Guilford Press.

Gerbner, G., Gross, L., Morgan, M., & Signorielli, N. (1981). Health and medicine on television. *New England Journal of Medicine, 305*, 901–904.

Granther, J. H., Post, G., & Zaynor, L. (1985). The prevalence of bulimia and binge eating in adolescent girls. *International Journal of Eating Disorders, 4*, 29–42.

Gray, J. J., Ford, K., & Kelly, L. M. (1987). The prevalence of bulimia in a black college population. *International Journal of Eating Disorders, 6*, 733–740.

Herzog, D. B., Norman, D. K., Gordon, C., & Pepose, M. (1984). Sexual conflict and eating disorders in 27 males. *American Journal of Psychiatry, 141*, 989–990.

Hsu, L. K. G. (1987). Are the eating disorders becoming more common in blacks. *International Journal of Eating Disorders, 6*, 113–124.

Huon, G. F. & Brown, L. B. (1986). Attitude correlates of weight control among secondary school boys and girls. *Journal of Adolescent Health Care, 7*, 178–182.

Katz, J. L. (1986). Long distance running, anorexia nervosa and bulimia: Two cases. *Comprehensive Psychiatry, 27*, 74–78.

King, M. B. & Mezey, G. (1987). Eating behaviour of male racing jockeys. *Psychological Medicine, 17,* 249–253.

Klesges, R. C., Mizes, J. S., & Klesges, L. M. (1987). Self-help dieting strategies in college males and females. *International Journal of Eating Disorders, 6,* 409–417.

Morton, R. (1694). *Phthisiologica: Or a Treatise of Consumptions.* London: Smith and Walford.

National Center for Health Statistics, C.A. Schoenborn. (1988). Health promotion and disease prevention. United States, 1985. *Vital and Health Statistics.* Series 10, No. 163. DHHS Pub. No. (PHS) 88–1591. Public Health Service. Washington, D.C.: U.S.Government Printing Office.

Pope, H. G., Hudson, J. I., & Jonas, J. M. (1986). Bulimia in men. A series of fifteen cases. *The Journal of Nervous and Mental Disease, 174,* 117–119.

Pope, H. G., Champoux, R. F., & Hudson, J. I. (1987). Eating disorders and socioeconomic class: Anorexia nervosa and bulimia in nine communities. *The Journal of Nervous and Mental Disease, 175,* 620–623.

Rosen, J. C. & Gross, J. (1987). Prevalence of weight reducing and weight gaining in adolescent girls and boys. *Health Psychology, 6,* 131–147.

Rowley, S. (1987). Psychological effects of intensive training in young athletes. *Journal of Child Psychology and Psychiatry, 28,* 371–377.

Schneider, J. A. & Agras, W. S. (1987). Bulimia in males: A matched comparison with females. *International Journal of Eating Disorders, 6,* 235–242.

Schwartz, H. (1986). *Never Satisfied: A Cultural History of Diets, Fantasies and Fat*. New York: The Free Press.

Silverman, J. A. (1987). An eighteenth century account of self–starvation in a male. *International Journal of Eating Disorders, 6,* 431–433.

Slothower, J. (January 1988). Mean mental muscles: The psychological price of steroids. *Health,* 20.

Steen, S. N., & Brownell, K. D. (1986). Weight loss and dietary practices in collegiate wrestlers. Presented at the annual meeting of the American Dietetic Association, Las Vegas.

Steen, S. N., Oppliger, R. A. & Brownell, K. D. (1988). Metabolic effects of repeated weight loss and regain in adolescent wrestlers. *Journal of the American Medical Association, 260,* 47-50.

Sterling, J.W., & Segal, J.D. (1985). Anorexia nervosa in males: A critical review. *International Journal of Eating Disorders, 4,* 559–572.

Szmukler, G. I. (1985). The epidemiology of anorexia nervosa and bulimia. *Journal of Psychiatric Research, 19,* 143–153.

Yates, A., Leehey, K., & Shisslak, C. M. (1983). Running—an analogue of anorexia? *New England Journal of Medicine, 308,* 251–255.

4

Sexuality in Males with Eating Disorders

David B. Herzog, Isabel S. Bradburn, and Kerry Newman

The sexual sphere is particularly salient in attempting to elucidate features unique to eating disorders in males. The clinical picture of anorexia nervosa and bulimia nervosa appears to differ for men and women in this domain, with more eating-disordered men exhibiting gender dysphoria and/or a homosexual orientation than their female counterparts. The low representation of men manifesting what are commonly considered "feminine" disorders highlights the need to investigate gender identity themes and biological factors in these men.

The literature on sexuality in eating-disordered males parallels the prevalence rates of these disorders in men: relatively few reports have been published. Most of the studies to date concern anorexia nervosa and are largely theoretical and anecdotal in nature. In addition to the problem of small samples, the paucity of studies addressing sexuality may reflect the difficulty of researching this topic in adolescent populations, when sexual identities often have not yet consolidated.

Several theories have been advanced that discuss the role of sexuality in the etiology of eating disorders in men. Early psychoanalytic literature speculated on the anorexic's ambivalent desire to remain in an infantile, dependent relationship with his mother and on his fear of the masculine role. Starvation was seen as a wish to kill the incorporated mother by starving her out, and to remove the fat associated with the female form (Falstein et al., 1956). Other researchers have proposed that psychosexually immature males, like females, may develop anorexia nervosa to ward off adolescent maturational conflicts, specifically regarding sexual feelings and behavior (Crisp & Toms, 1972).

Similarly, guilt or fear regarding a homoerotic experience may also precipitate an eating disorder (Crisp, 1970).

Research on males has attempted to identify sexual attitudes and behaviors that parallel what has been described in eating-disordered women. Reports have focused on patients' sexual anxiety, limited sexual experience, and ambivalence toward their roles and identities as males. Studies have also looked at the loss of sexual interest in eating-disordered patients from a biological perspective, noting the endocrine changes that are associated with weight loss and dietary disturbance.

The following chapter will review sexuality as an associated clinical feature, a prognostic factor, a precipitant, a risk factor, and an endocrine marker of eating disorders in men. The emphasis is on three major areas: sexual attitudes and behavior, gender dysphoria and homosexuality, and endocrine dysfunction.

SEXUAL ATTITUDES AND BEHAVIOR

Anorexic males display a considerable degree of anxiety with regard to sexual activities and relationships. Fichter and Daser (1987) compared 29 male anorexics to 23 female anorexics, using the *Structured Interview for Anorexia Nervosa and Bulimia* (SIAN) developed by Fichter (1985). Most subjects were more than 18 years of age, with the majority being in their early twenties. Males displayed significantly more sexual anxieties than did females. Fifteen patients (75%) reported a high degree of "disgust" towards sexual relationships and several felt anxious about "getting involved too closely" or becoming "trapped." Patients also expressed considerable shyness and lack of confidence with respect to women.

Fichter and Daser (1987) noted signs of sexual repression, as 80% of a subsample of their patients (16/20) grew up in families that regarded sex as a taboo subject. Dally (1969) reported that three of six male patients disliked discussing sexual subjects and were apprehensive about forming a sexual relationship; two additional subjects showed no sexual interest. One of Hasan and Tibbetts' (1977) six patients had an "intense fear" of sexuality. Similarly, Burns and Crisp (1984) studied 27 male anorexics (mean age, 22) and concluded that the majority admitted "obvious relief" at the diminution of their sexual drive during the acute phase of their illness.

Corresponding with the reported sexual anxiety, studies have noted low levels of sexual activity among anorexic males, before and during the illness. Fichter and Daser (1987) found that only six of their 29 male patients had ever engaged in sexual intercourse prior to their illness, only five others had experienced "petting," and 95% reported "attempts to suppress sexual drive." Thirteen anorexic and 14 bulimic males presenting for evaluation at the Massachusetts General Hospital Eating Disorders Unit (EDU) were compared with a control sample of eating-disordered females of similar age. The male sample differed significantly from the female sample in terms of sexual experience (Herzog et al., 1984). Males with eating disorders were significantly less likely to have had premorbid sexual relations or to be involved in a sexual relationship at the time of evaluation than were females with eating disorders, even though the mean age at onset for the males was slightly higher.

Limited premorbid sexual activity among eating-disordered males has also been noted by Crisp et al. (1986), although the low activity levels did not differ significantly from anorexic women. The researchers compared the clinical characteristics of a consecutive series of 36 male anorexics to 100 female anorexic patients. The mean age of both groups was approximately 20 years. Among the males, they found that premorbid sexual activity was absent in 13 patients (36%), "unremarkable" in 15 (42%), marked but fantasized in four (11%), and high in four (11%). Hasan and Tibbetts (1977) also noted circumscribed premorbid sexual behavior, and loss of sexual interest during the anorexic episode characterized patients in other samples (Beumont et al., 1972; Dally, 1969; Hall et al., 1985; Herzog et al., 1984; Margo, 1987).

Bulimic males, however, appear to be more sexually active than anorexic males, both premorbidly and at the time of their illness. Although Russell's (1979) two patients were "extremely limited" in their premorbid sexual experience, Pope et al. (1986) found that 11 of 14 male bulimic patients (79%) described regular premorbid sexual activity; four later became sexually inactive while bulimic. While three patients reported no sexual activity, two of them were only 16 years old and described having sexual fantasies and/or girlfriends. Male bulimics presenting at the EDU were also more likely to report current regular sexual activity than male anorexics. More than half (54%) of the 24 bulimic patients aged 18 or older were actively involved in a sexual relationship at presentation, compared to 14% (2/14) of the anorexics. Similarly, more anorexics than bulimics had never had a serious sexual relationship and were not interested in developing one; 64% of the anorexics (n=9) fell into this group, while only 20% (n=5) of the bulimics did. No differences existed between the groups in terms of age at presentation.

Outcome of male anorexia nervosa has been shown to be significantly associated with frequency of premorbid sexual activity. Burns and Crisp (1984, 1985) found that absent or minimal premorbid sexual fantasy and activity (predominantly masturbation and flirting) were associated with poor outcome. Moreover, at follow-up, only two of the 16 patients with stable weights of at least 85% of matched population mean weight (MPMW) were not sexually active. The eight patients with complete "absence of sexual feelings" were all underweight.

These reports indicate that anorexia nervosa is associated with sexual inactivity. However, it is not clear to what extent morbid sexual inactivity is fueled by sexual conflicts that give rise to anorexia nervosa and to what extent it is a response to the starvation state. We will first discuss possible premorbid sexual precipitants and then turn to a review of endocrine studies.

GENDER DYSPHORIA AND HOMOSEXUALITY

Conflict over gender identity or over sexual orientation may precipitate the development of an eating disorder in many males. Crisp (1983) originally observed that gender identity uncertainty was frequently present at the commencement of anorexia nervosa in males. In his experience with 40 male patients, men "develop shape consciousness either within this context [uncertainty in gender identity] or else within massive adolescent obesity" (p. 25). Crisp has since modified this view, concluding that eating-disordered males are no more confused about their gender identity than women with these disorders (Burns & Crisp, 1985). Hasan and Tibbetts (1977) noted that their male anorexic patients exhibited a "notable lack of assertive masculinity or identification" with other males, and concluded that fear of "manhood, with particular reference to the heterosexual role" (p. 151), formed a noteworthy feature of anorexia nervosa in males.

Fichter and Daser (1987) suggested the very low ("superfeminine") scores obtained by their sample of anorexic males on the "masculinity-femininity" scale of the Freiburger Personality Inventory indicated disturbed gender identity development.* Interviews with these patients revealed that they saw themselves and were seen by others as more feminine than other men, both in attitudes and behavior. Many indicated that as children they had preferred traditionally feminine activities to games favored by boys (65%), and four (20%) would have rather been girls. In general the patients appeared to identify more closely with their mothers than with their fathers. Using a semantic differential test design, the investigators asked patients to rate

---

*The items contributing to the "femininity" factor of the Freiburger Inventory are: "reserved-ness, shyness, inhibition, depressed mood, timidity, low self-esteem, somatic and psychosomatic disturbances, dizziness, constipation, irritability and sensitivity to changes in weather" (Fichter and Daser, personal communication). While these items may represent stereotypic manifestations of distress in females, it is unclear why they should be considered "feminine" per se.

themselves, their mothers, and their fathers on a 16-trait, bipolarity scale. The patients rated themselves as more similar to their mothers than to their fathers on most items, especially on being "sad," "guilty," and "soft." Several patients stated that they saw themselves as similar to their mothers in emotional expression, sensitivity, and moodiness. Although this study indicates patients identified with their mothers, the connection between a strong maternal identification and conflicted gender identity is not one that can simply be assumed. Further data are needed before such a link can be supported. Additional studies might also examine the relationship between maternal identification and eating disorders, independent of gender identity.

Several eating-disordered males evaluated at the EDU also expressed gender conflicts. For example, one stated during evaluation he wished he were a woman and another desired to be a lesbian in order to "be a woman but still make love to a woman." In the experience of the Johns Hopkins Eating Disorders Unit, adolescent males tend to present with gender dysphoria, while older males manifest more work-related conflicts (Andersen, personal communication).

Although cross-gender behavior and atypical gender identity in childhood do not necessarily lead to homosexual orientation in adulthood, several reports show an association between them (Green, 1985). Several authors have noted that homosexual conflict preceded the onset of the eating disorder in up to 50% of male patients (Crisp, 1967; Dally, 1969; Crisp & Toms, 1972; cf. Scott, 1986). One of Burns and Crisp's (1984) anorexic patients avoided sexual activity because of ego-dystonic homosexuality, and two bulimic patients in the EDU reported that their eating disorders developed around the time they began to think of themselves as homosexual.

Homosexuals are also overrepresented in many samples of eating disordered men. While the proportion of male homosexuals in the general population crossculturally is estimated to be 3%-5% (Whitam, 1983), samples of eating-disordered men are commonly twice as high or greater. One of Langdon-Brown's (1931) four male anorexic patients was homosexual. Two of Dally's (1969) patients had "homosexual features," as did one patient of Hasan and Tibbetts (1977). Five of 20 (25%) of Fichter and Daser's (1987) male patients reported having had homosexual contacts, leading the authors to conclude that "homosexual tendencies" were common among male anorexics. One-third of a sample of nine male bulimics was homosexual (Robinson and Holden, 1986).

Another study that matched male and female bulimics on age, duration of illness, and frequency of self-induced vomiting, found that eight of 15 (53%) males were homosexual or bisexual, compared to none of the women

TABLE 1

Percentage of Males with Homosexual Orientation

Anorexia Nervosa	
Dally (1969)	33% (n = 6)
Fichter & Daser (1987)	25% (n = 20)
Hasan & Tibbetts (1977)	17% (n = 6)
Herzog et al. (1984)	15% (n = 13)
Langdon-Brown (1931)	25% (n = 4)
Bulimia Nervosa	
Dunkeld Turnbull et al. (1987)	0% (n = 5)
Hall, Delahunt, & Ellis (1985)	0% (n = 9)
Herzog et al. (1984)	50% (n = 14)
Pope, Hudson, & Jonas (1986)	7% (n = 14)
Robinson & Holden (1986)	33% (n = 9)
Schneider & Agras (1987)	27% (n = 15)

(Schneider & Agras, 1987). Significantly more anorexic and bulimic males presenting to the EDU several years ago were homosexually oriented than eating-disordered females (Herzog et al., 1984). A recent record review of 44 males 18 years of age and older who presented for evaluation at the EDU (including males from the previously published study who were more than 18 years old) revealed that 13 (30%) identified themselves as homosexual and two (4%) as bisexual. All but one of these patients were diagnosed as having bulimia nervosa.

These findings suggest that homosexuality is common in males with eating disorders. However, clinic samples may underrepresent heterosexual men, who may be more reluctant than homosexual men to seek help for what are popularly considered female disorders. At the EDU, for example, 67% of the male homosexual patients were self-referred, compared to 29% of the heterosexual patients. Other studies have failed to find a similar high prevalence of homosexuality in their male patients. None of Hall et al.'s (1985) nine male anorexics or Dunkeld Turnbull et al.'s (1987) five bulimic patients were homosexual, and only one of Pope et al.'s (1986) 14 male bulimics was homosexual. Homosexual men may also be overrepresented in most psychiatric populations. Nonetheless, the fact that so many samples included sizeable proportions of homosexuals stimulated exploration of the relationship between eating disorders and male homosexuality, an association that is particularly intriguing in light of the infrequent reports of homosexuality in the female eating-disordered population.

Crisp (1970) has suggested that conflict over homosexual feelings in male eating-disordered patients plays a role comparable to that of heterosexual conflict in female patients. By reducing their sexual drive through starvation, patients can temporarily resolve their sexual conflicts. Indeed, many eating-disordered males appear to view their homosexual orientation disfavorably. Fichter and Daser (1987) reported that of the five patients in their study who had experienced homosexual contacts, only one viewed this experience positively. Another patient was relieved by his lowered sex drive because of concerns over his possible homosexuality (Burns & Crisp, 1984). For some of the EDU patients, both the homosexual and eating-disordered behaviors are experienced as shameful, repugnant, and essentially unwilling compulsions.

While some patients have a stable homoerotic orientation, some—particularly adolescent patients—fleetingly engage in homosexual behaviors. For these patients, homosexual activity may represent sexual experimentation or a way of "acting out." One EDU patient presented his promiscuous homosexual behavior, as well as his bulimia, in rebellious terms, as a way of wresting control away from his overbearing parents. Future studies should attempt to distinguish between sexual behavior and sexual identity in these men.

THE ROLE OF THE FAMILY

Some researchers have associated specific family dynamics with gender conflicts or homosexual preference in males with eating disorders, although the data to support this are scanty. Many anorexic males were raised in families with poor parent-child relationships similar to what has been described in the literature for some male homosexuals. Distant or hostile relationships between fathers and sons have been described for anorexics (Dally, 1969) and homosexuals (Freund & Blanchard, 1983). In the EDU sample, homosexual men generally reported worse familial relationships than heterosexual men. Eight of 10 homosexual patients on whom family biographies were available described histories of early family trauma, including sexual or physical abuse, abandonment, or death of an important relative. Another suffered from sexual abuse by schoolmates.

In contrast, none of the 30 heterosexual male patients with family history records reported abandonment or abuse during childhood or early adolescence. Perhaps not surprisingly, the heterosexual group also reported more positive feelings toward their fathers than the homosexuals: 12 of the heterosexual patients (40%) felt close to their fathers, while only one (10%) of the homosexual men did.

Fichter and Daser's (1987) anorexic patients also experienced poor or nonexistent relationships with their fathers. Nearly one-third did not live with their fathers while growing up and the death rate for these fathers of sons younger than 15 was twice that of a community sample. Those fathers who remained with the patients' families often played peripheral roles and marital conflict was common.

Some clinicians have observed that homosexual male patients have close relationships with domineering, overprotective mothers (Bieber et al., 1962; Thompson et al., 1973), although this finding has not been convincingly documented in the general homosexual population (Freund & Blanchard, 1983). Some families of male eating-disordered patients also demonstrate the same pattern, leading to speculation regarding the association between this mother-child constellation and a son's eating disorder. Crisp and Toms (1972) proposed that their male anorexic patients, most of whom had been overprotected and overnurtured in childhood, were ill-equipped to handle the demands of maturation and turned to "nurturant means" to meet their growing pains. Fichter and Daser (1987) observed that the "close and intimate relationship" exhibited by most of their male anorexics and their mothers would lead to a "symbiotic family network" in the absence of a strong paternal presence, and is suggestive of gender identity disturbance. At this point, the connection between family dynamics and a son developing an eating disorder and homoerotic orientation is highly speculative.

SOCIOCULTURAL FACTORS

Homosexual men may be at an increased risk for developing an eating disorder because of cultural pressures within the homosexual community to be thin (Schneider & Agras, 1987). Yager and colleagues (1988) found that male homosexual college students reported higher prevalences of bulimic behaviors and fears of weight gain than did a control group of college men. The homosexual men also scored higher on many Eating Disorder Inventory scales (Garner et al., 1983).

In order to determine if there exists greater concern about a thin shape and low weight among homosexual men compared to heterosexual men, we investigated differences in standards of current and ideal weight and body satisfaction between these two groups. Our non-clinical, community-wide sample consisted of 43 homosexual and 32 heterosexual men between the ages of 18 and 35. Based on their answers to a self-report questionnaire and selected figure drawings,* we found that the homosexual men weighed significantly less than the heterosexual men, and were more likely to be underweight and to desire an underweight ideal weight (based on Metropolitan Life Tables, 1983). Compared to the heterosexuals, homosexual men

---

*These drawings are based on those used by Fallon and Rozin (1985).

were less satisfied with their body build and, like Yager et al.'s subjects, scored significantly higher on the "Drive for Thinness" scale of the Eating Disorders Inventory. "Drive for Thinness" was negatively correlated with masculinity (Bem, 1974, 1981) and with self-esteem (Rosenberg, 1965) for homosexual subjects.

The finding that a non-clinical sample of homosexual men was underweight and considered a thin figure ideal supports the notion that "gay" male culture places greater value on men being slender than does "straight" culture. That the homosexual men were also more dissatisfied with their bodies than their heterosexual counterparts suggests a motivational factor for developing an eating disorder that may be different from, and place them at higher risk than, other men.

It is interesting to note in this context that more male homosexual patients at the EDU were premorbidly obese than male heterosexuals, and that on average they weighed significantly more. Perhaps, as with female patients, the homosexual men feel increased pressure to slim down as their weight deviates more markedly from what is culturally valued, and this pressure contributes to the etiology of their eating disorder.

As it does with so many women, dissatisfaction with appearance may be a salient theme in puberty with homosexual men. In a retrospective study, Prytula et al. (1979) found that homosexual men recalled greater dissatisfaction with their general physical characteristics, body image, and self-concept during their adolescence than did heterosexual males. The authors propose that early negative feedback on body characteristics from peers and/or family may be involved in the development of a homosexual preference. These factors may also predispose an individual to develop an eating disorder. It is also likely that homosexual youths internalize pejorative social messages about homosexuality, thus contributing to a negative self-image.

The findings presented indicate that psychosexual and gender identity conflicts, as well as sociocultural pressures for homosexuals, may contribute to the development of eating disorders in men. We turn now to biological studies that outline the physical complications of eating disorders on the sexual system.

ENDOCRINE DYSFUNCTION

The lack of sexual interest and the diminution of sexual functioning in males during the acute phase of anorexia nervvosa may be attributable, in part, to an endocrine dysfunction analogous to that underlying amenorrhea in females (Beaumont et al., 1972). little is known about the reproductive hormone profile in male anorexics, as few endocrine studies have been reported and all have been hampered by small sample sizes. Most studies have examined the reduction in gonadotropin secretion in male patients, analogous to the hypogonadotropic hypogonadism observed in female patients.

Beumont et al. (1972) found that the output of urinary testosterone in six anorexic patients prior to refeeding was significantly below the normal range. All but one of the patients had reported a marked reduction in libido duringthe illness, often with the cessation of masturbation and disappearance of morning erections. Serial sampling showed testosterone output increased with weight gain. However, patients' weights and testosterone output both remained below normal levels two months after the commencement of the study. Thus, it is unclear whether reduced urinary testosterone levels return to normal following a full return to normal weight.

Total pituitary gonadotropin activity (TGA) was measured in three patients in Beumont et al.'s study and serial estimations were performed on two. TGA decreased when body weight was low, but rose on refeeding, although it still fell below normal values. However, these abnormalities of gonadotropin secretion have also been observed in simple starvation (Copeland, 1985), making it difficult to establish whether such disturbances are not simply due to malnutrition.

Results similar to those of Beumont et al. have been reported by Lemaire et al. (1983), who found that plasma testosterone and serum follicle stimulating hormone (FSH) concentrations were significantly lower in eight anorexic males at the time of maximum weight loss than in a control group of aged-matched males. Serum luteinizing hormone (LH) concentrations were lower in four. Lemaire et al. also examined gonadotropin response to luteinizing hormone-releasing hormone (LHRH) and observed that in four of the five patients there was no gonadotropin response to the infusion. In the fifth patient, the heaviest in the sample, basal concentration of LH and its response to LHRH were normal, but basal concentration of FSH and its response to LHRH were decreased. As patients' weights rose from 70% to 80% MPMW, plasma testosterone and serum gonadotropins and their response to LHRH increased. Increases in serum testosterone concentrations correlated significantly with weight gain.

Initially low concentrations of plasma testosterone and serum LH levels have been found to increase significantly with weight to reach that of matched population mean concentrations in 12 male anorexics (Crisp, Hsu, et al., 1982). Testosterone concentrations at target weight, however, were still below normal in some subjects. LH response to LHRH was absent at low body weight, enhanced at a transitional early/mid-pubertal body weight, and normal at the newly restored adult body weight. Unlike Lemaire's study, however, FSH response to LHRH in this series was retained even at very low weights and serum FSH was not correlated with body weight. Crisp et al. propose that the hyper-response of LH, occurring at approximately 45 kg, was due to the relative lack of negative feedback caused by low circulatory testosterone concentrations and is related more to actual weight than to the MPMW of an individual. This hyper-response of LH to LHRH at intermediate low weights has also been observed in females (Sherman et al., 1975).

Lemaire et al. suggest that malnutrition and weight loss alone cannot explain the decrease of testosterone in all cases and that specific hypothalamic anomalies may exist independently of malnutrition. They observed that two patients' plasma testosterone concentrations remained low even when weight was normalized and in three others testosterone concentrations decreased again despite weight being greater than 90% of MPMW. The researchers propose that the psychological features of anorexia nervosa may explain some of the decrease in testicular steroid output in their patients.

A similar process in females is manifested in a delayed recovery of menses. These women may persist in abnormal eating behavior despite maintenance of body weight (Falk & Halmi, 1982), which may explain the delayed response in men as well. Lemaire et al. also suggest that patients whose weight loss begins in adulthood may have hypothalamic pituitary centers more resistant to undernutrition than those whose weight loss begins during puberty. This hypothesis was based on the results of one late-onset patient who showed only very mild hormonal anomalies despite emaciation comparable to the others in the series.

Thus, it appears that in male anorexics total gonadotrophins are decreased, with serum LH perhaps more affected than FSH, suggesting that decreased pituitary stimulation leads to decreased output of testosterone. Although the search is ongoing for biological markers for these disorders, the bulk of the literature to date suggests that the endocrinological disturbances noted in males are secondary to the disordered eating and weight loss, and normalize upon weight gain and stabilization of dietary pattern.

CONCLUSIONS

The literature on eating-disordered males points out that sexual issues are important in the evaluation and treatment of these patients. While there is no one pattern that characterizes the sexual activity of eating-disordered men, the data show several trends. Males, especially those who develop anorexia nervosa, report limited promorbid sexual interest and experience, a high degree of sexual anxiety, and aversion towards sexual relationships. Positive outcome in male anorexics is associated with regular sexual activity pre-morbidly and at follow-up.

The conflicts around gender identity and sexual orientation that many patients exhibit may precipitate their eating disorders. Homosexual men appear to be at increased risk for developing eating disorders, at least in part due to sociocultural pressures and internalized negative body image. Eating-disordered men have endocrine abnormalities similar to those of eating-disordered women, with lowered concentrations of gonadotrophins. As with female patients, it remains unclear as to what extent the sexual conflict of these men propels the loss of sexual drive noted in these patients, and to what extent the sexual disinterest is the consequence of undernutrition and a disruptive diet.

The question asked most frequently about eating disorders is: Why are they so much more common in women than in men? The most obvious answer is that women face greater pressures to be thin than do men. Preliminary research indicates that homosexual men feel similar cultural pressures toward slenderness. Future research should attempt to outline features common to both at-risk groups. It is also worth exploring why there are so few female homosexuals in study populations. Have studies simply not addressed female sexual orientation, or are lesbians reluctant to utilize traditional therapeutic settings, thereby skewing clinic samples? An alternate explanation is that homosexual women are protected against developing eating disorders. Future studies should also address gender dysphoria in eating-disordered men. Insight into gender conflicts in these patients may explain why some men are vulnerable to these disorders and aid in their evaluation and treatment.

REFERENCES

Bem, S. L. (1974). The measurement of psychological androgyny. *Journal of Consulting and Clinical Psychology, 42*, 155-162.

Bem, S. L. (1981). *The Bem Sex Role Professional Manual*. Palo Alto, CA: Consulting Psychologists Press.

Beumont, P. J. V., Beardwood, C. J., & Russell, G. F. (1972). The occurrence of the syndrome of anorexia nervosa in male subjects. *Psychological Medicine, 2*, 216-231.

Bieber, I., Dain, H., Dince, P., Drellich, M., Grand, H., Gundlach, R., Kremer, M., Rifkin, A., Wilbur, C., & Bieber, T. (1962). *Homosexuality: A Psychoanalytic Study*. New York: Basic Books.

Burns, T. & Crisp, A. H. (1984). Outcome of anorexia nervosa in males. *British Journal of Psychiatry, 145*, 319-325.

Burns, T. & Crisp, A. H. (1985). Factors affecting prognosis in male anorexics. *Journal of Psychiatric Research, 19*, 323-328.

Copeland, P. M. (1985). Neuroendocrine aspects of eating disorders. In S. W. Emmett (Ed.), *Theory and Treatment of Anorexia Nervosa and Bulimia: Biomedical, Sociocultural, and Psychological Perspectives* (pp. 51-72). New York: Brunner/Mazel.

Crisp, A. H. (1967). Anorexia Nervosa. *Hospital Medicine, 1*, 713-718.

Crisp, A. H. (1970). Anorexia, nervosa, "feeding disorder," "nervous malnutrition," or "weight phobia"? *World Review of Nutrition and Dietetics, 12*, 452-504.

Crisp, A. H. (1983). Some aspects of the psychopathology of anorexia nervosa. In P. L. Darby, P. E. Garfinkel, D. M. Garner, & D. C. Coscina (Eds.), *Anorexia Nervosa: Recent Developments in Research* (pp. 15-28). New York: Alan Liss.

Crisp, A. H., & Burns, T. (1983). The clinical presentation of anorexia nervosa in males. *International Journal of Eating Disorders, 2*, 5-10.

Crisp, A. H., Burns, T., & Bhat, A. V. (1986). Primary anorexia nervosa in the male and female: A comparison of clinical features and prognosis. *British Journal of Medical Psychology, 59*, 123-132.

Crisp, A. H., Hsu, L. S., Chen, C. N., & Wheeler, M. (1982). Reproductive hormone profiles in male anorexia nervosa before, during and after restoration of body weight to normal. *International Journal of Eating Disorders, 1*, 3-9.

Crisp, A. H. & Toms, D. A. (1972). Primary anorexia nervosa or weight phobia in the male: Report on 13 cases. *British Medical Journal, 1*, 334-338.

Dally, P. (1969). *Anorexia Nervosa*. London: Heinemann Medical Books.

Dunkeld Turnbull, J., Freeman, C. P. L., & Annandale, A. (1987). Physical and psychological characteristics of five male bulimics. *British Journal of Psychiatry, 150*, 25-29.

Falk, J. R. & Halmi K. A. (1982). Amenorrhea in anorexia nervosa: Examination of the critical body weight hypothesis. *Biological Psychiatry, 17*, 799-806.

Fallon, A. E. & Rozin, P. (1985). Sex differences in the perceptions of desirable body shape. *Journal of Abnormal Psychology, 94*, 102-105.

Falstein, E. J., Feinstein, S. C., & Judas, I. (1956). Anorexia nervosa in the male child. *American Journal of Orthopsychiatry, 26*, 751-772.

Fichter, M. M. (1985). *Magersucht und Bulimia*. Springer Verlag: Heidelberg, New York.

Fichter, M. M., & Daser, C. (1987). Symptomatology, psychosexual development and gender identity in 42 anorexic males. *Psychological Medicine, 17*, 409-418.

Freund, K. & Blanchard, R. (1983). Is the distant relationship of fathers and homosexual sons related to the sons' erotic preference for male partners or to the sons' atypical gender identity or to both? *Journal of Homosexuality*, 7-25.

Garner, D. M., Olmstead, M. P., & Polivy, J. (1983). Development and validation of a multi-dimensional Eating Disorder Inventory for anorexia nervosa and bulimia. *International Journal of Eating Disorders, 2*, 15-34.

Green, R. (1985). Gender identity in childhood and later sexual orientation: Follow-up of 78 males. *American Journal of Psychiatry, 142*, 339-341.

Hall, A., Delahunt, J. W., & Ellis, P. M. (1985). Anorexia nervosa in the male:

Clinical features and follow-up of nine patients. *Journal of Psychiatric Research, 19*, 315-321.

Hasan, M. K. & Tibbetts, R. W. (1977). Primary anorexia nervosa (weight phobia) in males. *Postgraduate Medical Journal, 53*, 146-151.

Herzog, D. B., Norman, D. K., Gordon, C., & Pepose, M. (1984). Sexual conflict and eating disorders in 27 males. *American Journal of Psychiatry, 141*, 989-990.

Langdon-Brown, W. (1931). *Anorexia Nervosa*. Individual Psychological Publications, Medical Pamphlet 2.

Lemaire, A., Ardaens, K., Lepretre, J., Racadot, A., Buvat-Herbaut, M., & Buvat, J. (1983). Gonadal hormones in male anorexia nervosa. *International Journal of Eating Disorders, 2*, 135-144.

Margo, J. L. (1987). Anorexia nervosa in males: A comparison with female patients. *British Journal of Psychiatry*, 151, 80-83.

Metropolitan Life Insurance Company. (1983). Height and weight tables. *Statistical Bulletin, 41*, 3-5.

Pope, H. G., Hudson, J. I., & Jonal, J. M. (1986). Bulimia in men: A series of fifteen cases. *Journal of Nervous and Mental Disease, 174*, 117-119.

Prytula, R. E., Wellford, C. D., DeMonbreun, B. G. (1979). Body self-image and homosexuality. *Journal of Clinical Psychology, 35*, 567-572.

Robinson, P. H. & Holden, N. L. (1986). Bulimia nervosa in the male: A report of nine cases. *Psychological Medicine, 16*, 795-803.

Rosenberg, M. (1965). *Society and the Adolescent Self-Image*. Princeton University Press.

Russell, G. F. M. (1979). Bulimia nervosa: An ominous variant of anorexia nervosa. *Psychological Medicine, 9*, 429-448.

Schneider, J. A., & Agras, W. S. (1987). Bulimia in males: A matched comparison with females. *International Journal of Eating Disorders, 6*, 235-242.

Scott, D. W. (1986). Anorexia nervosa in the male: A review of the clinical, epidemiological and biological findings. *International Journal of Eating Disorders, 5*, 799-819.

Sherman D. M., Halmi K. A., & Zamudio R. (1975). LH and FSH response to gonadotropin-releasing hormone in anorexia nervosa: Effect of nutritional rehabilitation. *Journal of Clinical Endocrinology Metabolism, 41*, 135-142.

Sterling, J. W. & Segal, J. D. (1985). Anorexia nervosa in males: A critical review. *International Journal of Eating Disorders, 4*, 559-572.

Thompson, N. L., Schwartz, D. M., McCandless, B. R., & Edwards, D. A. (1973). Parent-child relationships and sexual identity in male and female homosexuals and heterosexuals. *Journal of Consulting and Clinical Psychology, 41*, 120-127.

Whitam, F. L. (1983). Culturally invariable properties of male homosexuality: Tentative conclusions from cross-cultural research. *Archives of Sexual Behavior, 12*, 207-226.

Yager, J., Kurtzman, F., Landsverk, J., & Wiesmeier, E. (1988). Behaviors and attitudes related to eating disorders in homosexual male college students. *American Journal of Psychiatry, 145*, 495-497.

5

Men, Body Image, and Eating Disorders

Ann Kearney-Cooke
and Paule Steichen-Asch

That the earliest human experience is somatic is a widely held view in the literature on body image, psychosexual, and psychosocial development (Chodorow, 1978; Erikson, 1950; Freud, 1933; Greenacre, 1958; Kestenberg, 1975; Piaget, 1954; Schilder, 1950). These theorists generally agree that body image, a cognitive construct, forms as the infant becomes capable of distinguishing and integrating sensations. The body image is particularly complex because it appears to include surface, depth, and postural pictures of the body as well as the attitudes, emotions, and personality reactions of individuals to their bodies (Kolb, 1959). In addition, it incorporates cultural attitudes.

Body image is crucial to the early personality formation in the child, especially to the differentiation of the self from the world, as the sense of body boundaries is formed. Because the body is the only object in a person's perceptual field which simultaneously is perceived and is part of oneself, theorists have proposed an equation between body feelings and personality patterns (Fisher, 1966; Schilder, 1935). The unique closeness of the in-

The first author would like to thank (1) Paule Steichen-Asch, Ph.D. for analyzing the data and writing the results section of this chapter, (2) Len Lansky, Ph.D. (University of Cincinnati), for consulting on the data analysis, in particular advising on splitting the normal sample to normals and at-risk men, and (3) Mala Matacin, M.A. for assistance in collecting the data and Nancy Cooper, M.A. for coding the data.

dividual's body to his identity maximizes the likelihood that it reflects and shares his most important preoccupations. Fisher (1966) states that the body, like all significant objects, can become a convenient "screen" on which one projects one's most intense concerns.

Disturbance of body image is a multidimensional phenomenon, including such issues as distortion of body size, dissatisfaction with body size, concern with body shape, and insensitivity to introceptive cues (Cooper & Taylor, in press; Garner & Garfinkel, 1981). The purpose of this chapter is to identify the body image concerns of men and to discuss the ways in which personality development and body image development may interact to leave a male at risk for concerns about body shape and for an eating disorder. We will also suggest treatments which might address these issues. In particular, we will address the following questions: Do male eating-disordered patients suffer body image disturbance? If they do so, what is the nature of the disturbance? How do normal, noneating-disordered college men feel about their bodies? What factors in demography, body image history, and personality structure might predispose a man to develop an eating disorder? What factors in development seem to leave some men vulnerable about their bodies? Why do many men aspire to a full-chested, lean-waisted look while others attempt to make their bodies thin?

The answers to these questions will come in part from a study of 16 men with eating disorders and 112 male college students. The remainder of this chapter consists of a description of the research study, discussion of research findings, and recommendations for treatment. We end with a summary and some suggestions for future research.

DESCRIPTION OF RESEARCH STUDY

Subjects

The noneating-disordered group comprised 112 male college students from introductory psychology courses in a university in the Midwest. The average age of the subjects was 20.3 years (range 17 to 37). Participants were predominantly single (97%) and white (89%). Forty-four percent were raised Catholic, 30% Protestant, and 2% Jewish; 10% had no religious training. Participation was voluntary, although subjects received class credit.

The 112 college men were divided into two groups: the "at-risk" group (n = 28), those men with scores on the Body Shape Questionnaire that were within the range of the eating-disordered patients' scores, and the "normal" group (n = 84), those who scored below the lowest of the eating-disordered patients' scores on the same test.

The 16 males who made up the clinical sample were recruited from clinicians who treat eating disorders in private practice, support groups, or hospital programs. To be included in the study, a patient had to meet the minimal criteria for diagnosis of anorexia or bulimia as established by the Diagnostic and Statistical Manual of Mental Disorders (DSM-III, American Psychiatric Association, 1980). As documentation of these symptoms, it was shown later that each participant had scored above 30 on the Eating Attitudes Test (EAT), the clinical level for eating disorders set by Garner and Garfinkel (1980).

The average age of the clinical group was 27.4 (range 15 to 51). Subjects were all single and white. They were reared in the Catholic (19%), Protestant (50%), or Jewish (25%) religion.

Instruments

The Eating Attitudes Test (EAT), which measures abnormal eating attitudes and behavior, is a 40-item scale in which subjects are asked to respond to a variety of questions related to eating and dieting behaviors. Items on the EAT are rated on a six-point frequency scale ranging from always to never. Scores above 30 are considered in the clinical range (Garner & Garfinkel, 1980).

The Body Shape Questionnaire (BSQ) is a self-report measure of concerns about body shape, particularly the phenomenal experience of "feeling fat." The items which constitute the measure were derived by conducting semistructured interviews among various groups of women, including patients with anorexia and bulimia. The concurrent and discriminant validity of the measure has been shown to be good. The BSQ is a 34-question scale that uses a one to six scoring system ("never" = 1; "always" = 6). The mean score for females struggling with bulimia was 136.9 (SD = 22.5) (Cooper, Taylor, Cooper, & Fairburn, 1987). For this study we changed the gender where appropriate. Item 9, for example, was changed from "Has being with thin women made you feel self-conscious about your shape?" to "Has being with thin men made you feel self-conscious about your shape?"

The Millon Clinical Multiaxial Inventory (MCMI) is a 175-item inventory based on Millon's theory of personality (Millon, 1969, 1981). It was also developed to parallel and complement the DSM-III diagnostic system. The MCMI has 20 scales; the first eight assess personality styles or traits, the next three assess more pathological personality patterns, and the last nine address issues of clinical symptomatology. Scores on the MCMI are reported as base rate (BR) scores, which are transformed scores designed to maximize correct diagnostic classification by optimizing valid-positive to false-positive ratios. A BR score of 75 indicates that a particular trait is likely to be present, while a BR score of 35 represents the median score of a normal or nonclinical group (Millon, 1982).

The demographic questionnaire was designed by the first author to examine body image history. It included questions about memories of parents' attitudes towards their own and the subject's body, peers' reactions to bodies, importance of relationships, preferred body shape for men and for women, and earliest memory of feeling shame about the body. The open-ended answers were classified in categories and coded.

Procedure

The noneating-disordered group of subjects was recruited through the subject pool of the University of Cincinnati's Psychology Department. During the first week of classes, we made a standard announcement soliciting participation in an experiment on body image for males. After students signed up, they met with the research assistant in a large group testing session. They were asked to fill out a demographic questionnaire and instruments asking questions about body image, eating disorders, and personality patterns. After completing the tests in the research packet, the students were told that they could receive the results of the study if they wished.

For the clinical population, patients were recruited through individual therapists, support groups, and hospital units specializing in the treatment of eating disorders. After the clinician determined that a male patient met the diagnostic criteria for an eating disorder, the therapist gave the patient the research packet to fill out. The completed packet then was forwarded to the first author to be coded for research.

RESULTS

Concerns of Contemporary Men: Summary of Responses to Open-Ended Questions

With regard to body parts of which one is ashamed, the response given by most men in all three groups was "stomach, gut, belly," followed by "upper and lower extremities."

In regard to the ideal male body shape for contemporary men, the normal group (Group 1) and the at-risk group (Group 2) most often gave the response "muscular, strong, and broad shoulders." By contrast, the men with eating disorders (Group 3) most often described the "lean, toned, thin" shape as their ideal.

In regard to the ideal female body shape, the response given most often by all three groups was "thin, slim, slightly underweight." In the normal and the at-risk group, the next most frequent response was "shapely, well-proportioned." For men with eating disorders, however, the second most popular response was "big breasts, voluptuous, or firm and solid."

Analysis of Variances

A group of analyses of variance was computed comparing normal, at-risk, and eating-disordered men on the following variables. Table 1 summarizes the results.

On parental variables, the groups showed no differences with regard to father's positive attitude toward his own body. For two other variables, however—amount of contact with father and closeness to parents—we noted significant differences among the three groups; the means were most normal for Group 1 and least normal for Group 3.

On variables related to peers' reactions to their bodies, we found significant differences among the three groups in the directions expected. Men struggling with eating disorders (Group 3) reported that they were teased more about their bodies while growing up and were preferred less for athletic teams. Their sexual preferences included homosexuality and bisexuality, whereas all the subjects in Groups 1 and 2 reported being heterosexual.

On the variable related to body satisfaction, there was a significant difference among the three groups in the expected direction. Results were also as expected for the summary score on the Eating Attitudes Test: men in Group 3 scored the highest.

Table 2 presents the results of the personality variables data. It displays the mean base rate (BR) scores for the MCMI from the three groups. Base rate scores are obtained by transforming raw scores to reflect known personality and syndrome prevalence rates (Millon, 1982). For general interpretive purposes, a BR score of 75 or more identifies the presence of a trait or disorder. F-ratios are displayed in Table 2.

For the basic personality pattern scales, with the exception of compulsive, all results were highly significant in the expected direction. Group 1 (normal) scored highest on histrionic/gregarious, narcissistic, and antisocial/aggressive. Group 3 (eating-disordered men) scored highest on avoidant, dependent, and passive-aggressive.

TABLE 1

Analysis of Variance for Three Groups: Normal Controls, At-Risk Males, and Eating-Disordered Males Parental Variables, Peers' Reactions, and Body Satisfaction

	Normal Mean Std.Dev.		At Risk Mean Std.Dev.		Eating-Disordered Mean Std.Dev.		Statistical Significance	
Parental Variables								
Father's Body Feelings	1.35	.48	1.41	.50	1.40	.51	.15	NS
Mother's Body Feeling	1.44	.50	1.74	.45	1.62	.50	4.06	<.05
Attention to Body-Child	1.56	.50	1.22	.42	1.44	.51	5.12	<.01
Contact With Father	2.34	1.08	2.33	1.00	2.69	1.78	2.88	NS
Closeness to Parents	2.02	1.09	2.63	.74	2.88	.81	7.63	<.001
Peers' Reaction								
Teasing as Child	1.55	.50	1.41	.50	1.19	.40	4.56	<.01
Negative Attitude Toward Body	4.93	2.45	3.81	1.98	3.31	2.33	3.15	<.05
Chosen for Athletic Teams	1.74	.73	1.89	.85	2.69	.60		
Sexual Preference	1.12	.77	1.41	1.22	1.62	1.20	2.67	NS
Body Satisfaction								
Weight Perception	2.87	.60	3.44	.70	3.12	.89	8.47	<.001
Body Dissatisfaction	2.16	.72	2.85	.99	3.88	.96	25.54	<.001

TABLE 2

Analysis of Variance for Three Groups: Basic Personality Pattern and Pathological Personality Disorder

Item	Normals Group 1 (N = 84)		At Risk Group 2 (N = 27)		Bulimics Group 3 (N = 16)		F	p
	Mean	Std.Dev.	Mean	Std.Dev.	Mean	Std.Dev.		
Basic Personality Pattern								
Schizoid	32.19	22.31	42.38	28.29	59.53	33.09	8.60	<.001
Avoidant	34.42	24.01	48.50	28.09	71.47	28.85	14.48	<.001
Dependent	46.08	26.10	61.38	31.67	73.13	31.30	7.58	<.001
Histrionic	72.65	17.83	69.85	24.51	52.40	31.78	5.71	<.005
Narcissistic	72.59	17.13	66.50	22.83	50.93	22.18	8.42	<.001
Antisocial	67.30	19.70	63.88	24.78	44.87	24.27	6.98	<.001
Compulsive	56.54	14.28	54.54	17.67	54.87	11.44	.27	NS
Passive Aggressive	45.54	23.24	57.04	24.28	67.33	18.76	7.00	<.001
Pathological Personality Disorder								
Schizotypal	40.93	16.36	46.65	19.92	60.07	17.02	8.10	<.001
Borderline	48.32	16.90	53.69	13.90	60.67	9.82	4.46	<.01
Paranoid	62.69	14.21	63.92	17.29	54.47	16.69	2.14	NS

Note: High score means high syndrome. A score of 75 or more is interpreted as pathological.

Discriminant Analysis Among Normal, At-Risk, and Bulimic Men

We used a multiple discriminant function to determine whether selected variables were effective in discriminating among the normal, at-risk, and bulimic men. For obvious reasons, the Eating Attitudes Test and body dissatisfaction were not considered as predictors.

Variables were selected on the following grounds: (1) we believed that a limited number of predictors should be used because Group 3 contained only 16 cases; (2) the variables which were selected were highly significant in the preceding analysis of variance; and (3) variables were selected so as to represent dimensions mentioned earlier, namely family, peers, and personality.

In the analysis among the three groups (see Table 3), seven variables were

TABLE 3

**Discriminant Analysis Using Seven Items
as Discriminating Variables Among Normal,
At Risk, and Bulimic Men**

Canonical Discriminant Functions

Function	Eigenvalue	% of Variance	Cum. %	Canon. Correl.	X^2	DF	Sign
1	.47	91.12	91.12	.56	50.63	14	.0001
2	.05	8.88	100	.21	5.27	6	NS

**Canonical Discriminant Functions
Evaluated at Group Means (Group Centroids)**

Group	Function 1	Function 2
Normal	−.42	−.07
At Risk	.43	.39
Bulimic	1.57	−.29

Classification Table

		Predicted Group Membership		
Actual Group Cases		Normal	At Risk	Bulimic
Normal	83	66.3%	22.9%	10.8%
At Risk	26	26.9%	46.2%	26.9%
Bulimic	15	0%	26.7%	73.3%

Percent of "grouped" cases correctly classified: 62.90%

entered. The maximum of two discriminant functions was calculated; the resulting combined X^2 [(14, N=124) = 50.63, $p < .0001$] was significant. The canonical correlation between the first discriminant function and group membership was .56 (between-group variability accounted for 91% of the variance).

After removal of this first discriminant function among the three groups, there was no significant discriminating power associated with the second function (X^2 (6, N=124) = 5.27). An examination of the group centroids of the first descriminant function among the three groups discriminated between at-risk (*C* = .43) and eating-disordered (*C* = 1.57) men, but also between at-risk and normal (*C* = -.42) men.

On the basis of this discriminant analysis, 63% of the cases (124 cases) would have been classified correctly into the appropriate group. More specifically, 66.3% of the normal men, 46.2% of the at-risk men, and 73.3% of the eating-disordered men would have been classified correctly into the appropriate group on the basis of the first discriminant function (the second did not explain much additional variability among groups). Thus, sensitivity (ability to detect eating-disordered men) was slightly better than specificity (accuracy in identifying normal cases). Variables correlated most highly with the first discriminant function were avoidant personality, rejection from athletic teams, absence of a narcissistic pattern, and dependent personality (see Table 4). The remaining variables (lack of closeness to parents, a passive-aggressive character, and a history of having been teased) also correlated with the function.

TABLE 4

Discriminant Analysis for Normal, At Risk, and Bulimic Men

	Correlation with Discriminant Function			
Variables	Function 1	Function 2	Univariate F-Ratio	Sign
Avoidant personality	.71	−.13	14.53	.0001
Rejection in athletic teams	.57	−.51	9.94	.0001
Narcissistic personality	−.54	.30	8.42	.0004
Dependent personality	.51	.24	7.58	.0008
Lack of closeness to parents	.50	.52	7.78	.0007
Passive-aggressive pers.	.49	.17	7.00	.001
History of being teased	−.37	−.07	3.89	.02

DISCUSSION

Body Image Concerns of College Men

This study found that the preferred body shape for contemporary men without eating disorders was the V-shaped body, whereas the eating-disordered group strove for the "lean, toned, thin" shape.

It is puzzling that most men still prefer the full-chested, thin-waisted body shape, as well as the look of strength and agility. Lipman (1962) states that the early American value system, which stressed the attributes of physical prowess for men, made sense then because it was anchored in and related functionally to the frontier and rural society. He suggests that the perpetuation of this old rural ideal of manliness represents one of the most serious cultural lags of our time; certainly, male physical strength and prowess are not prerequisites for success in most careers, as they were in the past. This particular shape seems to gain importance during adolescence.

For the adolescent, the changes in physique, a developing ability to think abstractly, and the subsequent capacity for self-reflection mark the beginning of a period of extreme physical and psychological self-consciousness. At the same time as the adolescent male is attempting to integrate the somatic changes of puberty, he is trying to understand the meaning of becoming a man in our culture. From birth, most boys learn that being a man entails a certain set of attitudes and behaviors, including independence, competitiveness, toughness, aggressiveness, and courage. This set of values may explain in part why noneating-disordered men scored highest on the antisocial, narcissistic, and histrionic scales of the Millon inventory. Although some of these traits certainly are desirable, others can be problematic, lead to emotional isolation, and limit the development of a boy's potential.

Through their peers and through the media, young men are confronted daily with a definition of manhood which is distorted, dysfunctional, and potentially destructive. The popular ideal overemphasizes physical strength, force, and athletic skills. Yet where else can adolescent boys turn to understand their emerging manhood?

Fogel (1986) proposes that masculinity often is defined in relation and in contrast to women. During the last 20 years, however, popular conceptions of women's role in society have begun to change dramatically in American culture. One important component of this change is women's increased participation in economic and professional life, particularly in occupations and at levels reserved previously for men. Consequently, a man's career, which formerly played a major role in his identity, now is often a source of anxiety and tension. In addition, turning to women to gain a better understanding of masculinity is more difficult today because women are reassessing their own roles and because their own identity is in flux.

Researchers have found that increased achievement and competence among women due to the designation of occupations by gender presents problems for men (Bowman, Worthy, & Greyser, 1965). Pleck (1973) points out that traditional norms for male-female relations and sex-role socialization have not prepared men to interact with achieving women either as partners in marriage or as peers at work. Could women's entry into economic and professional life be generating a "male backlash"? Is this backlash being expressed in part through an idealization of the powerful V-shaped body and the recent trends in men's fashions? In the February 1, 1988, edition of *Newsweek*, one of the top stories was titled "Sylvan Chic: The Marketing of Masculinity." The editor introduces the story by reporting that the "pseudo-sportsman" look has become "a big hit in the upscale urban jungle," where "men who never leave the sidewalk" are buying (among other items) expensive rubber-soled shoes. The editor proposes that "designers are cashing in on the nostalgia for a time when men were men."

With both males and females reassessing their sex roles, it is not surprising that adolescence, a time of transition, is the period when many persons of both genders develop eating disorders and obsessions with their bodies. Because we are focusing on males, we are left with questions about the meaning of the ideal male shape. Do the presentation of a powerful body type and the trend toward rugged fashion make a statement about men's longing for a time when men were in charge? Do the men who feel threatened by the women's movement need to "flex their muscles" in an attempt to be sexually dominant as their traditional masculine prerogatives ebb away?

Men with Eating Disorders

Although there are many paths to the development of an eating disorder, a preliminary risk factor model emerged through the discriminant function analysis. Men with eating disorders tend to have dependent, avoidant, and passive-aggressive personality styles, and to have experienced negative reactions to their bodies from their peers while growing up. They tend to be closer to their mothers than to their fathers. The discussion that follows will describe the overall group profile that emerged and the ways in which personality and body image development may interact to place a man at risk for concerns about body shape and for an eating disorder.

With regard to the personality profile, men with eating disorders score highest on the dependent, avoidant, and passive-aggressive scales on the MCMI. These patterns, according to Millon (1982), reflect relatively enduring and pervasive traits that typify a person's style of behaving, perceiving, thinking, feeling, and relating to others. Millon (1981) describes these personality styles in the following ways.

Dependent personalities are distinguished from other pathological patterns by their marked need for social approval and affection and by their willingness to live in accord with the desires of others. They adapt their behavior to please those on whom they depend; their search for love leads them to deny thoughts and feelings that may arouse the displeasure of others. Such individuals avoid asserting themselves lest their actions be seen as aggressive. Dependents may feel paralyzed when alone, and need repeated assurance that they will not be abandoned. Unable to draw on themselves as a major source of comfort and gratification, they must arrange their lives to ensure a constant supply of nurturance and reinforcement from their environment. To protect themselves from losing the affection and protection of those on whom they depend, dependents submit quickly and comply with others' wishes, or make themselves so pleasing that no one could possibly want to abandon them.

Millon (1981) describes the avoidant personality as an "actively" detached person who is oversensitive to social stimuli and hyperreactive to the moods and feelings of others, especially those moods and feelings that portend rejection and humiliation. Their extreme anxiety not only intrudes into their thoughts and interferes with their behavior but also disposes them to distance themselves from others as a protection against the psychic pain they anticipate.

A distinguishing feature of the passive-aggressive personality is the belief that those who suffer from it were subjected to appreciably more than their share of contradictory family messages. Their eroticism and capriciousness, their tendency to shift from agreeableness to negativity, simply mirror the inconsistent models and reinforcement to which they were exposed. They have deeply rooted feelings of ambivalence about themselves and others. The name of this disorder is based on the assumption that such individuals are expressing covert aggression passively.

What factors in development might explain why eating-disordered men develop such a passive-dependent approach to life and why controlling their body becomes their avenue to gain control? In what ways do body image and psychosocial development interact to leave a man vulnerable to concerns about his body?

Speculations About the Interaction Between Personality and Body Image Development

Our findings followed logically from the work of previous researchers. Fisher, Fisher, and Stark (1980), for example, proposed that body image development begins before birth. It involves the parents' preconceived image of which sex they would like the baby to be and what they want the baby to look like. This image is an ideal one, which is influenced by the parents' own body image history (Kearney-Cooke, in press). Fisher et al. (1980) state that when the baby is born, the parents will welcome it into the world if enough similarities exist between their ideal image and the baby's actual appearance. The baby's emotional needs then can be met by a loving environment, which leads to feelings of personal worth; these feelings, in turn, are the basis of a secure body image.

According to Mahler, Pine, and Bergman (1975), the child has increased external perception at the age of four or five months, and begins to differentiate his own body from his mother's. He distinguishes his body from other objects in the environment through kinesthetic, visceral, and motor sensations. Adequate somatic sensory stimulation, such as touching, rocking, and water play, are important for the development of body image in the infant. Blaesing and Brockhaus (1972) state that if the infant does not receive adequate tactile and vestibular stimulation his ego development will be impaired, his level of anxiety will increase, and he will have a poor foundation for reality testing. By the end of the first year, the child develops the ability to move away physically from his mother; eventually he can walk and distinguish his body from the rest of the world.

Mahler et al. (1975) describe the period from approximately 18 to 22 months as a time when the child wants to explore the world and move away from his mother, but is in conflict. He fears engulfment on the one hand and loss of the love object on the other. Boys become aware during this stage that girls do not have a penis; consequently they develop a more distinct awareness of their own bodies and their relation to other people's bodies.

Erikson (1950) describes the toddler stage as lasting from one to three years of age. Mastery of body and environment are major tasks of this stage; toddlers struggle to acquire motor skills, language skills, and bowel training. The parents' approval or disapproval of the toddler's more autonomous behavior and appearance has a significant effect on the child's developing sense of self and body image. Depending on the parents' reactions, the children may regard the body and its parts as good or bad, pleasing or repulsive, clean or dirty, loved or disliked. If a child's strivings toward independence, often expressed somatically, are accepted by his family during this period, he will accept himself and his body and will not overvalue or devalue his body. If he feels that there is something wrong with his interest in venturing out on his own, however, he will develop feelings of shame, helplessness, and inadequacy.

In examining the personality profile of eating-disordered men, we would speculate that these men had a parent or parents who discouraged independence and possibly set up barriers to keep their child from gaining autonomy. They may have been overprotective and may have made few demands for self-responsibility; they may have rewarded their sons for remaining more dependent. As a result, these boys failed to develop a cohesive sense of self separate from their parents. Their intense dependence on others may have robbed them of the opportunity to do things for themselves, to go out and discover their real strengths and weaknesses. Failure to become more autonomous may have deprived them of the experiences needed to develop attributes that would distinguish them as individuals. Thus, in a culture that emphasizes thinness, having the perfect lean body could provide an opportunity for these men to attain an identity.

Sex typing and sex-role identification also are major tasks of the toddler stage. In our culture, muscular build, overt physical aggression, competence at athletics, competitiveness, and independence generally are regarded as desirable for boys, whereas dependency, passivity, inhibition of physical aggression, smallness, and neatness are seen as more appropriate for females. Boys who later develop eating disorders do not conform to the cultural expectations for masculinity; they tend to be more dependent, passive, and nonathletic, traits which may lead to feelings of isolation and disparagement of body.

Schilder (1950) proposed that an individual develops conscious and unconscious attitudes about his or her body through identification with another person. In regard to closeness with each parent, the findings of our study support what Sours (1950) and Dally (1969) found in their research: men with eating disorders report feeling close to their mother and having little contact with their fathers. Sours (1950) hypothesized that this increased identification with mother might play a role in the eating-disordered man's need to rid the body of all fat. This notion fits what one bulimic man wrote in response to the question on the demographic questionnaire about the time when he felt most ashamed of his body: "I was doing wash with a friend. He pulled a pair of jeans out of the machine and didn't know who they belonged to. They were so big, my friend said they must belong to my mother—they were mine."

As a child leaves home and enters school, the reaction of peers also plays a role in body image development. For the first time the child enters a group that has no special interest in him. The members of the group are at an age where they must compete and assert their own ability to survive outside their homes. Often, popularity and leadership are based largely on appearance (Fisher et al., 1980). We found that most of the men with eating disorders reported negative reactions from their peers. They reported being the last ones chosen for athletic teams and often cited being teased by peers about their bodies as the times when they felt most ashamed of their bodies. Unfortunately, the sense of ineffectiveness and inferiority about their appearance and body competencies often was confirmed as they ventured out of the home. Feelings of unattractiveness and inadequacy may have resulted in more social humiliation and self-doubt. The result may have been to retreat further into the home and to attempt to change their bodies to gain a sense of power and control.

In response to the preliminary findings presented here, we obtain the following profile of the man who develops an eating disorder. When we look at this personality profile, this man appears to lack a sense of autonomy, identity, and control over his life. He seems to exist as an extension of others and to do things because he must please others in order to survive emotionally. We speculate that he came from an environment which is unable to validate his strivings for independence, a situation which leaves him at risk for symptom formation later in life. He has a history of experiences around his body (such as being teased about his body shape) which leaves him vulnerable about his body image. He tends to identify with his mother rather than with his father, a pattern which leaves his masculine identity in question andestablishes a repulsion of "fat" which he associates with femininity. He also lives in a culture which emphasizes thinness and fitness, and exaggerates the importance of body image as a result.

RECOMMENDATIONS FOR TREATMENT

On the basis of the results of this study, the authors find Hilde Bruch's (1973, 1978) conceptualization of eating disorders most helpful in planning the overall treatment.

Therapy must assist the eating-disordered male in developing a more cohesive sense of self, a true self in which all aspects of his personality can be expressed, not only those which his family found acceptable. Separation issues also must be addressed, including the separateness of his own body image from the bodies of significant others, which would help these patients to have a less distorted view of fat. The patient also must work through the issue of control through self-knowledge and expression versus the pseudocontrol experienced through weight loss. In addition, therapy must address his vulnerability around body image and its relationship to the development and maintenance of an eating disorder.

Because these men struggle for acceptance by others even at the cost of silencing themselves, the authors suggest that the body image work take place in a group. This format would provide them with a place to experiment with more direct, more honest communication while exploring the history of their body image development and the meaning of male body types.

Guided imagery can be used in the treatment of body image disturbance. Before presenting the two theme-centered guided imageries, we would like to describe this technique briefly.

During the past two decades, there has been a proliferation of research and reports about the clinical application of guided imagery in treating an extensive range of disorders, including body image (Hutchinson, 1983; Kearney-Cooke, in press; Schultz, 1978; Wooley & Kearney-Cooke, 1986). It has been found that guided imagery is a powerful tool when used in treatment approaches ranging from psychoanalytic psychotherapy (Reyker, 1977) to behaviorism (Wolpe, 1958).

Guided imagery is a fantasy-inducing process which combines deep muscle relaxation and the suggestion of images. It is a powerful technique for psychic reconstruction whereby repressed material around the body can be brought to the surface. This technique can provide patients with a detailed picture ofkey parental attitudes, developmental periods, and relationships that affected their body image. For eating-disordered men who tend to be focused externally, guided imagery is especially powerful because it teaches patients to look within and to trust their own responses. Finally, the symbolic nature of imagery permits greater freedom of exploration into the highly charged area of "body."

The following two theme-centered guided imageries can be used to explore the psychodynamic meaning of male eating-disordered patients' preferred body shape and their compulsion to rid their bodies of fat.

Guided Imagery: Meaning of Male Body Shapes

Van Der Velde (1985) hypothesizes that body image provides three social functions. It enables men to project how others see them by means of their appearance and actions; it enables them to control selectively the establishment and preservation of a desirable view of themselves; it enables them to create within others impressions that may not reflect their actual selves. We developed the following guided imagery to allow men to examine the meaning of the three body types (V-shaped, thin, and fat) and to determine the deeper meaning of the particular image they are trying to project.

Patients are asked to imagine that when they wake up the next morning and look in the mirror, each one sees that his body has a thin, lean shape. They are asked to go through the day and to be aware of how it is to be in the world with this new body. They are instructed to watch how they eat, how they dress, how they move, how they interact with others, how others respond to them, and what they do with their free time. As they go through the day, they are asked to be aware of what their body says to their parents, to other males, to females, and so on before they open their mouth. (Examples: Does it say I am powerful, in control, out of control, masculine, feminine, virile, etc.?) Do they act differently with a body of this particular shape?

The patients then are taken through the same imagery with the other two shapes (V-shaped and fat). Then they are asked to sculpt or draw the shape to which they aspire and to write the statement which that particular shape makes to the world about them. Finally, they discuss the meaning of this statement.

Guided Imagery: The Meaning of Fat

Sours (1980) speculates that fat means different things to males and to females. Whereas fat in a girl is likely to represent femininity (the development of breasts and hips), to a boy it is more apt to be related to thoughts of babyhood and weakness. Sours states that the presence of gender confusion helps to explain the increased seriousness of anorexia when it does occur in males, because increased identification with the mother would decrease the ability to differentiate self from mother and would increase the identification with the mother's rounded body shape. This fear of identification would lead, in turn, to controlling vigorously any hint of fat.

In an attempt to clarify the psychodynamic meaning of "fat" for eating-disordered men so they might be able to view weight gain more realistically, we have developed the following imagery.

The patients is asked to imagine that he is given a magic laser which can remove all the fat from his body painlessly. Then he is asked to visualize his body and to use the laser to rid the body of fat. He is to see the fat dropping off him and landing in front of him in a puddle. How does he feel as he looks at the fat in the puddle? Is he relieved to experience it as separate from him or does he miss it?

Now this fat in the puddle is coming to life and taking shape. What does it turn into? What does this newly formed animal, person, or object do? Whatdoes it say about itself? Does the patient like it?

The patient then is asked to talk to the "fat creature" and to learn what it is about. Does it represent part of himself that he's disowned? Does it remind him of his mother, from whom he struggles to separate? Is it a burden?

The fat now melts back into the puddle. The patient has a choice: to leave the fat behind, to integrate it back into his body, or to carry it with him in a sack. How does he feel about his choice? What will he lose and what will he gain with this choice?

After the imagery is completed, the patient is asked to draw what the fat turned into during the imagery. Under the drawing he is asked to write a description of what it turned into (what it looked like physically, how it acted during the imagery, and how it responded to the patient's decision at the end of the imagery). Then the patient is asked to discuss the possible meaning of "fat" for him.

SUMMARY

Although the subject of eating disorders has received a great deal of attention in both popular and scholarly literature, research on males with eating disorders is limited. Culturally, men may be less subject to the factors which move women toward eating disorders, but they are not immune to the present emphasis on fitness and dieting or to the kind of underlying psychopathology which provides the foundation for the symptoms of eating disorders. Thus, more attention to the male eating-disordered patient is warranted.

The role of personality organization and functioning in eating disorders has not been fully established. Some theorists suggest that personality factors may play a more important role in the development of eating disorders in men than in women (Andersen, 1988), but empirical studies addressing this hypothesis do not exist. In this study, males with eating disorders did not score in the psychopathological range for personality disorders (such as borderline or narcissistic), but did emerge with a personality style characterized by dependency, avoidance, and passive-aggressiveness.

In this chapter, the authors offer some suggestions for the treatment of body image disturbance among eating-disordered patients. More research is needed for the development and evaluation of techniques to treat body image disturbance. Better understanding of the ways in which the image and functions of the body are employed in psychic conflict offers the possibility of enhancing the conceptualization and treatment of eating disorders. Whether the value of the treatment lies in the resolving of body image disturbance per se or in the psychodynamic issues which emerge through the body image work, further development of techniques is warranted. In addition, the role of body image parameters in mediating outcomes of treatments for males or females with eating disorders remains fertile ground for scientific study.

The study described in this chapter is descriptive; it does not purport to make conclusive statements regarding the etiology of eating disorders in men. Instead it provides information on the body image concerns of normal and eating-disordered men and offers a preliminary risk factor model which needs further validation. These preliminary results must be viewed with caution because of the correlational nature of the data and the small sample size of the clinical group. In the future, it would be advisable to validate these results with additional measures and a broader population.

REFERENCES

American Psychiatric Association. (1980). *Diagnostic and Statistical Manual of Mental Disorders* (3rd ed.). Washington, D.C.: Author.

Andersen, A. E. (1988). Anorexia nervosa and bulimia in males. In D. Garner & P. Garfinkel (Eds.), *Diagnostic Issues in Anorexia Nervosa and Bulimia Nervosa*. New York: Brunner/Mazel.

Blaesing, S. & Brockhaus J. (1972). The development of body image in the child. *Nursing Clinics of North America, 7* (4), 597-607.

Bowman, G. W., Worthy, N. B., & Greyser, S. A. (1965). Are women executive people? *Harvard Business Review, 43* (4), 14ff.

Bruch, H. (1973). *Eating Disorders*. New York: Basic Books.

Bruch, H. (1978). *The Golden Cage: The Enigma of Anorexia Nervosa*. New York: Random House.

Chodorow, N. (1978). *The Reproduction of Mothering: Psychoanalysis and the Sociology of Gender*. Berkeley: University of California Press.

Cooper, P. J. & Taylor, M. J. (In press). Body image disturbance in bulimia nervosa. *British Journal of Psychiatry* (Supplement).

Cooper, P. J., Taylor, M. J., Cooper, Z., & Fairburn, C. G. (1987). The development and validation of the body shape questionnaire. *International Journal of Eating Disorders, 6* (4), 485-494.

Dally, P. J. (1969). *Anorexia Nervosa*. New York: Grune & Stratton.

Erikson, E. (1950). *Childhood and Society*. New York: W. W. Norton & Company.

Fisher, G., Fisher, J., & Stark, R. (1980). The body image. Chapter in *Aesthetic Plastic Surgery* (pp. 1-32). Boston: Little, Brown and Company.

Fisher, S. (1966). Body attention patterns and personality defenses. *Psychological Monographs: General and Applied, 80*, 9 (617), 1-29.

Fogel, G. I. (1986). Introduction: Being a man. In G. I. Fogel, F. M. Lane, & R. S. Liebert (Eds.), *The Psychology of Men*. New York: Basic Books.

Freud, S. (1933). The psychology of women. In *New Introductory Lectures on Psychoanalysis*. New York: W. W. Norton & Company.

Freud, S. (1959). Some psychological consequences of the anatomical distinction between the sexes. In *Collected Papers*, Vol. 5. New York: Basic Books, Inc.

Garner, D. M. & Garfinkel, P. E. (1980). The eating attitudes test: An index of the symptoms of anorexia nervosa. *Psychological Medicine, 9*, 273-279.

Garner, D. M., & Garfinkel, P. E. (1981). Body image in anorexia nervosa: Measurement, theory and clinical implications. *International Journal of Psychiatry in Medicine, 11*, 263-284.

Greenacre, P. (1958). Early physical determinants in the development of the sense of identity. *Journal of the American Psychoanalytic Association, 6*, 612-627.

Hutchinson, M. G. (1983). Transforming body image: Your body, friend, or foe? *Women and Therapy, 1*, 59-67.

Kearney-Cooke, A. M. (In press). Reclaiming the body: Using guided imagery in the treatment of body image disturbance among bulimic women. Chapter prepared for L. Hornyak & E. Baker (Eds)., *Handbook of Experiential Techniques in the Treatment of Eating Disorders*.

Kestenberg, J. (1975). *Children and Parents: Psychoanalytic Studies in Development*. New York: Jason Aronson.

Kolb, C. (1959). Disturbance of body image. In S. Arieti (Ed.), *American Handbook of Psychiatry* (pp. 749-769). New York: Basic Books.

Lipman, A. (1962). Cultural lag and masculinity. *Journal of Educational Psychology, 35*, 216-220.

Mahler, M., Pine, F., & Bergman, A. (1975). *The Psychological Birth of the Human Infant*. New York: Basic Books, Inc.

Millon, T. (1969). *Modern Psychopathology*. Philadelphia: Saunders.

Millon, T. (1981). *Disorders of Personality: DSM-III, Axis II*. New York: Wiley Press.

Millon, T. (1982). *Millon Clinical Multiaxial Inventory Manual* (2nd ed.). Minneapolis: National Computer Systems.

Piaget, J. (1954). *The Construction of Reality in the Child*. New York: Basic Books, Inc.

Pleck, J. H. (1973). Male threat from female competence: An experimental study in college dating couples. (Doctoral Dissertation, Harvard University).

Reyker, J. (1977). Spontaneous visual imagery: Implications for psychoanalysis, psychopathology, and psychotherapy. *Journal of Mental Imagery, 2*, 253-274.

Schilder, P. (1935). *The Image and Appearance of the Human Body*. New York: International Universities Press.

Schilder, P. (1950). *The Image and Appearance of the Human Body*. New York: International Universities Press.

Schultz, D. (1978). Imagery and the control of depression. In J. L. Singer & K. S. Pope (Eds.), *The Power of Human Imagination*. New York: Plenum.

Sours, J. A. (1980). *Starving to Death in a Sea of Objects: The Anorexia Nervosa Syndrome*. New York: Jason Aronson.

Van Der Velde, C. D. (1985). Body image of one's self and of others: Developmental and clinical significance. *The American Journal of Psychiatry, 142* (5), 527-537.

Wolpe, J. (1958). *Psychotherapy by Reciprocal Inhibition*. Palo Alto, CA: Stanford University Press.

Wooley, S. C., & Kearney-Cooke, A. (1986). Intensive treatment of bulimia and body image disturbance. In K. D. Brownell & J. P. Foreyt (Eds.), *Psysiology, Psychology and Treatment of Eating Disorders*. New York: Basic Books.

SECTION II

Clinical and Psychometric Studies

6

Primary Anorexia Nervosa in the Male and Female: A Comparison of Clinical Features and Prognosis

Arthur H. Crisp and Thomas Burns

This chapter draws on two reported studies of the comparison between male and female anorectics. In 1986, Crisp et al. reported a comparison of presentation and long term follow-up characteristics of 36 males and 102 females. In 1987, Fichter and Daser described and compared presentation characteristics of 29 male and 23 female cases of primary anorexia nervosa.

Prevalence

The rarity of male anorexia nervosa is widely commented upon, but many authorities claim that up to 10% of all cases are male and some claim that the condition is getting more common in the male. These views contrast with the first author's experience. Thus, in 1967 he reported 60 cases of anorexia nervosa which had been assessed without preferential selection based on gender over the period 1960-1964 (Crisp, 1967). Five of them were male. Since then he and his colleagues have documented about 850 female cases. Until 15 years ago, about one in three of female patients referred was seen, up to a maximum of two consultations per week. Since then, referrals have increased from 10 to 15 or more per week, but it is still possible to accept only two. Under these circumstances, selection factors could have affected the kind of female patients seen. However, criteria governing such selection have been mainly geographical. Thus, if local patients needed to be seen and the clinics were already fully booked three months ahead, then those referred from outside have not been considered. The overall pattern has been that the clinic serves severely ill female anorectics whose characteristics do not seem to have changed over the 30 years in question. Patients seen in this way would have been assessed at length in the first instance and then usually taken into treatment.

In contrast to the above practice in respect to female patients, the first author has very rarely turned away a male case, simply because they are so rare and, therefore, of special research interest. In this way, around 80 male cases have also been carefully documented, representing no more than 1 in 100 of all referrals.

Whatever the precise sex distribution ultimately turns out to be, it is likely to remain highly skewed to an extent rarely seen in disease processes other than those specifically based in the reproductive apparatus itself. Such an observation invites scrutiny of the condition in males and its relationship to anorexia nervosa in the female in a search for understanding of the condition. It has been suggested, for instance, that the fundamental difference between male and female "fatness" prompted by puberty and with implications for biological and gender roles thereafter may be important. Young females often become preoccupied with those aspects of their shape determined by such "fatness" and with its reproductive, biological, and social significance. In contrast, young males are less concerned about their superficial fatness and more concerned about lean body mass and its significance for strength, dominance, and masculinity.

Thus, the first indicator for puberty in girls, apart from the earlier height spurt, is the beginning of breast development. Next, pubic hair begins to appear, hips begin to increase in size, and subcutaneous fat deposition on buttocks, anterior abdomen, thighs, upper arms, etc., in particular confer the typical biological mature contour. Axillary hair is a later development. Such changes are dependent upon the newly emerging female sex hormone pattern and it has been suggested that this female fatness has important biological significance in evolutionary terms, as well as its social significance.

Any fatness present in the pubescent boy is less intimately a feature of the pubertal processes. Although it can be shown that boys do increase their fat deposition during this period, the increase is modest. For instance, at a height of 5 ft 11 ins (180 cm), fat mass averages 20 lbs (9 kgs). In contrast, a girl of similar height would on average contain 44 lbs (20 kgs) of fat. In contrast to the hip development of the pubescent female, in the male there is a major increase in shoulder width as part of a male-based proportionately greater increase in lean body mass at this stage (see Crisp, 1980). Only those males with gender identity doubt might, despite being normal in body weight, be more likely to get caught up with sensitivity to their roundness and femininity and set out, like young females, to regulate its energetic aspects by calorie restraint (Crisp, 1980).

This latter view has recently found some support from the systematic study by Fichter and Daser (1987). They concentrated on this aspect, using standardized instruments, and reported in 20 cases that: "The topic of sexuality was taboo in the families of 16 cases (80%) and was rejected in one further case. Almost all patients (95%) had attempted to suppress their sexual drive and were relieved by the loss of libido following weight loss. The average age of first nocturnal emission was 13.4 years. Sexual anxieties appeared to be present with respect to hetero- as well as homosexual behavior. In addition, there were indications of childhood and adolescence cross-gender behavior. Thus, during their childhood, 13 patients (65%) preferred cooking, sewing, playing with dolls, and cleaning to tougher and more boyish games. Seventeen patients (85%) reported of themselves that they were "anything but a daredevil" in childhood. Four patients (20%) would have preferred to be a girl. Five patients (25%) said they had never (and nine additional cases said that they had only rarely) been in love with a girl. At the time of assessment, 21 out of all 29 primary anorexia nervosa patients (72%) were aged 18 years or over. Nevertheless, only six patients (30%) had not had a genuine relationship with a girl. Fifteen patients (75%) reported a very high degree of anxiety and disgust with regard to heterosexual relationships and intercourse. In addition to shyness and lack of confidence with respect to women, several patients reported anxiety about getting involved too closely or becoming trapped by a woman.

In this chapter, the authors again present their own comparative data on males and females at presentation, highlighting in the discussion similarities and differences with the findings of Fichter and Daser. In addition, they describe: 1) aspects of treatment effects on subsets of the two groups, and 2) some comparative information concerning long-term outcomes in the two sexes.

METHODOLOGIES OF PRESENTATION AND FOLLOW-UP STUDIES

Criteria for diagnosis in the female and male have been outlined elsewhere (Crisp, 1967; Crisp & Toms, 1972). In this chapter, a series of 102 females, first seen between 1968 and 1972 and reported on elsewhere (Crisp et al., 1980), is now compared with the first 36 of the male cases in respect of clinical characteristics at presentation (Crisp & Burns, 1983). Twenty-seven of the male cases, with a follow-up period of at least two years and in some cases as much as 20 years since initial presentation (Burns & Crisp, 1984), are also compared in respect of follow-up status with 100 cases similarly followed up within the female series and where the duration of follow-up was 4-7 years. The relationship between clinical features at presentation and long-term outcome status in the two groups is also compared.

Features at Presentation

The method of data collection previously applied to the 102 female cases was applied to the male cases. Thus the medical records (including nursing records and social workers' reports) of all the patients were studied systematically and clinical data in the following categories were recorded:

1. clinical features at presentation;
2. history of present illness;
3. personal history;
4. premorbid relationship with family;
5. family history and premorbid parental relationship;
6. treatment and outcome at one year after presentation.

For those patients who were no longer attending St. George's Hospital at one year after presentation, information on the last category was gathered at the time of follow-up.

Follow-up

Details of the follow-up method for the female cases have been reported elsewhere (Hsu et al., 1979). The duration of follow-up of these cases had been 4-8 years (mean 5.9). The duration of follow-up of the 27 male cases, assessed in a similar way to the female cases (Burns & Crisp, 1984), ranged from two to 20 years (mean 8.0 years).

Assessment of outcome was partly based on an outcome measure described by Morgan and Russell (1975)—the average outcome score. This score is based, for the female, on the outcome in five areas: nutritional status, menstrual function, mental state, sexual adjustment and socioeconomic status. For the males, the menstrual function scale was omitted. The ratings on the scales are based on the six-month period immediately preceding the interview and the final score for each patient represents an average of the ratings for the scales. The authors also defined a general outcome category based on the patient's body weight during the six months preceding follow-up. Three categories of outcome were defined: (1) *good*: weight within 10% of matched population mean weight (m.p.m.w.) (Kemsley, 1952); the grounds for choosing this cut-off point are elaborated upon later in this chapter; (2) *intermediate*: body weight 10-20% below m.p.m.w.; (3) *poor*: body weight below 80% of m.p.m.w.

Statistical Analysis

The statistical tests used in comparing features of the male and female samples were two-sample t tests in the case of continuous variables, and chi-squared tests in the case of categorical or dichotomous variables. In the latter, where necessary, Yate's correction was utilized. In addition, though t tests were robust to departures from normality, on the few occasions where sample sizes were small, the distribution of the continuous variable was checked before performing a t test.

PRESENTATION STUDY

Features at Presentation

1. All patients, male and female, were "weight phobic" with concern about "fatness" and characterized by related avoidance behavior.
2. Mean age at presentation was similar in males and females, being in the 21st year (Table 1).
3. There was no parental social class difference (Registrar-General's Classification of Occupation); there was a tendency for more of the females to have been married/divorced (Table 1).
4. The age of onset of the illness was very similar between males and females (Table 2) but males were significantly more overweight at the onset.
5. Maximum degree of overweight ever was the same for the two populations, with both showing on average a maximum weight 10% above their mean matched population mean weight (m.p.m.w.) (Kemsley, 1952). There was a slight tendency for the males to be relatively lower in body weight (taking height into account) at presentation, with a mean of 73.6% of m.p.m.w. compared with 77% for females, and for

TABLE 1

Age, Social Class, and Marital Status of Samples

	Age (Years) at Presentation	Social Class (%)					Marital Status (%)	
		1	2	3	4	5	Single	Married/Divorced
Females (*n* = 102)								
Mean	20.8	28	40	20	7	5	84.5	15.5
SD	±6.2							
Males (*n* = 36)								
Mean	20.4	29	37	14	20	0	94.4	5.5
SD	±5.3							

Reprinted with permission from Crisp, Burns, and Bhat (1986). Primary anorexia nervosa in the male and female: A comparison of clinical features and prognosis. *British Journal of Medical Psychology, 59*, 123–132.

males also to report a relatively lower weight than the females at some stage during their illness (Table 2).

6. The mean duration of the illness at the time of presentation was similar for males and females (Table 2).

Personal History

Birth order

Of the females, 14 were only children, 27 were first-born, and 41 were youngest children. Of the males, five were only children, eight were first-born, and 13 were youngest children. There is no difference between the sexes in this respect.

Eating patterns in childhood

Nine females (9%) were reported as having had a generally poor appetite in childhood and 53 (53%) as having had a big appetite. This contrasted with seven males (19%) with poor appetite and only eight (22%) with a big appetite prior to puberty. This difference between the sexes is significant at p < 0.01.

Premorbid obsessionality and athleticism

Twenty-four percent of the females showed very high levels of conscientiousness in their work at school premorbidly compared with 50% of the males

TABLE 2

Weight, Age of Onset, and Duration of Illness and Dietary Characteristics

| | Maximum Premorbid Weight | | Onset of Illness | | Mean Duration of Illness (Years) at Time of Presentation | Dietary Complications Additional to Abstinence[b] | | | | Lowest Weight During Illness So Far (kg)[a] | Weight at Presentation (kg)[a] |
	Age (Years)	kg[a]	Age (Years)	kg[a]***		Bulimia	Vomiting	Laxative Abuse*	Anxiety in Eating with Others		
Females (n = 102)											
Mean	15.6	57.6	17.3	52.3	3.5	46	43	59	42	37.4	40.6
SD	±3.2	±9.1 (109.1)	±4.0	±7.6 (99.3)	±4.3	(45)	(42)	(57)	(41)	±5.6 (72.0)	±7.4 (77.0)
Males (n = 36)											
Mean	16.7	64.2	17.1	61.7	3.3	14	13	8	8	42.0	47.0
SD	±2.9	±13.9 (110.0)	±3.7	±11.8 (108.7)	±3.04	(39)	(37)	(24)	(26)	±7.0 (68.5)	±8.3 (73.6)

*P < 0.05; **P < 0.001.

[a]Percentage m.p.m.w. given in parentheses.

[b]Percentage of total sample given in parentheses.

Reprinted with permission from Crisp, Burns, and Bhat (1986). Primary anorexia nervosa in the male and female: A comparison of clinical features and prognosis. *British Journal of Medical Psychology, 59,* 123–132.

(p < 0.005). Only 23% of the females compared with 39% of the males showed a very high level of interest in sports (p <0.025).

Peer relationships during childhood

Twenty-three females patients (22%) were reported to have been excessively shy during childhood compared with seven male patients (19%). Half the patients in both groups were reported as having had few or no friends during childhood and in a quarter of the patients in each group this had persisted through to the onset of the illness.

Premorbid sexual activity

In 24 of the females this was judged to have been absent, in 21 unremarkable, in 21 marked at a fantasy level, and in 28 it was judged to have been high. Amongst the males it was absent in 13, unremarkable in 15, marked but fantasized in four, and four of the patients had been highly active. There were no significant differences between the two groups in this respect. However, in respect of actual sexual experience and of deriving pleasure from it as a premorbid experience, this characterized one-third of the males compared with only one-fifth of the females and this difference was significant at the p < 0.025 level. Either at an active or a fantasy level, roughly a quarter of the male patients described doubt about their masculinity and some had been actively homosexual prior to their illness.

Academic attainment

Of the females 23 were 16 years or under in age. Of the remaining 80, all but 17 had at least one O-level pass (General Certificate of Education, UK) whilst 37 had at least one A-level pass. Of the males, 11 were 16 years of age or under. Of the remaining 25, 16 had at least one O-level pass whilst 13 had at least one A-level pass.

Family History and Relationships

Amongst the females, one or both parents of 86 of the patients were interviewed on at least one occasion. Of the remaining 16 patients, the husbands of 10 of them were interviewed on at least one occasion, and in only five instances was the patient the only informer about family history and relationships. A similarly high proportion of relatives of the male patients was interviewed.

Mental illness in parents

Taking general practitioner consultations as the minimum criterion for mental illness, a positive history in one or other or both parents was found in a quarter of both the male and female groups. The illness usually took the form of depressive disorder—rarely manic-depressive illness but much more often neurotic-depressive illness. Other diagnoses included agoraphobia and alcoholism.

Weight disorders in the family

Amongst the females, low body weight was present in a family member in 29 cases (mother 14, father nine, siblings seven). Three of the mothers were judged to have or have had anorexia nervosa. Major obesity was present in 10 instances in one or other parent, most often the mother. So far as the males were concerned, one father and four mothers were recorded as having had definite anorexia nervosa; this was also the case for a number of siblings (Crisp & Toms, 1972). Ten of the fathers and seven of the mothers had been markedly obese. In one family, both the mother and the father had a definite history of anorexia nervosa.

Premorbid parental relationships

Amongst the females, 96 of the patients had been brought up by their natural mothers and fathers. Ninety-one sets of parents still lived together, one couple was separated, four were divorced, and in six instances one of the parents had died. Amongst the males, 34 of the patients had been raised by natural mothers and fathers, while two had stepfathers. Thirty-two sets of parents still lived together, one pair was separated, and one pair divorced, whilst in two instances one of the parents had died and the survivor lived alone.

TREATMENT

The authors have always made the diagnosis of anorexia nervosa at three levels (see Crisp, 1967). The first is the behavioral and readily available experiential level (e.g. resistance to eating, battery of associated defenses, stigmata of starvation). The second is the often denied but always present phobia of normal adult body weight and its avoidance, the fully fledged syndrome being present at weights below 80% of the mean matched population weight. The third is the identification of the underlying maturational conflict, often never articulated, now no longer present, having been prompted by puberty and its immediate or delayed social consequences and then aborted by the illness.

The authors' intervention involves preliminary assessment of these matters, together with the anoretic and important family members, concurrently enabling the majority to contemplate thereafter, at least temporarily, the real change. Thereafter, elective entry into a treatment program occurs in which behavioral control of the anorectic defenses passes to the therapist, enabling weight gain to mean matched population levels within the context of individual and family psychotherapy. The majority of patients engage in this total process.

To the authors' minds, the first level of diagnosis is very similar for both sexes and the systematic comparative studies reported here confirm them in this view. The second level of diagnosis, the weight phobia and avoidance stance, would also seem to be very similar pathological mechanisms in both sexes and further evidence for this is presented below in this section. However, it may be that the basis of the phobia, in terms of meaning of adult body shape, is significantly often different between the sexes as well as having different meanings within each group. This is most obviously true in terms of the probable greater degree of gender identity doubt which the first author has commented on in the past and which Fichter and Daser (1987) emphasized. However, the authors believe that this may not be a major factor of a qualitative kind distinguishing males and females so far as the maturational pathogenesis of the condition is concerned. Meanwhile, they have always addressed it as simply another facet of separation/individuation based in the challenges of puberty. To this end, the individual and family psychotherapeutic intervention has taken a similar form for both sexes throughout the last 30 years.

So far as the psychoendocrinology of the condition is concerned, over the years the first authors and various colleagues have studied the relationship between weight gain and hormonal changes in patients with anorexia nervosa undergoing treatment involving weight gain to fully adult levels. Because of the distorting impact of massive dehydration due to laxative abuse and vomiting, these studies have been undertaken on patients with the abstaining pattern of ingestive avoidance subserving normal body weight avoidance.

Typically, in females such weight gain leads to restoration of low normal levels of LH and of estrogen (see Figures 1 and 2 as illustrative), although exceptions arise when major premorbid obesity has been present (Crisp et al., 1973). In contrast, FSH response to weight gain is usually more muted in the first instance (Crisp et al., 1982).

The same findings characterized male anorectics as they gain weight (Figures 3 and 4).

These changes, which the authors believe are of profound psychological significance for anorexia nervosa for both the male and female, need to be recognized as they occur clinically within treatment. Thus, as puberty is rekindled, patients become sexually aware of themselves and self-conscious, and often begin to blush again. Acne may reemerge. If these changes are not recognized as the preamble to reactivation of the particular original developmental psychopathology of the case, then the patient (often with their parents' collusion) will discharge themselves from further care there and then.

In fact, the underside of this biological threshold in weight terms is remarkably similar for the majority of anorectics both male and female, apart from those whose anorexia nervosa has been of very early onset and which has then induced severely stunted growth. Palmer et al. (1975) revealed this weight as around 42-46 kgs in a study of 12 female and two male cases and Crisp et al. (1982) subsequently confirmed it was marginally higher in a number of male cases. This threshold weight for reactivation of incipient puberty in the vast majority of cases, male and female, is substantially lower than the weight at which menstruation (a much later pubertal event) returns in females. Anorectics are often reported as achieving a weight of around 45 kgs in treatment as evidence of substantial recovery. However, the authors believe that by avoiding further weight gain the patients are managing to sustain their anorectic posture and thereby will not have engaged in meaningful psychotherapy concerning their adolescent problems. This, in their experience, holds equally true for female and male anorectics.

FOLLOW-UP STUDY

The details of the male anorexia nervosa follow-up study have been reported elsewhere and are recapitulated in Chapter 10 of this volume. Here the authors describe the follow-up comparisons undertaken, as outlined earlier in this chapter.

In respect of percentage matched population mean weight at follow-up, Table 3 (see p. 93) reveals that 15 males were less than 90% and 11 were between 90% and 110% at follow-up, whereas amongst the females 43 were below 90% and 51 between 91% and 110%. In addition, one male and six females were greater than 110% matched population mean weight at follow-up. It can be seen that there was a tendency for more of the males than the females to be less than 90% of matched population mean weight at follow-up. However, this did not achieve statistical significance. The majority of both populations had been involved in intensive treatment of a kind

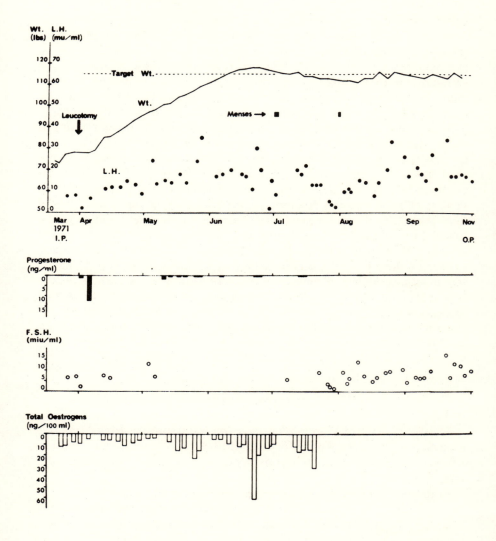

Figures 1 and 2. In these two cases, there are marked increases in plasma gonadotrophins coincidental with weight gain during treatment. The first case also showed evidence of steroid and goadotrophic cyclicity consistent with early restoration of menstruation. These two patients had normal premorbid body weights. Reprinted with permission from Crisp, Hsu, Chen, and Wheller (1982), Reproductive hormone profiles in male anorexia before, during and after restoration of body weight to normal. *International Journal of Eating Disorders, 1,* 3-10.

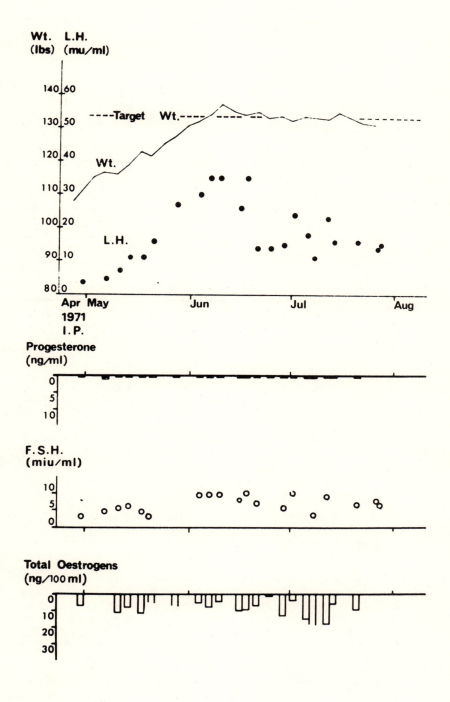

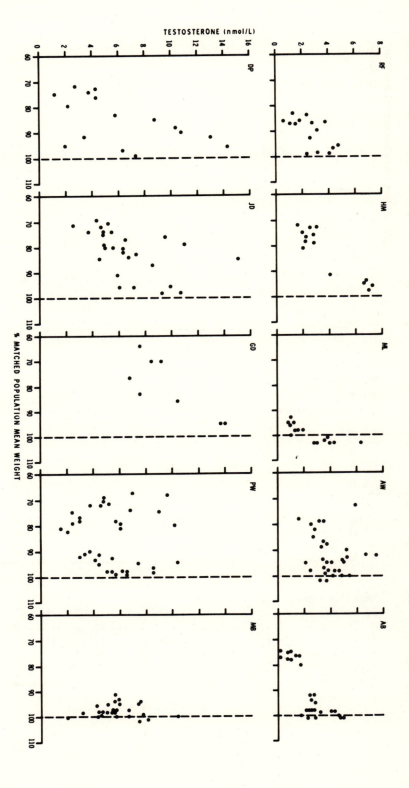

Figure 3. Plasma testosterone levels in 10 males with anorexia nervosa studied during the time that they gained weight to normal (matched population mean weight) levels.

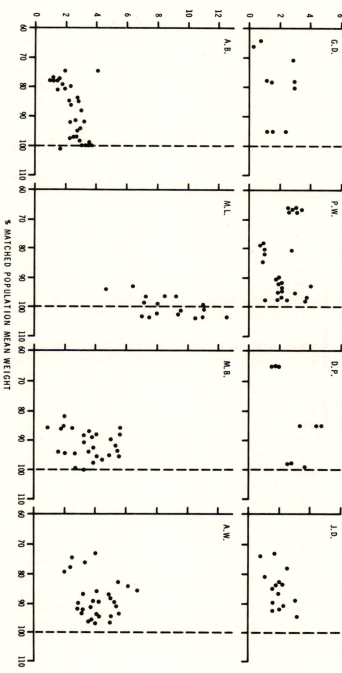

Figure 4. Plasma luteinizing hormone levels in 8 males with anorexia nervosa studied during the time that they gained weight to normal (matched population mean weight) levels.

described elsewhere (Crisp, 1967, 1980) and in contrast to the females, two of whom had died from the condition at follow-up, none of the males had died.

When outcome is examined in terms of individual outcome scores (range 1-4 with 4 being better outcome) similar to those used by Morgan & Russell (1975) but excluding the menstrual function scale, then it can be seen (Table 4) that, if the male and female groups are broken down into those whose weight is 80% or less matched population mean weight (bad outcome), 80%-90% matched population mean weight (intermediate outcome) and 90%-110% matched population mean weight (good outcome), then there is a highly significant association in all instances (p < 0.001) between outcome in terms of their body weight outcome categories and the other measures of outcome.

There is also a tendency for males who have done well in respect of weight also to do significantly better than the females in other respects. This issignificantly so in respect of mental state and of their socioeconomic status as shown in Table 4. However, those males who have done badly in respect ofbody weight do significantly less well than the female counterparts in respect of the nutritional scale and the socioeconomic scale. There is also a significant difference for the intermediate groups on the psychosexual scale, where the males did less well than the females.

Table 5 catalogues these factors, using the 15% below mean matched population weight criterion for recovery as stated in Chapter 10, together with those found to be significantly associated with outcome in the male population (Burns & Crisp, 1984). It can be seen that there are differences between the two populations. Some of the factors significant in the larger population of female subjects did not emerge as significant amongst the smaller population of males. However, the smaller population of males yielded other factors significantly associated with good outcome. Also especially noteworthy is the fact that, whereas bulimia and vomiting are associated with poor outcome in the females, this is not so in the case of males.

DISCUSSION

The main conclusion to be drawn from this study is that males and females afflicted with anorexia nervosa are similar in terms of both premorbid characteristics and illness features, including prognosis. Some minor differences do emerge and will be commented on with the knowledge that, in a multivariate study of this kind, some of them could have arisen by chance whilst others may be due to selection factors and, in respect of the follow-up studies, somewhat different ranges of duration of follow-up.

TABLE 3

Follow-up Status in Terms of Body Weight (wt)[a]

	Wt < 80%	80% ⩽ wt < 90%	90% ⩽ wt < 110%	Wt > 110%	Total
Male	6	9	11	1	27
Female	16	27	51	6	100

[a]Weight is expressed as percentage of matched population mean weight.
Reprinted with permission from Crisp, Burns, and Bhat (1986). Primary anorexia nervosa in the male and female: A comparison of clinical features and prognosis. *British Journal of Medical Psychology, 59,* 123–132.

TABLE 4

Overall Outcome Characteristics Related to Follow-up Body Weight Status

Scale	Outcome Category		
	Wt < 80%	80% ⩽ wt < 90%	90% ⩽ wt < 110%
Nutrition			
Male	1.33 ± 0.42 (6)	2.74 ± 1.00 (9)	3.67 ± 0.52 (11)
Female	1.90 ± 0.38 (16)	2.57 ± 0.50 (27)	2.93 ± 0.36 (51)
	$P < 0.01$	n.s.	$P < 0.001$
Socioeconomic			
Male	1.98 ± 0.62 (6)	3.09 ± 0.53 (9)	3.21 ± 0.51 (11)
Female	2.56 ± 0.53 (16)	2.83 ± 0.47 (27)	2.81 ± 0.61 (51)
	$P < 0.05$	n.s.	$P < 0.05$
Psychosexual			
Male	1.72 ± 0.49 (6)	2.26 ± 1.01 (9)	3.27 ± 0.68 (11)
Female	1.96 ± 0.87 (16)	3.21 ± 0.57 (27)	3.10 ± 0.84 (51)
	n.s.	$P < 0.01$	n.s.
Mental state			
Male	2.68 ± 0.82 (6)	3.33 ± 0.71 (9)	3.91 ± 0.30 (11)
Female	2.50 ± 0.63 (16)	3.36 ± 0.86 (25)	3.38 ± 0.81 (51)
	n.s.	n.s.	$P < 0.05$

Note: Probability values refer to *t* tests ascertaining whether male and female scale scores differ significantly within each outcome category.
Reprinted with permission from Crisp, Burns, and Bhat (1986). Primary anorexia nervosa in the male and female: A comparison of clinical features and prognosis. *British Journal of Medical Psychology, 59,* 123–132.

TABLE 5

Factors Associated with Poor Long-Term Outcome of Anorexia Nervosa

Factor	Male ($n = 27$)	Female ($n = 100$)
Lower social class		****
Poor childhood social adjustments	*	***
Poor relationship between parents	—	***
Activity disturbed premorbid relationship with parents	**	***
Older age of onset		
Of severe dieting	*	**
Of amenorrhea	—	**
Older age at presentation	*	****
Married at presentation	—	**
Long duration at presentation		
Of illness	**	****
Of amenorrhea	—	****
Previous psychiatric treatment	**	****
Symptoms at presentation		
Absence of bulimia	*	
Bulimia		***
Vomiting		*
Purging	*	
Anxiety on eating with others	*	****
Lower body weight (50% m.p.m.w. and below)		
During illness	***	***
At presentation	*	**
Poor outcome one year after presentation (or any subsequent treatment)	—	****
Absence of premorbid sexual activity		
General	**	—
Masturbation	***	—
Fantasy	****	—

*$P < 0.10$; **$P < 0.05$; ***$P < 0.01$; ****$P < 0.001$.
—, Not examined.
Reprinted with permission from Crisp, Burns, and Bhat (1986). Primary anorexia nervosa in the male and female: A comparison of clinical features and prognosis. *British Journal of Medical Psychology, 59,* 123–132.

The similarities include similar social class backgrounds and remarkably similar ages of onset of the condition. The former finding contradicts a previous report based on smaller numbers that males with anorexia nervosa tend to come more often from working-class backgrounds than do females (Crisp, Douglas, et al., 1970). Both groups displayed the same central, though often readily denied, preoccupation with body weight and shape and panic at the prospect of weight gain. Defenses against weight gain were similar, except that females more often abused laxatives whilst males were more likely to have been premorbidly athletic. The assumption here is that, in anorexia nervosa, such premorbid behavior has often been associated with the same fundamental psychopathology to do with bodily control and adolescentdisplacement activity, albeit without, at the time, the major weight loss based on avoidance mechanisms which characterizes anorexia nervosa itself.

Meanwhile, evidence of similarity between male and female anorectics comes from other reports (Crisp, Jones, et al., 1978; Crisp & Bhat, 1982) that, as groups, they score similarly on the CCEI (Crown-Crisp Experiential Index), a self-report psychoneurotic inventory (Crown & Crisp, 1979). In seemingly comparable non-anorectic male and female populations, female scores usually significantly exceed male scores on this instrument. The authors believe that such findings serve to confirm their view that anorexia nervosa is not the existentially and individualistically self-fulfilling state that some claim it to be. Rather it is, beneath the individual bravura and "back-to-the-wall" stance, a regressed and diminished state of body and mind characterized by loss of identity and desperation—even the differences between male and female have become blurred.

The similarity between male and female anorexia nervosa also holds, in the main, for follow-up characteristics except that bulimia and also vomiting as a defense against weight gain are not associated with a poor prognosis in the males. Vomiting in females is, of course, a not uncommon defense; indeed, it is a time-honored defense against weight gain at normal body weight. Vomiting is also said to occur predominantly in females in relation to suppressed anger (Hill, 1972) and can be observed to accompany reactions such as extreme disgust. The prevalence of functional vomiting in males within the general population is less well studied and possibly occurs most commonly following consumption of excessive amounts of alcoholic fluids. Suffice to say that functional vomiting probably often has a different origin in males and females and this may account for the difference in its prognostic significance for male and female anorectics.

Differences also include the absence of death occurring during the follow-up in respect of the males. Two of the authors' female patients had died despite their intensive interventions. This finding is of interest given that the series of male anorectics was unselected and many of them were followed up for a substantial period of time (mean 8.0 years). In most female series, mortality over a number of years is of the order of 5% and in one instance has been reported as being as high as 17% for a major series of female patients followed up for 20 years (Theander, 1983). More recently, one of the authors' male patients has died from suicide.

The sex difference in prevalence of anorexia nervosa is remarkable. The disorder is likely to be even more rare in the male population relative to the female than some reported series have suggested. Certainly, when the present comparisons are corrected for the factor of acceptance for consultation, then the male prevalence rate in the population of those anorectics who have presented to this clinic is no more than 1% of the female rate.

Of course, it may be that there is more masked anorexia nervosa amongst males within the general population, although there is no doubt that such hidden disorder is also common in the female. In this connection this study has shown that premorbid involvement in athletics has been found to characterize male anorectics and perhaps some fully fledged male anorectics lurk undetected amongst the welter of male athletes and, perhaps also, the population of joggers (Yates et al., 1983). Male anorectics also make good chefs and, in the authors' experience, may survive in such roles many years without too much comment.

In the authors' view, male anorexia nervosa may hold important clues to our understanding of the nature of anorexia nervosa. What, for instance, characterizes those males who become sensitive about their "fatness" and embark on the calorie restrictions that burgeon to characterize the condition? Crisp, Matthews, et al. (1986) have demonstrated that, for the female, the key biological and perceptual factor suggesting that fully established anorexia nervosa, in terms of its being an avoidance posture, lies at 20% or more below mean matched population weight. However, the amount of and proportion of fat within the body is twice as much for females as males and it may be that the male threshold is, say, 10% below mean matched population weight.

The authors do not agree with the current Feighner et al. (1972) criteria in respect of necessary weight characteristics for anorexia nervosa. They believe that these matters should not be arbitrarily determined but instead related to psychobiological changes and that, for the present, the debate should be broadened to allow meaningful identification of the necessary weight/fatness characteristics for definition of anorexia nervosa in males and females. Meanwhile, in this chapter, in contrast to the less stringent criteria used in Chapter 10 (i.e., good outcome in weight terms defined as being within 15%

of mean matched population weight), they have chosen the cut-off point of less than 10% below mean matched population weight as an indicator of recovery.

So far as the biological and perceptual weight thresholds for males are concerned, Crisp (1967) suggested that male anorectics were characterized by often having been wrestling with gender identity problems involving a sense of female self and concern about feminine aspects of shape determined by fat rather than lean body mass. Whether or nor this affects biological as well as perceptual forces at work needs to be explored. This view concerning gender identity doubt in males has now also been expressed by Fichter and Daser (1987). The present authors continue to recognize this characteristic, but are impressed that, in their follow-up study, those male anorectics who have recovered nearly all display developed heterosexual adjustments. Of course, it may be that the minority not recovered comprise those with unresolved gender identity doubt which characterized their precipitating conflicts. The authors propose to reexamine these data in this way but doubt that they will find such an outcome.

The factor of calorie restraint which characterizes all anorexia nervosa can sometimes seemingly arise in both male and female cases in association with sensitivity over obesity rather than concern about shape at normal body weight. It is noteworthy that, in the female, such premorbid obesity confers a bad prognosis despite the fact that the original calorie restraint seems not to have been overdetermined by concern about gender role whereas, in the male, premorbid obesity does not confer a poor prognosis. It may be that the habitual concerns about regulation of the self in normal weight females, translated into concern about shape and consequent dieting behavior, are in fact also a feature of the obese females but submerged by the obesity. Thus, it is usually the basis of complaint by those obese females who seek help on account of their obesity. In contrast, obese males much less commonly seek help for treatment of their obesity.

Concerning the gender identity issue, the authors believe that homosexual preoccupations are more likely to be a feature of adolescent sexual conflict in the male or are more likely to be latched onto by those intervening. Homosexuality in the male is often borne of passivity and fear of females, especially in such cases as the authors are discussing here. This may reflect itself more generally in the developmental psychopathology which is being addressed in a clinical situation.

In the authors' experience many female anorectics are equally uncertain, timid, inexperienced, and sometimes undifferentiated in relation to their gender roles. Biological and sociocultural forces combine to render it less likely that this be construed in terms of gender identity doubt, although the reality is that this exists. The authors believe that such doubts are common in adolescence and that anorexia nervosa often precipitates out early on in the face of such challenges in those who are otherwise vulnerable. They believe that this view is upheld by the comparative findings of the follow-up studies.

Like the females, the male anorectics tend to be slightly premorbidly obese but no more than can often be mainly accounted for by rapid growth to puberty (Crisp et al., 1970). Perhaps rapid precipitation into puberty and hence adolescence is itself a risk factor for anorexia nervosa (Crisp, 1970); such rapid growth characterizes females more than males who, on average, grow more slowly. It may be, as has previously been suggested, that any dieting behavior within adolescence provides a mechanism for those who are otherwise vulnerable to develop the condition. Such vulnerabilities doubtless vary between the sexes with, for instance, the female experiencing "fatness," as distinct from obesity, as inseparable from her sexuality, whereas for the adolescent male it is aggression that is perceived as associated with obesity (Crisp et al., 1970). However, it seems that very few males ever seriously contemplate dieting at this age, whereas the majority of females do (Crisp, 1967).

REFERENCES

Burns, T. P. & Crisp, A. H. (1984). Outcome of anorexia nervosa in males. *British Journal of Psychiatry, 145,* 319-325.

Crisp, A. H. (1967). Anorexia nervosa. *Hospital Medicine,* May, 713-718.

Crisp, A. H. (1970). Premorbid factors in adult disorders of weight, with particular reference to primary anorexia nervosa (weight phobia). A literature review. *Journal of Psychosomatic Research. 14,* 1-22.

Crisp, A. H. (1980). *Anorexia Nervosa: Let Me Be.* London: Academic Press.

Crisp, A. H. & Bhat, A. V. (1982). 'Personality' and anorexia nervosa—the phobic avoidance stand. *Psychotherapy and Psychosomatics 38,* 178-200.

Crisp, A. H. & Burns, T. P. (1983). The clinical presentation of anorexia nervosa in males. *International Journal of Eating Disorders, 2,* (4) 5-10.

Crisp, A. H., Douglas, J. W. B., Ross, J., & Stonehill, E. (1970). Some developmental aspects of disorders of weight. *Journal of Psychosomatic Research, 14,* 313-320.

Crisp, A. H., Hsu, L. K. G., Chen, C. N., & Wheeler, M. (1982). Reproductive hormone profiles in male anorexia nervosa before, during and after restoration of body weight to normal: A study of 12 patients. *International Journal of Eating Disorders, 1,* No. 3, 3-9.

Crisp, A. H., Hsu, L. K. G., Harding, B., & Hartshorn, J. (1980). Clinical features of anorexia nervosa (a study of a consecutive series of 102 female patients). *Journal of Psychosomatic Research, 24,* 179-191.

Crisp, A. H., Jones, G. M., & Slater, P. (1978). The Middlesex Hospital Questionnaire: A validity study. *British Journal of Medical Psychology, 51,* 269-280.

Crisp, A. H., MacKinnon, P. C. B., Chen, C. N., & Corker, C.S. (1973). Observations of gonadotrophic and ovarian hormone activity during recovery from anorexia nervosa. *Postgraduate Medical Journal, 49,* 584-590.

Crisp, A. H., Matthews, B., Norton, K. R. W., & Oakey, M. (1986). Weight-related attitudes and behaviour in anorexics, recovered anorexics and normals. *International Journal of Eating Disorders, 5,* 789-798.

Crisp, A. H. & Toms, D. A. (1972). Primary anorexia nervosa or weight phobia in the male: Report on 13 cases. *British Medical Journal, 1,* 334-338.

Crown, S. & Crisp, A. H. (1979). *Manual of the Crown-Crisp Experiential Index.* Sevenoaks, Kent: Hodder & Stoughton.

Feighner, J. P., Robins, E., Gaize, S., Woodruff, R., Winokur, G., & Munoz, R. (1972). Diagnostic criteria for use in psychiatric research. *Archives of General Psychiatry, 26,* 57-63.

Fichter, M. M. & Daser, C. (1987). Symptomatology, psychosexual development and gender identity in 42 anorexic males. *Psychological Medicine, 17,* 409-418.

Hill, O. W. (1972). Functional vomiting. *Hospital Medicine, 1,* 755-759.

Hsu, L. K. G., Crisp, A. H., & Harding, B. (1979). Outcome of anorexia nervosa. *Lancet, i,* 62-65.

Kemsley, W. F. F. (1952). Body weight at different ages and heights. *Annals of Eugenics, London, 16,* 316-334.

Morgan, H. C. & Russell, G. F. M. (1975). Value of family background and clinical features as predictors of long term outcome in anorexia nervosa: 4-year follow-up of 41 patients. *Psychological Medicine, 5,* 355-371.

Palmer, R. L., Crisp, A. H., MacKinnon, P. C. B., Franklin, M., Bonnar, R., & Wheeler, M. (1975). Pituitary sensitivity to 50 ug LH/FSH-RH in subjects with anorexia nervosa in acute and recovery stages. *British Medical Journal, 1,* 179-182.

Theander, S. (1983). Long-term prognosis of anorexia nervosa: A preliminary report. In P. L. Darby, P. E. Garfinkel, D. M. Garner, & D. V. Cosina (Eds.) *Neurology and Neurobiology.* New York: Alan R. Liss. *3,* 441-442.

Yates, A., Leehey, A., & Shisslak, C. M. (1983). Running— An analogue of anorexia? *New England Journal of Medicine, 308,* 251-255.

7

Eating Disorders in Males: Insights from a Clinical and Psychometric Comparison with Female Patients

D. Blake Woodside, David M. Garner, Wendi Rockert, and Paul E. Garfinkel

Although the first medical description of anorexia nervosa (AN) consisted of both a male and female case (Morton, 1694), the nature of the disorder in males has been poorly understood because of its relative rarity. Despite parallels in the clinical description of the disorder in both sexes, some have proposed psychological theories which suggest that AN could not exist in males (Cobb, 1950; Nemiah, 1950; Selvini-Palazzoli, 1965). Moreover some sets of diagnostic criteria have excluded males by a requirement for amenorrhea (Cobb, 1950; Kidd & Wood, 1966; Nemiah, 1950).

Nonetheless, clinical reports of AN in males have continued to appear and a number of authors from centers specializing in eating disorders have published relatively large series of male cases. Similarly, while the predominant

Dr. Woodside was supported by a fellowship grant from the National Institute of Nutrition (Canada).

interest in bulimia nervosa (BN) has been in females, there have been recent reports of the expression of this disorder in males (Andersen, in press; Gwirtsman et al., 1984; Mitchell & Goff, 1984; Pope et al., 1986; Robinson & Holden, 1986; and Turnbull et al., 1987).

This chapter describes a series of cases of males suffering from AN and BN. The description will include information on the clinical, psychological, and biological characteristics of this sample in relation to the more typical female patients.

REVIEW OF THE LITERATURE

An early summary of this literature by Beaumont et al. (1972) contained 250 possible cases which were derived from 31 reports. It was concluded that there was a consistent clinical picture in males that was similar to the picture seen in females. Vandereycken and Van der Broucke (1984) reviewed all cases reported between 1970 and 1980 and reached similar conclusions—that the cases reliably reported were indistinguishable clinically from those reported in females. The literature on AN in males has recently been comprehensively reviewed by Scott (1986) and Sterling and Segal (1985). It was concluded in both reviews that there are no significant gender-dependent differences between males and females with AN with regard to the clinical picture, epidemiology, endocrinology, and outcome of the syndromes.

Crisp et al. (1986) compared a sample of male anorexics to a female sample, matched in terms of clinical characteristics and prognosis, and found no significant differences between the two groups in terms of outcome. Numerous other reports of smaller samples have come to the same conclusion (Fichter et al., 1985; Hall et al., 1985; Andersen & Mickalide, 1985). Margo (1987) reported a sample of 13 males with eating disorders and a comparison group of females, and found no significant differences clinically between the two groups, aside from increased hyperactivity in the male sample. Their finding of a tendency towards increased premorbid weight in the male patients was likely obscured by the failure of this report to distinguish between patients with AN and BN.

Nevertheless, some have argued that there are differences between male and female cases of AN. The issue of sexual orientation in male patients with eating disorders is one such area and it remains controversial. Earlier reports (Crisp, 1967; Crisp & Toms, 1972; Dally, 1969) had suggested that there was an increased incidence of homosexuality in males with eating disorders. Schneider and Agras (1987), Herzog et al. (1984), and Robinson and Holden

(1986) supported this view, based on observations of their own samples.

However, other recent reports (Hall et al., 1985; Crisp et al., 1986; Pope et al., 1986; Turnbull et al., 1987) did not indicate any increase in homosexual orientation. Margo (1987) noted a marked lack of sexual interest in about one-half of his sample. Fichter et al. (1985) also reported marked sexual disinterest in their sample, which they attributed to reduced levels of testosterone. They found that increasing levels of testosterone correlated with increasing sexual drive upon weight normalization. Burns and Crisp (1985) demonstrated a correlation between increased premorbid sexual activity and better prognosis, but did not differentiate between heterosexual and homosexual sexual activity.

More recently, there have been numerous reports of the occurrence of BN in males (Andersen, in press; Gwirtsman et al., 1984; Mitchell & Goff, 1984; Pope et al., 1986; Robinson & Holden, 1986; Schneider & Agras, 1987; Turnbull et al., 1987). These reports have included observations of bulimic behaviors in samples of college students (Pyle et al., 1983). Generally, these reports support the previous observations in undifferentiated samples that clinically these patients are indistinguishable from their female counterparts. However, Schneider and Agras (1987) reported that in their sample of 15 cases, the males were significantly heavier than the females in terms of percentage of ideal body weight, both past and current, and were significantly more likely to have problems with alcohol and social deviancy.

There is very limited literature describing the psychological characteristics of male patients using standardized psychometric measures. Gwirtsman et al. (1984) reported elevated scores on a number of depression scales in their small sample of bulimic men. Fichter et al. (1985) compared a group of male patients with AN and BN to an unselected group of female patients on a variety of psychometric measures, and found that on the Freiburger personality inventory the profiles of these two groups were identical except for "superfeminine" scores by the males on the "masculinity-femininity" subscale.

Three recent studies have utilized the Eating Attitudes Test (EAT; Garner et al., 1982) and the Eating Disorders Inventory (EDI; Garner et al., 1983) to assess the symptoms of AN and the typical psychopathologies of male patients. Turnbull et al. (1987) found that five male bulimics did not score within the pathological range on the EAT and their EDI profiles did not demonstrate the elevations typically seen in female patients with eating disorders. However, males did display elevated scores compared to non-eating disordered men.

By contrast, Andersen (in press) reported that, overall, male patients had elevated scores on both the EDI and the EAT. Profiles were also examined within diagnostic subgroup (restricting AN, AN with bulimic complications, bulimia with a history of AN, and normal weight bulimia). Mean EDI profile scores generally fell well within the pathological range on all subscales for all diagnostic subgroups. On a small subgroup of patients, both pre- and post-treatment scores were available, demonstrating a reduction in EDI scores after treatment.

Finally, Schneider and Agras (1987) reported on a matched sample of 15 male and female bulimics, all of whom were administered an extensive psychometric battery, which included the EAT and the EDI. There were no differences between males and females on these psychometric measures.

In summary, there are several conclusions that can be drawn from the literatures on eating disorders in males. First, there is a broad consensus that the illness in males is clinically similar to, if not indistinguishable from, that in females. Second, while the number of reports is small, the majority of evidence indicates that males have similar psychometric profiles to females on measures of eating pathology. Finally, there is no clear answer to the question of whether there are fundamental disturbances in sexual identity which may distinguish male from female cases of eating disorders.

DESCRIPTION OF THE SAMPLE

Methods

Our sample consists of all males referred to the authors with a provisional diagnosis of eating disorders since 1973. The procedure for assessing these individuals has varied over the years. Currently, all are interviewed initially by one of us (BW) and a psychometric screening battery is administered, which includes the EAT-26 (Garner et al., 1982), the EDI (Garner et al., 1983), and an adapted version of the Berscheid Body Dissatisfaction Scale (Berscheid & Hohrnstedt, 1973). The psychometric battery has evolved over the years and smaller amounts of information are available for earlier patients.

Diagnoses were made according to DSM-III-R criteria (American Psychiatric Association, 1987). All males seen before the publication of DSM-III-R have been rediagnosed accordingly by database review. In our center, bulimic patients are further subdivided according to whether they currently also suffer from anorexia nervosa (AN-B), have suffered from anorexia nervosa in the past (BNphxAN), or have bulimia alone (BN). We make these distinctions as per the suggestions of Russell (1987), and Fairburn and Garner (1986). Of the 53 males seen, 34 met DSM-III-R criteria for a diagnosis of an eating disorder. The diagnoses of our 34 patients with eating disorders are listed in Table 1. Ten patients were diagnosed with restricting AN, six with AN and BN concurrently, six with BNphxAN, eight with BN, and four with eating disorders not otherwise specified (ED-NOS). An example of the last category would be as follows:

Al was a 28-year-old, married man. He had been premorbidly obese, weighing 245 pounds at 6'4 in height. He had decided to diet shortly after the death of a brother, when he was also experiencing significant financial problems. He lost 67 pounds over the course of six months by means of excessive dieting and vigorous exercise. He experienced significant starvation-related complications, including impaired cognition and bloating. At 178 pounds, he had an intense desire to lose weight, was eating less than 500 calories per day, and was exercising vigorously to lose more weight. He was briefly hospitalized, where he lost to 173 pounds. At this time his EAT-26 score was 50, and he showed a marked drive for thinness on the EDI. While he otherwise fit the diagnostic criteria for AN, his weight loss was just short of the required criteria, and thus he was assigned a diagnosis of ED-NOS.

Nineteen of our patients did not qualify for a diagnosis of an eating disorder. Their diagnoses are listed in Table 2. For comparison purposes, similar information on our female referrals from 1981 to 1987 is given in Table 3. In all cases, the diagnoses given are the primary diagnosis. Examples of some of these other cases are as follows:

Bill was an 18-year-old from the Middle East. Known to be suffering from delayed puberty and a learning disability, he had attained a height of 5' and a weight of 100 pounds by age 17. Shortly after his 18th birthday, he had begun to restrain his food intake and lost 15 pounds. On interview, he denied a drive for thinness and claimed that he wished to gain weight. He did admit to very restrained food intake, but related this to an episode of peptic ulcer disease that he had experienced in the previous year. His gastroenterologist had told him after the episode that he should avoid spicy and fatty foods or he would suffer a recurrence of his illness. In his household, this amounted to an extremely restrained diet, and he cut out most foods specifically for the purpose of avoiding his ulcers.

In this case, a diagnosis of conversion disorder was made because of the clear psychologic etiology of the physical symptoms. The only intervention required was to reassure him that he should be able to eat all foods and to suggest to him that he would be more likely to have a recurrence of his ulcer

TABLE 1

**Diagnoses of Male Patients
with Eating Disorders**

Anorexia Nervosa	10
Anorexia Nervosa/Bulimia	6
Bulimia-past history AN	6
Bulimia Nervosa	8
Eating Disorder NOS	4
Total	34

TABLE 2

**Diagnoses of Patients Who Failed to Qualify
for an Eating Disorder Diagnosis**

Affective Disorder	3
Conversion Disorder	3
Schizophrenia	3
Phobic Disorder	2
Personality Disorder	1
Diagnosis Unclear	7
Total	19

TABLE 3

**Females Who Failed to Qualify
for an Eating Disorder Diagnosis (1981–1987)**

Affective Disorder	8
Conversion Disorder	29
Schizophrenia	8
Phobic Disorder	3
Personality Disorder	5
Diagnosis Unclear	26
Other Diagnoses	10
Total	89 of 895 referrals

from worrying about what he was eating. He promptly returned to his premorbid pattern of eating and when last seen had returned to his usual weight.

The following is a slightly more complex case:

Charles was a 30-year-old man, a refugee from Eastern Europe. He was referred for assessment of low weight, and appeared very upset about how low his weight was. He described a cyclical course of increase and decrease in weight associated with changes in food intake. He had been an acrobat as a teenager, and had always been aware of his appearance. During the interview, it became apparent that this man was markedly hypomanic, with grandiose, paranoid ideas and some mildly psychotic thinking. A review of his weight history suggested that his episodes of weight loss corresponded to episodes of mania, several of which had required hospitalization. During these episodes he would lose interest in food and restrict his eating. He had not experienced any episodes of depression. A diagnosis of unipolar mania was made.

Demographic and clinical information for the AN and the combined BN and BNphxAN groups is provided in Table 4. Compared to a larger group of females with similar diagnoses, there are no significant between group differences on age of presentation, duration of illness, or weight at presentation as a

TABLE 4

Clinical Features

MALES AND FEMALES WITH ANOREXIA NERVOSA			
	Males	Females	p
	(n = 8)	(n = 163)	
Age	30.0 (5.7)	25.8 (7.0)	0.10
Weight at diagnosis as % average	74.5 (9.0)	75.2 (7.8)	ns
Duration of illness (mos)	96.4 (85.5)	65.9 (65.9)	ns
MALES AND FEMALES WITH BULIMIA NERVOSA			
	Males	Females	p
	(n = 11)	(n = 368)	
Age	27.7 (9.2)	24.4 (5.1)	ns
Weight at diagnosis as % average	106.8 (14.5)	102.7 (14.8)	ns
Duration of illness (mos)	73.8 (101.2)	70.7 (54.6)	ns

Numbers in parentheses are standard deviations.

TABLE 5
EAT Scores Comparing Matched Male and Female Eating Disorder Samples

	Females (n = 20)	Males (n = 20)	p
Total EAT score	39.0 (12.54)	31.15 (15.56)	0.087
Subscale scores			
Dieting	23.2 (8.03)	16.75 (10.12)	0.032
Bulimia	10.65 (3.45)	9.60 (3.99)	ns
Oral control	5.15 (4.63)	4.80 (5.08)	ns

Numbers in parentheses are standard deviations.

percentage of matched population mean weight (Health and Welfare Canada, 1954).

With the above in mind, we have collapsed a sample of 20 males who meet DSM-III-R criteria for AN or BN and matched them with a sample of females on the following variables: diagnostic subgroup, age, weight at presentation as a percent of matched population mean weight, duration of illness, and year of presentation. Male patients who engaged in binge eating and/or vomiting were also matched with females on the frequency of these behaviors. The male patients selected are the subset of patients on whom complete psychometric data is available.

Table 5 displays a comparison of the matched male and female samples on the EAT-26. Males (x=16.75, SD=10.12) had significantly lower scores than females (x=23.2, SD=8.03) on the Dieting subscale but were indistinguishable on the Bulimia and Oral Control subscales. There was a trend for total EAT-26 scores to be higher in the female group, although similar proportions of males (75.0%) and females (90.0%) scored above the cut-off score of 20.

Table 6 indicates EDI subscale means for the two comparison groups. Of the eight EDI subscales, the only significant group difference was on the Drive for Thinness subscale, with males (x=11.57, SD=6.91) reporting less pathological scores than females (x=17.15, SD=3.89). This is consistent with the above-mentioned pattern on the EAT-26 Dieting subscale. Although there are trends for males to have lower mean scores on the Body Dissatisfaction and Interoceptive Awareness subscales, these do not reach statistical significance.

Table 7 presents data on sexual orientation in 28 of our sample of male patients. Twenty-two (78.6%) of the patients reported exclusively heterosexual orientation, while six (21.4%) reported either bisexual or exclusively homosexual orientation. This is a statistically significant elevation from the 13% rate

TABLE 6

EDI Scores

	Females (n = 19)	Males (n = 19)	p
Drive for thinness	17.15 (3.89)	11.57 (6.91)	0.005
Bulimia	10.47 (6.65)	8.10 (4.98)	ns
Body dissatisfaction	18.21 (8.82)	13.10 (8.62)	0.08
Ineffectiveness	12.94 (8.20)	10.21 (8.12)	ns
Perfectionism	8.78 (5.38)	7.63 (5.58)	ns
Interpersonal distrust	5.00 (4.43)	7.05 (4.77)	ns
Interoceptive awareness	13.21 (6.81)	9.47 (5.75)	0.076
Maturity fears	5.00 (6.02)	3.84 (3.09)	ns

Numbers in parentheses are standard deviations.

TABLE 7

Sexual Orientation—Males

	ANR n = 5	ANB n = 6	BNphxAN n = 5	BN n = 8	ED-NOS n = 4	Total
Exclusively heterosexual	5 (100%)	5 (83%)	2 (40%)	6 (75%)	4 (100%)	22 (78.5%)
Bisexual/ homosexual	0	1 (17%)	3 (60%)	2 (25%)	0	6 (21.5%)

Numbers in parentheses are percentages.

TABLE 8

Sexual Orientation—Females

	ANR n = 68	ANB n = 77	BNphxAN n = 175	BN n = 170
Exclusively heterosexual	62 (91.2%)	70 (90.9%)	158 (90.3%)	163 (95.9%)
Primarily heterosexual, some homosexual	2 (2.9%)	3 (3.9%)	8 (4.6%)	3 (1.8%)
Bisexual	1 (1.5%)	1 (1.3%)	1 (0.6%)	1 (0.6%)
Exclusively homosexual	0	0	2 (1.1%)	0
Asexual	3 (4.4%)	2 (2.6%)	2 (1.1%)	0
Autosexual	0	1 (1.3%)	4 (2.3%)	3 (1.8%)
Total with some homosexual orientation	3 (4.4%)	4 (5.2%)	11 (6.3%)	4 (2.4%)

Numbers in parentheses are percentages.

usually quoted for the general population (Kinsey et al., 1948; $X^2 = 6.239$, df=1, $0.01 < p > 0.02$). The highest rate of homosexual/bisexual orientation is among the BNphxAN group. As a comparison, Table 8 presents data on sexual orientation for a group of 467 female patients, showing a 4% rate of some homosexual orientation. Rates of nonheterosexual orientations are uniformly low in the female sample, and much lower than in our male sample when compared both globally and across diagnostic subgroups.

Table 9 compares the male patients to a much larger group of female patients with eating disorders on a variation of the Berscheid Body Dissatisfaction Scale. The percentages of patients receiving each of the eating disorder diagnoses (AN, BN, ANB, BNphxAN) in the male and the female group were similar. The scale is a six-point, forced choice scale, with responses ranging from "extremely satisfied" to "extremely dissatisfied." The numbers on this table refer to the percentage of respondents who are dissatisfied with specific parts of their body. In our data analysis, "dissatisfied" refers to the percentages of respondents who scored "somewhat dissatisfied," "quite

TABLE 9

Berscheid Body Dissatisfaction Scale Scores

Item	Males (n = 18)	Females (n = 137)	p
Weight	83.3	80.3	ns[1]
Facial attractiveness	22.2	33.1	ns[1]
Breasts	66.7[2]	50.0	ns[1]
Abdomen	94.1	74.5	ns[1]
Buttocks	72.2	75.9	ns[1]
Hips	66.7	77.2	ns[1]
General muscle tone	83.3	65.7	ns[1]
Overall body appearance	83.3	71.5	ns[1]
Total score	73.4 (11.85)[3]	75.1 (16.19)[3]	ns[4]

Numbers for individual body parts are percentages "dissatisfied" with the indicated item (see text).
Numbers for "Total score" are the actual averaged scores on the scale for each group.
[1]by chi-squared analysis.
[2]n = 9 for this item.
[3]numbers in parentheses are standard deviations.
[4]by t-test.

dissatisfied," or "extremely dissatisfied." There are no significant differences between our male and female samples.

Case Examples

We have generally found male patients to be no different from female patients either clinically or in terms of their responses to treatment or in clinical course. The following case examples illustrate some of the treatment issues encountered and also illustrate the change in diagnostic status that occasionally occurs over time.

Doug is a 28-year-old man of northern European origin. He has been living in Canada for nearly a decade. He was initially referred for assessment of his binge eating and vomiting. He reported a three-month history of extremely severe binge eating; his usual form of termination for a binge was to pass out because of the quantity of food consumed. This was in the context of many years, concern about his weight and shape, and several drastic and strenuous efforts at dieting that had recently brought him to his lowest weight, 156 pounds, 100% of mean matched population weight (MMPW). He was also preoccupied with his bowels, and used laxatives, daily enemas, and weekly colonic irrigations as methods of weight control. At the time of consultation, he was also receiving Human Chorionic Gonadotropin injections from a weight loss clinic. He was initially diagnosed as suffering from BN (DSM-III-R), but had never met weight criteria for AN.

He was given a brief, unsuccessful trial of outpatient treatment, and then was referred to an intensive day treatment program. During his three months in this program, he was able to control his bingeing and vomiting, cease laxatives, and eat comparatively normally. However, he openly admitted that he was restraining his eating on evenings and weekends to avoid gaining any weight, and was quite direct in expressing his opinion that he would need to continue dieting once he left the program.

Within one week after leaving the program, he had begun to binge and vomit again, and had reduced his caloric intake to about 500 cals/day. He openly admitted to an intense desire to be thinner, and finally noted that in retrospect he had probably been bingeing since he began to diet as a teenager. He continues to struggle with his dilemma—that his urges to restrict are totally ego-syntonic, while his bingeing and purging behaviors are very ego-dystonic.

When this man was originally assessed for Day Hospitalization, it was felt that he would be a good candidate, mainly because of the short duration of his bingeing and vomiting behaviors. As his treatment progressed, the very high degree of investment in a thinner shape became more apparent, as well as his real inability to shift this "nervosa" part of his illness. This man demonstrates an extreme investment in dieting and body shape, similar to that seen in many female patients with eating disorders.

Eric is a 26-year-old law student, who was referred for assessment of his bingeing and vomiting. He had an eight-year history of intense preoccupation with weight and shape, expressed for him through intensive weight-lifting programs, which included special diets. He had begun to binge and vomit in his early twenties.

Six months prior to consultation, he had lost one foot above the ankle in a motorcycle accident, and during his six-month rehabilitation had been symptom-free. During this time he had been hospitalized, and reported eating freely. He continued to lift weights while in the hospital. Shortly after his discharge, he again began to restrain his eating, and began to occasionally binge and vomit.

This man responded extremely well to a few psychoeducational sessions aimed primarily at identifying for him how he had been able to stop his symptoms while in the hospital. The effects of his amputation on his body image were also discussed, and he seemed to have had a reduction of his own investment in a "perfect" body shape since his accident. At three-month follow-up he was bingeing only rarely, and was eating essentially normally.

This man demonstrates the interesting effect of loss of a body part on body image. Our sense is that the loss of his foot made it more possible for him to consider eating normally and tolerating the possible attendant weight gain because of the reduced investment in body image needed to successfully grieve for his lost body part. The amputation and the subsequent enforced hospitalization also seemed somehow to give him permission to eat more normally while being rehabilitated, and he was able to use this experience to help process the other information that had been provided for him in his sessions.

Fred is a 27-year-old homosexual man who was referred for assessment of low weight and episodes of bingeing and vomiting. Clinically, he had suffered from both AN and BN for many years, but had managed to continue working quite successfully. His experience with relationships was less successful, including a disastrous marriage to a woman and a series of sadomasochistic homosexual relationships.

He was referred to the same intensive day program mentioned above, and had a very different course. After an initial period of intense resistance to treatment, he began to allow himself to gain weight, and his eating began to normalize. By 10 weeks into the program he had gained nearly 15 pounds and was no longer bingeing or purging. He had also agreed to be interviewed by our family therapist with his homosexual lover. At this point, he began to reveal to the patient group more details about his homosexual relationships, and abruptly discharged himself after revealing in graphic detail the precise nature of his sadomasochistic sexual activity with his lover. He refused further follow-up.

With this man, the importance of his sexual orientation as a perpetuator to his eating disorder did not become clear until his eating had normalized somewhat. While he had made superficial attachments to the other patients in the treatment center, he could not bring himself to connect with them in any way except sexually. Our sense was that the intense pressure to be open with the group about relationships eventually caused him to decide to disclose his sexual practices, but that he then found it impossible to remain in the group.

DISCUSSION

As in previous reports, the most notable finding in the current series is the failure to find differences between males and females with AN and BN. Our groups are indistinguishable on most clinical parameters.

The differences we have observed in terms of psychopathology may warrant speculation on the relative contribution of cultural factors for males and for females who develop the disorders. The relatively low scores by males on the Dieting (EAT) and Drive for Thinness (EDI) subscales could represent a culturally dependent difference between male and female attitudes towards dieting as a means of weight control. There was a trend for males to report less discomfort with their body on the EDI, which would be consistent with their reduced efforts to diet. However, this interpretation is difficult to reconcile with the failure to find gender-dependent differences on the Berscheid Body Dissatisfaction questionnaire. This scale measures attitudes towards a wide range of body parts, most of which are not the focus of clinical concern of most patients who present with eating disorders (ears, nose, etc.). It has been shown to correlate only 0.29 to the Drive for Thinness and to 0.55 to the Body Dissatisfaction subscales of the EDI (Garner, Olmsted, & Polivy, 1983).

Data from the current sample on sexual orientation indicate that homosexuality is increased in the male sample compared to the female sample. These results are less conclusive than some other reports. The results may indicate an increased level of disturbance in males with eating disorders, or may simply reflect a sampling bias regarding the males who were assessed at our center.

We have included case history data to demonstrate clinically observed similarities and differences between the male and female populations. For males, concerns about body shape seem to cluster more around looking "masculine" than around wishing to be thin. This is particularly true of the bulimic group. There is a group of restricting AN patients who simply want to be thin; this latter group is very similar to the female patients in this regard.

The fact that such a high proportion of male patients referred do not receive an eating disorder diagnosis is intriguing. Referring sources may be less familiar with the illness in males and refer a greater number of inappropriate patients, or it may be that the number of males suffering from symptoms which superficially resemble a true eating disorder may be proportionally greater in males compared to females. According to the current survey, the main distinguishing factor clinically between the eating-disordered group and the other group is the presence or absence of body image distortion and drive for thinness/avoidance of fatness.

In summary, it may be concluded that anorexia nervosa and bulimia nervosa are more alike than dissimilar in males and females, and that the differences in the indices of psychopathology are generally not indicative of differences in process. Further examination of psychopathological processes, using rigorous measures on a larger sample across diagnostic subgroups is needed to determine whether this conclusion is correct.

REFERENCES

American Psychiatric Association. (1987). *Diagnostic and Statistical Manual of Mental Disorders* (3rd ed. rev.) (DSM-III-R). Washington, D.C.: Author.

Andersen, A., Anorexia nervosa and bulimia nervosa in males.

Andersen, A. & Mickalide, A. (1985). Anorexia nervosa and bulimia. *Bull. Men. Clinic, 49* (3):227-235.

Berscheid, E., & Hohrnstedt, G. (1973). The happy American body: A survey report. *Psychology Today, Nov.,* 119-131.

Beaumont, P. J. V., Beardwood, C. J., & Russell, G. F. M. (1972). The occurrence of the syndrome of anorexia nervosa in male subjects. *Psychol. Med., 2,* 216-231.

Burns, T. & Crisp, A. H. (1985). Factors affecting prognosis in male anorexics. *J. Psychiatric Res., 19,*323-328.

Cobb, S. (1950). Borderlines of Psychiatry. Cambridge: Harvard University Press.

Crisp, A.H. (1967). Anorexia nervosa. *Hospital Medicine, 1,*713-718.

Crisp, A.H. & Toms, D.A. (1972). Primary anorexia nervosa or weight phobia in the male. *Br. Med. J., 1,*334-338.

Crisp, A.H., Burns, T., & Bhat, A.V. (1986). Primary anorexia nervosa in the male and female: A comparison of clinical features and prognosis. *Br. J. Med. Psychol., 59,*123-132.

Dally, P. (1969). *Anorexia Nervosa.* London: Heinemann.

Dally, P., Gomez, J., & Issacs, A.J. (1979). *Anorexia Nervosa.* London: Heinemann.

Fairburn, C.G. & Garner, D.M. (1986). The diagnosis of bulimia nervosa. *Int. J. Eating, Disorders 5* (3),403-419.

Fichter, M.M., Daser, C., & Postpischl, F. (1985). Anorexic syndromes in the male. *J. Psychiatric Res., 19,*305-313.

Garfinkel, P.E., Moldofsky, H., & Garner, D.M. (1980). The heterogeneity of anorexia nervosa. *Arch. Gen. Psych., 37,*1036-1040.

Garner, D.M., Olmsted, M.P., Bohr, Y., & Garfinkel, P.E. (1982). The eating attitudes test: Psychometric features and clinical correlates. *Psychol. Med., 12,*871-878.

Garner, D.M., Olmsted, M.P., & Polivy, J. (1983). Development and validation of a multidimensional eating disorder inventory for anorexia and bulimia. *Int. J. Eating Disorders, 2*(2),15-34.

Garner, D.M., Olmsted, M.P., & Garfinkel, P.E. (1985). Similarities among bulimic groups selected by different weights and weight histories. *J. Psychiatric Res. 19,*129-134.

Garner, D.M. Garfinkel, P.E., & O'Shaughnessy, M. (1985). The validity of the distinction between bulimia with and without anorexia nervosa. *Am. J. Psychiatry, 142,*581-587.

Gwirtsman, H.E., Roy-Byrne, P., Lerner, L., & Yager, J. (1984). Bulimia in men: A report of three cases with neuroendocrine findings. *J. Clin. Psychiatry, 45,*78-81.

Hall, A., Delahunt, J.W., & Ellis, P.M. (1985). Anorexia nervosa in the male: Clinical features and follow-up of nine patients. *J. Psychiatr. Res., 19,*315-321.

Health and Welfare Canada. (1954). Canadian Average Weights for Height, Age, and Sex. (Pamphlet). Ottawa: Nutrition Division of the Department of Health and Welfare.

Herzog, D.B., Norman, D.K., Gordon, C., & Pepose, M. (1984). Sexual conflict and eating disorders in 27 males. *Am. J. Psychiatry, 141,*898-990.

Kidd, C.B. & Wood, J.F. (1966). Some observations on anorexia nervosa. *Posgrad. Med. J., 42,*443-448.

Kinsey, A.C., Pomeroy, W.B., Martin, C.E. (1948). *Sexual Behavior in the Human Male.* Philadelphia: W.B. Saunders.

Margo, J.L. (1987) Anorexia nervosa in males. *Br. J. Psychiatry, 151,*80-83.

Mitchell, J.E., & Goff, G. (1984). Bulimia in male patients *Psychosomatics 25,*909-913.

Morton, R. (1694). *Phthisiologica: Or a Treatise of Consumption*. London: Smith and Walford.

Nemiah, J.C. (1950). Anorexia nervosa: A clinical study. *Medicine, 29*,225-268.

Pope, H.G., Hudson, J.I., & Jonas, J.M. (1986). Bulimia in men: A series of fifteen cases. *J. Nerv. Ment. Dis., 174*,117-119.

Pyle, R.L., Mitchell, J.E., Eckert, E.D., Halvorson, P.A., Neuman, P.A., & Goff, G.M. (1983). The incidence of bulimia in freshman college students. *Int. J. Eating Disorders, 2*,75-85.

Robinson, P.H. & Holden, N.L. (1986). Bulimia nervosa in the male: A report of nine cases. *Psychol. Med., 16*,795-803.

Russell, G.F.M. (1979). Bulimia nervosa: An ominous variant of anorexia nervosa. *Psychol. Med., 9*,429-448.

Russell, G.F.M. (1987). The diagnostic formulation in bulimia nervosa (in press).

Schneider, J.A. & Agras, W.S. (1987). Bulimia in males: A matched comparison with females. *Int. J. Eating Disorders, 6*,235-242.

Scott, D. (1986). Anorexia nervosa in the male. *Int. J. Eating Disorders, 5*,799-819.

Selvini-Palazzoli, M. (1965). The meaning of body for anorexia nervosa patients. Psychotherapeutic implications. *Proc.*—6th Int. Congr. Psychotherapy, London, 1964. Selected Lectures. Basel: Karger, pp. 96-103.

Sterling, J.W. & Segal, J.D. (1985). Anorexia nervosa in males: A critical review. *Int. J. Eating Disorders, 4*,559-572.

Turnbull, J.D., Freeman, C.P.L., Barry, F., & Annandale, A. (1987). Physical and psychological characteristics of five male bulimics. *Br. J. Psychiatry, 150*,25-29.

Vandereycken, W. & Van der Broucke, S. (1984). Anorexia nervosa in males. *Acta Psychiatrica Scandinavica, 70*,447-454.

8

Psychometric Testing in 76 Males with Eating Disorders

David H. Edwin and Arnold E. Andersen

Over a 10-year period, male inpatients and outpatients were referred to the Eating Disorders Treatment Service of the Psychiatric Consultation Service of the Johns Hopkins Hospital Department of Psychiatry because of tentative diagnoses of eating disorders made by referring physicians or therapists.

Full psychiatric evaluations were conducted with all patients, including comprehensive history and mental state examination as well as comprehensive weight and eating histories. All patients were also administered a number of psychological instruments, including the Eating Attitudes Test, the Eating Disorders Inventory, the General Health Questionnaire, and the Zung Depression Inventory. Inpatients were also administered the age-appropriate Wechsler IQ test, the Affects Balance Scale (ABS) (Derogatis, 1977), the SCL-90-R (Derogatis, 1975), and the Minnesota Multiphasic Personality Inventory (MMPI).

After thorough evaluation, patients were assigned to the following diagnostic groups:

Primary Eating Disorders

1. *Anorexia nervosa, restricting subtype (ANR):* These patients meet DSM-III-R criteria for anorexia nervosa, but have no history of bulimic behaviors. N=21.

2. *Anorexia nervosa with bulimic features (ANB):* These patients meet DSM-III-R criteria for anorexia nervosa, and acknowledge bingeing behavior as well. N=16.

3. *Normal-weight bulimia with a history of anorexia nervosa (BNHxAN).* These patients met DSM-III-R criteria for bulimia nervosa, and had histories of anorexia nervosa in the past. N=7.

4. *Normal-weight bulimia without history of anorexia nervosa (BN).* These patients met DSM-III-R criteria for bulimia nervosa, but had never met criteria for anorexia nervosa. N=12.

Secondary Eating Disorders (SED)

5. These patients were referred for evaluation of anorexia nervosa or bulimia, but ultimately diagnosed as suffering from other psychiatric disorders. Their diagnoses included depressive disorders, schizophrenia, anxiety disorders, and psychophysiological reactions. N=20.

Because of small numbers, patients were classed for some analyses as **Primary Eating Disorders** (Groups 1-4, N=56) or **Secondary Eating Disorders** (Group 5, N=20). Other analyses contrasted **Restricting Anorectics** (Group 1, N=21) with **all bulimic patients** (Groups 2-4, N=35). When too small for separate analyses of normal-weight bulimics with and without history of anorexia nervosa, these two groups were sometimes combined.

A reference group of 84 female eating disorder patients (49 ANR, 6 ANB, 16 BNHxAN, 13 BN) was matched for comparison purposes from successive consultations and admissions immediately after each of the males.

Group means were compared using the one-way analysis of variance. Individual group comparisons were made only when overall ANOVAs were significant at the .10 level. However, the number of fully examined male inpatients was small, so that the intergroup comparisons were not susceptible to statistical hypothesis testing. Therefore, the characterizations of those groups should be considered only suggestive and hypothetical, and are offered for discussion in part because substantial data exist about the same measures among female eating disorder patients.

RESULTS

Demographics and History (All Patients)

Table 1 describes the diagnostic categories of all patients referred. Fifty-six patients (73.7%) met DSM-III-R criteria for a primary eating disorder, while 20

TABLE 1

Diagnoses

Diagnosis	Females (%)	Males (%)	All
ANR	23 (32)	21 (28)	44 (30)
ANB	6 (8)	16 (21)	22 (15)
BN/HxAN	17 (24)	7 (9)	24 (16)
BN	13 (18)	12 (16)	25 (17)
Atypical E.D.	10 (14)	0 (0)	10 (7)
Psychogenic Dysphagia	0 (0)	4 (5)	4 (3)
Symptomatic E.D.	3 (4)	17 (22)	20 (14)
TOTAL	72 (49)	76 (51)	148

patients (26.3%) fell into other diagnostic categories. These proportions are similar to those described in published studies of females referred for consultation in this clinic.

Table 2 reveals no significant differences among groups on age or education, although all groups were older than is typically reported among female eating disorder patients.

Weights in patient histories (Table 3) were calculated as proportions of age- and sex-matched "ideal body weight." Males in general had higher maximum weights than females (mean of 130% IBW, versus 120%, $p < .06$). While women in general *felt fat* prior to dieting, men *were* medically or statistically *overweight* prior to the onset of their eating disorders. Diagnostic groups differed significantly, $p < .04$, with BN presenting the highest maximum weights. There were no differences in minimum weights or admission-consultation weights by sex. Among male subjects, diagnostic groups differed in minimum past weight, $p < .001$, with BN showing the least starvation by history, consistent with their diagnosis. Groups also differed in weight at referral or admission, $p < .001$, with anoretic groups (ANB, ANR) thinnest and BN patients heaviest. Patients differed in their own concepts of their ideal body weights, $p < .003$, supporting our clinical impression that women tend to seek lower body weights while men primarily seek change in body shape ("better physique").

Males did not differ significantly from females with respect to frequency of bingeing. Our male subgroups differed in their frequency of bingeing, $p < .002$; ANB patients averaged 35.5 binges per week, followed by BNHxAN (19.7),

TABLE 2

Demographics

	Age at Admit/Cons Mean (S.D.)	Yrs. Educ. Mean (S.D.)	White to Non-White	% Never Married	% Married	Sep/ Wid/ Div
ANR			41:3			
F	25.8 (8.8)	12.8 (3.1)		57	30	13
M	24.0 (9.9)	13.1 (4.1)		76	10	14
ANB			22:0			
F	17.3 (3.0)	11.7 (2.3)		100	0	0
M	26.6 (10.9)	19.9 (3.6)		75	13	13
BNHxAN						
F	26.8 (7.2)	13.2 (2.3)		53	24	24
M	27.7 (5.4)	14.0 (3.2)		71	14	14
BN			24:1			
F	24.9 (5.9)	14.3 (1.8)		77	23	0
M	30.4 (11.9)	15.8 (3.3)		33	42	25
Atypical E.D.			9:1	50	40	
F	27.5 (10.5)	11.3 (1.8)		50	40	10
M	—	—		—	—	—
Psychogenic Dysphagia			4:0			
F	—	—		—	—	—
M	30.0 (11.3)			25	75	0
S.E.D.			18:1	57.9	26.3	
F	22.3 (3.2)	12.0 (0)		67	33	0
M	26.6 (12.1)			56	25	19
All Pts.		13 (3)	141:7	62.2	24.3	
F	25.2 (7.9)	13 (3)	69:4	61.1	27.8	
M	26.8 (12.6)	13 (4)				

and BN (12.3). ANR and SED averaged less than .2 binges per week. The ANB and BNHxAN groups evidenced laxative abuse more frequently than ANR, BN, or SED patients, among whom this symptom was quite rare ($p < .05$). Across all of the primary eating disorder groups, about half of the patients acknowledged compulsive exercise; however, only one of the twenty SED patients reported this symptom. On the other hand, 25% of the SED patients reported that their initial weight loss was inadvertent, compared with no patients in any of the primary eating disorder groups, in which all patients had sought lower body weights.

TABLE 3

Weight Histories
Mean (SD) as Percent of Ideal Weight

	Highest Mean (S.D.)	Lowest Mean (S.D.)	Referral Mean (S.D.)	Ideal Self Mean (S.D.)	Inadvertent
ANR					
F	111 (21)	64 (9)	67 (11)	79 (9)	0
M	123 (30)	72 (12)	76 (10)	92 (14)	
ANB					0
F	112 (14)	78 (10)	82 (10)	84 (11)	
M	130 (48)	74 (14)	80 (10)	85 (19)	
BNHxAN					0
F	129 (23)	82 (14)	102 (28)	87 (7)	
M	146 (21)	76 (17)	95 (9)	92 (8)	
BN					1
F	121 (24)	91 (10)	107 (25)	90 (7)	
M	155 (24)	103 (9)	118 (17)	106 (7)	
Atypical E.D.					3
F	135 (48)	84 (15)	124 (9)	93 (21)	
M	—	—	—	—	
Psychogenic Dysphagia					
F	—	—	—	—	
M	119 (9)	90 (12)	99 (15)	—	
Symp					
F	124 (42)	86 (20)	89 (21)	89 (21)	
M	117	85	96.3	104 (14)	
All Pts.					
F	120 (27)	78 (15)	88 (25)	87 (10)	5:68
M	130 (36)	81 (18)	91 (22)	96 (16)	4:72

TABLE 4

Wechsler Full Scale IQ

	ANR M (SD)	ANB M (SD)	BNHxAn M (SD)	BN M (SD)
F	107 (15)	117 (17)	104 (11)	115 (9)
M	115 (20)	106 (12)	115 (12)	90 (9)

PSYCHOMETRICS

IQ (ED Inpatients Only)

SED patients were not admitted to the ED service, and thus were not tested for intelligence. The three ED groups with histories of weight loss (ANR, ANB, BNHxAN) achieved Full Scale Verbal, Performance and Full Scale Wechsler IQ scores in the upper Average to High Average ranges, while the normal-weight bulimics (BN) averaged in the lower part of the Average range. (See Table 4.)

GHQ, Zung (All Patients)

On the General Health Questionnaire, all groups substantially exceeded the cutting point for clinical distress (≥ four positive responses) with means ranging from 8-16 and without significant differences among groups. Scores on the Zung Depression Scale ranged from 51-68, with ANR patients scoring highest and SED scoring lowest, p < .02. There were no significant differences on either test by sex.

EAT (All Patients)

On the Eating Attitudes Test, patients differed by diagnosis, p < .02. SED patients scored lowest (M=23), considerably below the cut-off point in screening for eating disorders (> 30). This would be expected in the case of a validated screening test for primary eating disorders. Males did not differ significantly from females in their EAT scores. (See Table 5.)

EDI (All Patients)

Scores on the subscales of the Eating Disorders Inventory distributed differently across groups. Groups differed significantly on the Drive for

TABLE 5

Eating Attitudes Test

	ANR M(SD)	ANB M(SD)	BNHxAn M(SD)	BNsAN M(SD)	Atyp M(SD)	Symp M(SD)
F	66.8 (28.5)	40.8 (3.8)	53.5 (17.0)	47.2 (12.3)	29.6 (16.9)	42.0 (—)
M	57.3 (12.8)	38.8 (28.1)	61.3 (29.5)	38.3 (18.5)		23.1 (9.9)

Thinness scale, p < .001, with all Primary ED groups exceeding the SED group (p. 01), but no significant differences among the PED subgroups. Females scored higher than males, p < .08, providing modest additional support for the notion that female patients have a greater motivation for weight loss. Groups differed as well on the Bulimia scale, p. < .001; all bulimic groups (ANB, BNHxAN, BN) exceeded others (ANR, SED). Interestingly, both normal weight bulimic groups exceeded the ANB patients on the Bulimia scale as well. Males did not differ from females except on the Body Dissatisfaction scale; as expected, and consistent with their subjective weight histories, women were more dissatisfied with their bodies than men. (See Table 6.)

The Body Distortion scale did not discriminate among groups overall, although primary ED patients scored higher than SED patients, p < .04, and BN patients tended to score higher than other primary ED patients. Across groups, females again exceeded males, p < .001. The Ineffectiveness scale did not distinguish among all groups overall, or between sexes; however, SEDs again tended to score lowest. The Interoceptive Awareness scale distinguished among groups overall, p < .05, with BNHxAN patients scoring highest and SED patients scoring lowest; no significant sex differences emerged. No differences were apparent among groups or between sexes on the Perfectionism, Interpersonal Distrust, and Maturity Fears scales. Overall, then, the EDI is supported as a valuable tool for eliciting differences among subgroups of primary and secondary eating disorders.

ABS (ED Inpatients Only)

The Affects Balance Scale was administered only to patients admitted to the ED inpatient service. All ED patients demonstrated significant anhedonia, scoring more than a standard deviation below the mean on scales reflecting subjective joy, contentment, energy, and affection; there were, however, no significant differences among groups. Although females were more discontented and depleted of energy than males (p < .07 and .01 respectively), all means reflected clinically significant affective impoverishment. (See Table 7.)

Similarly, the groups tended to produce profiles elevated across the negative scales (Anxiety, Hostility, Guilt, Hostility), without significant differences by group or sex. The net balance between positive and negative affects was therefore highly skewed toward a negative and impoverished balance across all patient groups.

SCL-90-R (ED Inpatients Only)

Symptomatically, as well, all groups were quite troubled. All averaged more than two standard deviations above the mean on the Global Severity

TABLE 6

Eating Disorder Inventory Scores

	ANR M(SD)	ANB M(SD)	BNHxAN M(SD)	BN M(SD)	Atyp M(SD)	Symp M(SD)
Drive Thinness						
F	13.10 (6.5)	12.60 (5.5)	16.55 (4.0)	14.58 (3.9)	7.25 (7.8)	4.00 (5.66)
M	10.69 (7.8)	9.90 (6.2)	15.00 (6.5)	13.73 (4.6)	—	2.8 (3.8)
Bulimia						
F	1.50 (3.1)	5.20 (46)	11.36 (5.4)	10.83 (5.8)	0.25 (0.7)	0 (0)
M	2.62 (3.6)	5.50 (4.2)	9.80 (7.3)	9.00 (4.9)	—	1.07 (1.6)
Body Dissat						
F	16.60 (9.9)	9.00 (7.4)	19.09 (8.3)	19.92 (9.6)	12.13 (8.9)	11.50 (10.6)
M	10.54 (8.2)	8.40 (7.4)	12.00 (7.7)	14.36 (6.9)	—	8.73 (5.9)
Ineffectiveness						
F	14.20 (8.7)	6.20 (9.6)	14.64 (8.4)	9.17 (8.7)	9.88 (8.3)	3.00 (4.2)
M	12.39 (10.6)	9.00 (6.5)	16.00 (6.2)	7.36 (4.4)	—	5.33 (7.8)
Perfectionism						
F	8.90 (5.9)	7.80 (6.5)	8.46 (4.9)	10.00 (4.4)	6.50 (4.9)	3.00 (1.4)
M	9.15 (6.0)	7.50 (5.9)	9.20 (8.0)	7.55 (5.3)	—	7.87 (5.0)
Interpersonal Distance						
F	8.50 (4.5)	2.40 (2.5)	7.00 (5.7)	3.50 (4.3)	6.13 (4.2)	0 (0)
M	7.07 (5.3)	6.70 (4.9)	7.40 (2.7)	3.64 (2.1)	—	4.20 (5.1)
Interoceptive Awareness						
F	9.00 (7.3)	7.60 (3.6)	13.55 (7.4)	9.58 (5.9)	5.13 (4.5)	9.00 (11.31)
M	10.77 (7.7)	8.00 (8.1)	15.20 (7.3)	7.91 (4.8)	—	4.67 (5.2)
Maturity Fears						
F	5.90 (7.1)	5.00 (6.9)	2.72 (3.5)	4.67 (5.8)	1.38 (2.1)	4.00 (2.8)
M	6.92 (6.4)	4.80 (6.7)	5.80 (1.8)	2.82 (2.9)	—	4.00 (2.8)

TABLE 7

Affects Balance Scale
Mean (SD)

	ANR	ANB	BNHxAN	BN	Female	Male
JOY					29 (15)	34 (11)
F	27 (16)	33 (—)	28 (4)	30 (26)		
M	32 (11)	36 (13)	39 (13)	37 (9)		
CON					28 (14)	34 (10)
F	27 (17)	43 (—)	28 (3)	24 (14)		
M	32 (10)	35 (12)	43 (3)	34 (6)		
VIG					28 (15)	38 (13)
F	30 (18)	30 (—)	27 (6)	22 (16)		
M	36 (14)	42 (13)	34 (12)	45 (7)		
AFF					32 (14)	35 (13)
F	31 (17)	28 (—)	30 (5)	39 (20)		
M	32 (15)	36 (7)	41 (18)	39 (8)		
ANX					61 (23)	68 (11)
F	57 (29)	45 (—)	68 (11)	73 (8)		
M	68 (11)	66 (12)	70 (5)	57 (9)		
DEP					64 (23)	67 (13)
F	57 (29)	67 (—)	74 (6)	73 (3)		
M	68 (14)	69 (121)	63 (16)	59 (13)		
GLT					63 (23)	67 (10)
F	54 (28)	73 (—)	73 (3)	74 (6)		
M	66 (13)	69 (8)	67 (10)	67 (6)		
HOS					58 (23)	61 (11)
F	52 (28)	60 (—)	72 (11)	65 (9)		
M	63 (7)	60 (12)	54 (27)	62 (12)		
POS					28 (8)	32 (12)
F	32 (13)	30 (—)	25 (4)	30 (—)		
M	31 (12)	32 (16)	36 (10)	35 (4)		
NEG					70 (9)	65 (17)
F	69 (12)	64 (—)	74 (5)	74 (—)		
M	71 (13)	59 (24)	66 (13)	62 (11)		
BAL					31 (11)	30 (8)
F	33 (11)	30 (—)	24 (4)	27 (4)		
M	30 (11)	30 (—)	34 (11)	35 (4)		

Index summary scale of the SCL-90-R. Low-weight patients tended to complain of higher levels of somatic distress, although all groups approached clinical levels (T=63 or 90th percentile). All groups exceeded clinical levels on the Obsessive-Compulsive scale; not surprisingly, ANB and ANR patients scored highest, averaging about two standard deviations above the mean. All groups approached two SDS above the mean in scales reflecting Interpersonal

Sensitivity and symptomatic Depression. On the scale reflecting symptomatic Anxiety, the groups with histories of true anorexia (AN, BN, BNHxAN) were more than two SDs above the mean, while BN patients were one SD above the mean. On the scale reflecting hostile impulses and resentfulness, ANR patients approached two SDs above the mean, while both ANB and BN patients exceeded the mean by about 1 SD. (See Table 8.)

On the Phobic Anxiety scale, which taps into agoraphobic symptoms, all groups evidenced some avoidance (Mean T-scores 59-62), and ANR patients were clinically elevated (mean T-68). On the Paranoid Ideation scale, which at moderate levels reflects a suspicious and hypervigilant posture rather than frank paranoia, all groups evidenced significant elevations. The Psychoticism scale reflects an Eysenckian dimension characterized by increasing social alienation and idiosyncratic thinking (with very high elevations and certain item configurations betraying psychotic process); again, all patients were elevated. There were no significant differences on SCL-90-R scale T- scores by sex, although this may in part reflect differences between male and female norms.

MMPI (ED Inpatients Only)

All groups produced elevated MMPI profiles with serious characterologic implications; across all male groups, the mean profile was 278/287), with perhaps lower levels of distress reported by BNHxAN patients. This differs from observations among females that we have reported earlier (Edwin, Andersen, & Rossell, 1988). Similarly, validity configurations among males (but not females) were remarkable for low K (Defensiveness) scales, especially among normal-weight bulimics (BN). (See Table 9.)

Scale 1 (Hs) averaged about 70T, reflecting substantial somatic preoccupation, in all groups except BNHxAN, who were well within the normal range (p < .05). All groups reported very high levels of Depression (Scale 2), averaging 3-4 SD above the mean. Males produced higher T-scores than females, p < .03; this, again, may reflect normative differences. All groups were at least subclinically elevated on Scale 3 (Hysteria), with higher weight patients tending to report clinical elevations and no significant gender effects. ANR, ANB, and BNHxAN patients were elevated into the clinical range on Scale4(reflecting oppositionalism and/or impulsivity), with less elevated scores in those bulimics who had never been anorectic (BN). All groups differed from the population means on Scale 5 (reflecting for both sexes a denial of stereo typically masculine interests and identity). All groups and both sexes displayed a rather hypersensitive and suspicious disposition (Scale 6, Paranoia),with BNHxAN patients elevated into the clinical range.

TABLE 8

SCL-90-R
Mean (SD)

	ANR	ANB	BNHxAN	BN	Females	Males
SOM					65 (14)	63 (11)
F	60 (15)	59 (—)	72 (9)	70 (9)		
M	65 (13)	62 (11)	57 (11)	58 (8)		
OBS					73 (10)	70 (13)
F	71 (12)	70 (—)	73 (12)	78 (4)		
M	72 (13)	70 (12)	62 (17)	67 (20)		
INT					76 (10)	74 (9)
F	73 (13)	74 (—)	80 (3)	79 (3)		
M	75 (9)	72 (10)	78 (7)	68 (1)		
DEP					75 (10)	74 (10)
F	72 (13)	81 (—)	80 (3)	76 (4)		
M	75 (11)	75 (8)	73 (13)	67 (8)		
ANX					69 (13)	71 (11)
F	68 (16)	69 (—)	76 (9)	63 (10)		
M	72 (13)	71 (10)	71 (9)	61 (5)		
HOS					63 (9)	63 (13)
F	61 (10)	61 (—)	63 (6)	67 (6)		
M	67 (12)	61 (15)	52 (18)	61 (2)		
PHO					63 (16)	65 (10)
F	57 (18)	59 (—)	69 (14)	70 (8)		
M	67 (12)	63 (10)	59 (10)	62 (4)		
PAR					69 (12)	69 (9)
F	66 (14)	76 (—)	71 (9)	74 (5)		
M	72 (9)	64 (9)	66 (12)	74 (8)		
PSY					74 (10)	71 (11)
F	74 (14)	71 (—)	73 (9)	79 (—)		
M	71 (13)	72 (9)	70 (9)	69 (9)		
GSI					72 (9)	74 (11)
F	69 (11)	74 (—)	77 (5)	75 (5)		
M	74 (13)	73 (")	74 (")	69 (10)		
PSDI					67 (10)	70 (10)
F	65 (11)	62 (—)	72 (8)	-0-		
M	65 (9)	67 (13)	68 (4)	57 (10)		
PST					67 (10)	70 (10)
F	63 (10)	69 (—)	72 (8)	-0-		
M	71 (12)	70 (9)	68 (11)	70 (6)		

TABLE 9

MMPI Scale Scores
Mean (SD)

	ANR	ANB	BNc	BNs	F	M
L					47 (8)	49 (7)
F	46 (9)	51 (—)	46 (4)	50 (16)		
M	51 (7)	48 (7)	48 (9)	48 (3)		
F					62 (15)	64 (15)
F	57 (16)	55 (—)	72 (12)	71 (14)		
M	63 (20)	65 (11)	69 (10)	69 (20)		
K					52 (6)	46 (8)
F	54 (98)	44 (—)	52 (4)	50 (5)		
M	45 (10)	48 (7)	48 (10)	38 (7)		
1 (Hs)					65 (13)	69 (13)
F	58 (9)	63 (—)	72 (12)	78 (15)		
M	69 (14)	72 (12)	56 (5)	69 (19)		
2 (D)					76 (17)	88 (18)
F	66 (14)	81 (—)	86 (19)	87 (7)		
M	90 (20)	87 (17)	81 (3)	84 (32)		
3 (Hy)					65 (10)	69 (10)
F	60 (7)	57 (—)	69 (11)	77 (8)		
M	70 (9)	71 (10)	64 (6)	61 (14)		
4 (Pd)					73 (14)	72 (9)
F	66 (14)	64 (—)	83 (8)	87 (2)		
M	70 (8)	74 (10)	76 (12)	65 (1)		
5 (Mf)					43 (9)	71 (10)
F	44 (9)	59 (—)	43 (5)	36 (7)		
M	71 (8)	74 (14)	74 (6)	71 (11)		
6 (Pa)					65 (11)	65 (11)
F	59 (9)	68 (—)	73 (12)	71 (8)		
M	64 (13)	65 (8)	72 (12)	61 (11)		
7 (Pt)					70 (17)	77 (18)
F	61 (14)	62 (—)	81 (16)	82 (12)		
M	74 (22)	77 (15)	87 (7)	76 (19)		
8 (Sc)					69 (17)	77 (19)
	60 (16)	63 (—)	82 (13)	77 (17)		
	77 (25)	75 (15)	86 (17)	71 (12)		
9 (Ma)					59 (12)	62 (11)
	58 (14)	59 (—)	61 (12)	65 (5)		
	58 (10)	68 (13)	63 (6)	61 (4)		
0 (Si)					63 (16)	63 (15)
	59 (16)	46 (—)	72 (16)	67 (15)		
	64 (19)	59 (")	63 (3)	70 (13)		

All groups and both sexes were elevated at least two to three standard deviations above the mean on the scale reflecting obsessive anxiety (Scale 7, Psychasthenia), with BNHxAN patients almost 4 SD above the mean. The same distribution was observed on Scale 8 (Schizophrenia), which reflects among these patients a mixture of social alienation, peculiar bodily experiences, and impaired cognition, conation (or "will"), and impulse control. All groups and both sexes had moderate (subclinical) elevations on Scale 9 (Hypomania), reflecting some hyperactivity or drivenness; ANB patients tended to be highest, and were significantly more troubled than ANR patients (p < .05). All groups and both sexes were also subclinically elevated on scale 0 (Social Introversion), which can reflect either healthy and normal introversion or clinically significant social discomfort (Psychasthenia), with BNHxAN patients almost 4 SD above the mean. The same distribution was observed on Scale 8 (Schizophrenia), which reflects among these patients a mixture of social alienation, peculiar bodily experiences, and impaired cognition, conation (or "will") and impulse control. All groups and both sexes had moderate (subclinical) elevations on Scale 9 (Hypomania), reflecting some hyperactivity or driveness; ANB patients tended to be highest, and were significantly more troubled than ANR patients (p < .05). All groups and both sexes were also subclinically elevated on scale 0 (Social Introversion),which can reflect either healthy and normal introversion or clinically significant social discomfort.

DISCUSSION

As documented earlier, about three-fourths of patients referred to the Johns Hopkins University Eating Disorders service for consultation about possible eating disorders do indeed present primary eating disorders. These data suggest that males and females do not differ in this regard. However, males tend either to have a clear-cut eating disorder syndrome (ANR, ANB, BN, BNHxAN), or to present disordered eating behavior secondary to another, diagnosable psychiatric illness. In contrast, a significant proportion of females present atypical or mixed eating disorders. Both male and female patients tend to report past episodes of obesity. However, males have often been medically overweight, while females have more often suffered from the perception of being overweight (means of 123% of ideal body weight for males, compared with 111% for women at maximum).

Among males, as among females, weight histories and expectations were generally appropriate to eating disorder subtype: ANR patients were lower than ANB patients in their minimum past weight, highest past weight, admission weight, and desired weight. However, overall, males choose a preferred body weight about 90% of the population mean, while the desired weights of females averaged about 80%. This is certainly consistent with the female tendency to report feeling "obese" at lower weight levels.

These data certainly confirm the value of the Eating Attitudes Test (EAT) as an epidemiologic screen for primary eating disorder, distinguishing it from eating disorder secondary to other psychiatric and physical disorders. There was no significant difference in EAT scores by sex. Among males, a number of other indicators help to distinguish secondary from primary eating disorder patients. SED patients resemble ANR patients in that bingeing is extremely rare, but resemble BN patients (without weight loss histories) in setting reasonable weight goals for themselves. Compulsive exercise is common among primary EDs (50%), but very rare among SEDs. Inadvertent initial weight loss is reported by a quarter of SEDs, but was absent among primary EDs. Several scales of the Eating Disorders Inventory were also helpful in distinguishing secondary EDs: SED patients scored lower on Drive for Thinness, Bulimia, Body Distortion, Ineffectiveness, and Interoceptive Awareness. Thus, appropriate psychological instruments, along with the psychiatric history and mental status examination, lead to confident differentiation between primary and secondary eating disorders, as well as among PED subgroups.

Intellectual examination revealed average to high average intelligence among all primary eating disorder groups of both sexes, without significant differences. While this contradicts some conventional wisdom about the high intellect of eating disorder patients, it is generally consistent with recent reports and our clinical experience. Indeed, as the phenomenon of eating disorder has become more diffused, IQ values have drifted toward the mean. Further, the documentation of intellectual ability can at times be crucial for treatment. If a patient with an Average IQ has been anointed standard-bearer for the family, with expectations of postgraduate or professional education, documentation of true intellectual ability will facilitate the setting of more reasonable expectations.

All primary and secondary ED patients produced Affect Balance Scales remarkable for elevated negative affects as well as for an impoverishment of positive affects; there were no significant subtype effects, although women were more discontented and anergic than men. All groups were pan-symptomatic on the SCL-90-R, with peaks on Interpersonal Sensitivity and Depression. Low weight was associated particularly with somatic complaints, obsessional symptomatology, and anxiety symptoms. For the most part, these are indeed driven, joyless, and multiply symptomatic patients.

We have elsewhere discussed the differences among typical MMPI profiles of female ANR and ANB patients (Edwin, Andersen, & Rossell, 1988). Among males with primary eating disorders, the modal profile-type across all subtypes

SECTION III

Treatment and Outcome

9

Diagnosis and Treatment of Males with Eating Disorders

Arnold E. Andersen

DIAGNOSIS

The diagnosis of males with eating disorders (EDs) is usually a straightforward process, but as with appendicitis, you have to first think of it as a possibility. Accurate identification of anorexia nervosa (AN) or bulimia nervosa (BN) in males has been neglected for primarily two reasons: (1) because of its statistical scarcity, it is not as familiar to clinicians as eating disorders in women and so may not be recognized when it does occur; (2) theoretical biases in some diagnostic methods preclude it from existence. Some psychiatric formulations maintain, for example, that males cannot develop these disorders because they do not manifest a particular required psychodynamic theme, such as fear of oral impregnation, or because they do not have the amenorrhea required by some criteria.

The essential diagnostic criteria for AN may be summarized by the simple threefold requirement described by Russell: the *behavior* of self-induced starvation; the *psychopathological fear* of becoming fat that is out of all proportion to reality; and a *biologic abnormality* in reproductive hormone functioning which could apply to both men and women (Morgan & Russell, 1975). DSM-III-R gives somewhat more quantitative criteria for AN than Russell does by requiring specifically a loss of 15% in body weight, as well as amenorrhea for three cycles in the female, without specifying an analogous

TABLE 1

Diagnostic Criteria for Anorexia Nervosa*

A. Refusal to maintain body weight over a minimal normal weight for age and height, e.g., weight loss leading to maintenance of body weight 15% below that expected; or failure to make expected weight gain during period of growth, leading to body weight 15% below that expected.

B. Intense fear of gaining weight or becoming fat, even though underweight.

C. Disturbance in the way in which one's body weight, size, or shape is experienced, e.g., the person claims to "feel fat" even when emaciated, believes that one area of the body is "too fat" even when obviously underweight.

D. In females, absence of at least three consecutive menstrual cycles when otherwise expected to occur (primary or secondary amenorrhea). (A woman is considered to have amenorrhea if her periods occur only following hormone, e.g., estrogen, administration.)

---

*Reprinted with permission from the *Diagnostic and Statistical Manual of Mental Disorders* (3rd ed. rev.). Copyright © 1987 American Psychiatric Association.

reproductive hormone-related change in the male (American Psychiatric Association, 1987). The fact that the weight loss required for diagnosis of AN has diminished from 25% in DSM-III to 15% in DSM-III-R reflects the changing and essentially arbitrary nature of these quantitative criteria, rather than any change in the fundamental diagnostic requirements. From a clinical viewpoint, an individual can be considered to have AN, whether male or female, if a substantial amount of weight has been lost leading to a final state of being medically underweight, in the presence of an inappropriate fear of obesity, and in association with an abnormality of reproductive hormone functioning. Even this latter requirement may be nonspecific and may merely reflect substantial weight loss. Anorectics who not only restrict food intake (ANR) but also experience binge eating are usually referred to as having anorexia nervosa with bulimic complications, or as having AN, bulimic subtype (ANB).

Similarly, for bulimia nervosa, the process of diagnosis is relatively uncomplicated if the patient is open and honest on interview. In contrast to AN, which is a publicly visible disorder, BN is often a private and secretive disorder and usually requires cooperation from the patient to make a diagnosis. The term "bulimia" derives from the Greek words for "ox" and for "hunger." Diagnosis of BN, therefore, usually requires a history of ingestion of large amounts of food (often concentrated sweets and fats), eaten rapidly, against one's initial resistance and which is typically followed by feelings of being out of control, as well as by depression or guilt. There is a nonproductive debate between those who advocate using subjective criteria for a binge having taken

TABLE 2

Diagnostic Criteria for Bulimia Nervosa*

A. Recurrent episodes of binge eating (rapid consumption of a large amount of food in a discrete period of time).

B. A feeling of lack of control over eating behavior during the eating binges.

C. The person regularly engages in either self-induced vomiting, use of laxatives or diuretics, strict dieting or fasting, or vigorous exercise in order to prevent weight gain.

D. A minimum average of two binge eating episodes a week for at least three months.

E. Persistent overconcern with body shape and weight.

*Reprinted with permission from the *Diagnostic and Statistical Manual of Mental Disorders* (3rd ed. rev.). Copyright © 1987 American Psychiatric Association.

place (i.e., a patient perceives he has eaten in an out-of-control manner) and those who advocate "objective" criteria for the definition of a binge, for example that a certain number of calories of high density food be ingested in a defined period of time.

In fact, a continuum of bulimic behaviors exists between the extremes of the basically anorectic male with mild bulimic complications, who feels he has binged when he has eaten an extra salad against his will, and the other extreme of a normal weight bulimic who may ingest 8-10,000 extra calories of nutritionally dense food in a short time. We have found in our clinical experience wide variations in the extent of pre-ingestive struggle against appetite, and virtually every possible different amount, kind, and rate of food intake eaten by different bulimic individuals. The essential criteria for BN are, therefore, that binge eating takes place; that the binge eating makes the patient feel he is out of control and in danger of becoming fat; and that he feels he must compensate in some manner for the unwanted calories ingested, whether by self-induced vomiting, strenuous exercising, subsequent fasting, or abuse of laxatives/diuretics, etc.

The recently revised diagnostic criteria of the American Psychiatric Association for BN as described in DSM-III-R compared to those of DSM-III represent a helpful change by now specifying the frequency of binge episodes that must be present before a diagnosis of BN is allowed: an average of two binge eating episodes a week for three months (American Psychiatric Association, 1987). This quantitative requirement helps exclude from the bulimia nervosa diagnostic category any episodes of experimental binge eating, occurrences of short-term "copycat" bulimic behavior, or other transient abnormalities of eating behavior that do not deserve a diagnosis of true BN.

TABLE 3

Clinical Clues to Secretive Bulimia Nervosa

Hypokalemia of unknown cause or complications of hypokalemia (cardiac, renal, central nervous system).
Parotid gland or submandibular gland enlargement; esophagitis; esophageal bleeding or rupture.
Large weight fluctuations or weight loss of unknown origin.
Unexplained elevations of serum amylase.
Unexplained secondary amenorrhea.
Extensive loss of dental enamel or onset of many new caries.
Scars on the knuckles of the hand from manually induced vomiting.
Presence of Type I (insulin dependent) diabetes mellitus.
Other disorders of impulse control—alcoholism, drug abuse, borderline personality disorder.
Member of predisposed vocational groups—models, ballet, wrestlers, jockeys.

A common diagnostic error, incidently, is to use the term "bulimia" for a male who only induces vomiting of food but has not first eaten in a binge manner. The term BN is appropriately reserved for those males who first binge (bulimia = ox + hunger) whether or not they purge afterwards. On the other hand, the absence of self-induced vomiting or other mode of purging after binge behavior does not exclude a diagnosis of BN, if the required binge-eating and morbid fear of fatness are present.

Males who have an abnormality of eating behavior associated with the psychopathological fear of fatness but who do not meet full DSM-III-R criteria for either AN or BN are given the diagnosis of an "atypical" eating disorder or, more specifically, "Eating Disorder Not Otherwise Specified" (DSM-III-R: 307.50). Table 3 summarizes some of the signs of secretive bulimia that may alert the clinician to further inquire about the presence of hidden bulimic illness. Unexplained hypokalemia in a young person, rapid and frequent fluctuations in weight, and unexplained erosion of dental enamel are among the common medical tip-offs to undisclosed illness.

Why Diagnosis in Males Can Be Confusing

Eating disorders in males do occur less frequently than in females and this fact alone inclines the clinician to be less likely to even think of it as a diagnostic entity. There is a widespread but misleading stereotype of the kind of person who develops an eating disorder: young, white, upper middle class, and female. This stereotype may lead clinicians, especially those not accustomed to routinely treating disorders, to miss the diagnosis when it does occur, as it so often does, in *older* women, in *minorities*, or in *males* of any age.

Diagnosis in males can also be confusing because the clinician may find an increased incidence of males with eating disorders in a very different subset of the population than those commonly associated with a high incidence in females, such as ballet students (Garner & Garfinkel, 1980) or models. In males, for example, eating disorders occur more often in athletes, especially those whose sports demand weight control, such as wrestlers, jockeys, runners and swimmers. Also, males more often diet defensively when a sports-related injury takes place because of fear of weight gain from inactivity subsequent to injury. Further empirical research is needed to identify additional subgroups of males in which eating disorders occur at a higher than expected frequency so that early diagnosis can be made and preventive efforts can be implemented. Eating disorders appear to have an increased incidence in the subgroup of homosexual males, but no comparable observations have been made in homosexual females. (See Chapter 4 on sexuality.)

Diagnosis in males may additionally be confusing because the terms they use to express conflicts regarding body shape and size may differ from those commonly used by females. Men, for example, rarely complain about the number of pounds they weigh or the size of the clothes they wear. They are, instead, intensely worried about perceived abnormalities in body shape and form, and express intense desire to lose "flab" and to achieve a more classical male definition of muscle groups. We have not observed in males anything comparable to the psychological trauma some women suffer in going from a size 3 to a size 5, for example, or the overinvestment in a certain number of pounds, like staying in the "double digits" in weight, below 100 pounds.

Diagnosis of eating disorders in males may be further obscured because the reasons males give for dieting may sound on the surface medically plausible and even sensible. A subgroup of males in our clinical series heard warnings directed toward one of their parents that the parent should lose weight in order to improve the symptoms of a medical illness suffered, such as heart disease, diabetes, etc. A number of the males in our series who developed eating disorders personalized these warnings directed toward their parent and began to defensively diet to avoid for themselves the dire fate predicted for their parent because of excess weight.

For reasons that are not yet clear, women who go on to develop eating disorders very seldom begin to diet from fear of present or potential future medical illness. We have seen only one case in several hundred women who did diet to avoid a possible medical disease (and this was a woman in her 50s), but it is at least a not infrequent cause for dieting in men. We have reasoned that the male with eating disorders who defensively diets to avoid illness may have more obsessional traits, but this has not been empirically confirmed.

Another reason for diagnostic confusion in males is that the reproductive endocrine manifestation of eating disorders has no analog to the "on/off" criterion of amenorrhea in females. Testosterone gradually decreases in males with eating disorders and sexual function also gradually decreases *pari passu*. There is no equivalent step-like change in endocrine function in the male that triggers the same concern in parents and physicians that amenorrhea (primary or secondary) does in a female patient.

In summary, diagnosis of eating disorders in males may be accurately and promptly made by remembering that: a) eating disorders do occur in males, and b) the basic diagnostic criteria for males and females are similar, but the words boys and men use to describe their concerns for body shape and size and their reasons for dieting may differ from the terms girls and women use for the reasons they diet. Furthermore, males with eating disorders, when compared to females, often belong to different vulnerable subgroups that may predispose them to excessive dieting and the pursuit of thinness.

TREATMENT: BACKGROUND

The Nature of the Eating Disorders

Treatment of an illness should grow rationally from the clinician's understanding and conceptualization of the nature of the illness. It is therefore important to have a comprehensive and scientific understanding of the eating disorders (to the extent this information is available) in order to adequately treat these patients. Narrow concepts of etiology based on the belief that the eating disorders spring solely from a single abnormality of neurochemistry, from a specific abnormal family dynamic, or from a particular preexisting disease such as depressive illness will lead logically but unfortunately to restricted treatments that fail to appreciate the global nature of the disorder. In contrast, a multidimensional concept of origin that appreciates the interactive nature of at least several risk factors will lead to more appropriate comprehensive treatment. The following discussion (and Chapter 12 on mechanism) outlines our understanding of the eating disorders.

AN begins as an attempt at dieting for a variety of reasons and gains momentum so that the individual becomes unable and/or unwilling to reverse the trend and seek a healthy weight. We believe that this initial dieting practice is usually a voluntary behavior, but evolves by stages in predisposed individuals into a syndrome in which personal control is lost.

The exception to the concept of a voluntary onset of illness is made by the approximately 5 to 10% of cases in which there may be an inadvertent or iatrogenic onset. The term "inadvertent onset" means that the initial loss of weight is secondary to a preceding medical cause such as a peptic ulcer or a flu-like syndrome, or secondary to a physical injury or intervention such as having one's jaws wired after an automobile accident or having an abdominal surgery. Once some weight has been lost for medical/traumatic/surgical reasons, however, and the individual notices with pleasure that his weight is lower, he then takes over the control for additional weight loss on a voluntary basis. This happens most often in a person who has tried to diet previously but who had been unsuccessful in his past efforts at weight loss.

By "iatrogenic onset" is meant that the initial weight loss was recommended by a physician, or that the weight gain leading to psychological distress and dieting grew out of a prescribed medication or other treatment (i.e., out-of-date "ulcer diets"). Several males began dieting after taking prescribed corticosteroids or antidepressants which caused them to gain weight. Even if the onset of the weight loss is inadvertent or iatrogenic, it develops into a true primary eating disorder only after the individual takes over the process of additional weight loss, in which case it becomes indistinguishable from the more usual voluntary onset of AN or BN.

In our treatment program we conceptualize AN as being a disorder of *behavior* initially (as opposed to a primary disorder of mood or thinking), which then comes to serve a vital and stabilizing psychologic purpose in the individual's life and which is additionally stabilized by a variety of secondary biological mechanisms. These differing functions that AN comes to serve include, among others, stabilizing a crisis in development (especially for preteens and teenage males), dealing with crisis in marital or extramarital relationships (older onset males), ameliorating a mood disorder, and/or giving a boy or man a sense of control and effectiveness when life feels out of control. The perception of not being effectively in control may derive from an internal, implacable, perfectionistic personality trait, or from sources in the external world such as perceived demands of school, work, parents, friends, etc. Often, these reasons potentiate each other and the illness may then be called "over-determined" in that there are more forces present than needed to understand the tenacity of the illness.

While the illness initially begins as a voluntary behavior, eventually it takes on a life of its own through secondary mechanisms (see Chapter 12 on mechanism), including the formation of a social role (the "sick role") that becomes synonymous with, and dependent on, the continuation of the illness behaviors. Secondary medical mechanisms include such factors as weight gain from water retention after the patient has tried to stop vomiting or purging on his own. This unwanted weight gain leads to a renewed fear of fatness, distrust of the process of getting well, and the resumption of the vomiting or purging behavior.

Lastly, existential issues of identity may be involved in perpetuating the eating disorder. By identity issues is meant the formation of a personal sense of who one is that is so closely related to continued eating disorders symptomatology that the prospect of giving up the illness leads to fear of "nothingness" or a sense of anomie. Especially for chronically ill ED patients, getting better involves a leap of faith and the development of trust that a new and better identity will eventually result from treatment. The new pattern of healthy behavior in a healthy body may initially feel strange and awkward.

This brief explanation of how we view AN conceptually may make the treatment program described more coherent and scientifically plausible. Because BN can best be understood as growing out of an attempt at AN, rather than as a separate *de novo* disorder, the conceptualization of BN will be described in relationship to AN.

Relationship Between AN and BN

The close relationship between AN and BN needs to be understood in order to appreciate that these syndromes are points along a single continuous spectrum of illness rather than separate unrelated entities. Initial binge behavior is almost always an inadvertent and unplanned response to dieting behavior. Bulimic patients are basically potential anorectics, desiring thinness, who happened to have bodies and minds that didn't cooperate in achieving their goal of thinness. We have found in a series of more than 20 consecutive bulimic patients whose histories were closely examined that each one of them began binge eating only after some degree of preceding food restriction and/or weight loss, although the duration of the food restriction and degree of weight loss were quite variable, and preceded binge eating by a period of days, weeks, months, or, in some cases, years. After the binge behavior has been present for some time as a response to hunger, including hunger within the 24-hour day due to restriction/avoidance of food intake at breakfast and lunch (*Stage 1*), there occurs a gradual transition of the binge behavior from being a response to hunger to becoming an operantly mediated method of improving a variety of uncomfortable mood states (*Stage 2*).

Finally, the binge behavior may take on an autonomous and identity-giving quality (*Stage 3*). During this stage, it becomes unrelated to either hunger or to the improvement of abnormal mood states. Instead, it takes place in an autonomous, repetitive fashion, sometimes 20 or more times a day, and additionally confers a personal role and identity ("professional" anorexia or bulimia) (Woodall, Di Domenico, & Andersen, submitted for publication).

What distinguishes the otherwise identical people who all start by dieting but then go on differentially to AN vs. BN is a matter of great theoretical interest and practical concern. While the issue is far from settled, it appears that those individuals who are not able to drive their weight down by food restriction alone as the ANR group does, but in whom binge behavior breaks through, are individuals who differ from the pure food restrictors in personality, in sensitivity to inner distress, and in impulsivity. The person who goes on to become bulimic instead of anorectic is more often impulsive, a person who feels the psychologic distress of hunger more intensely, who is less tolerant of continued psychologic distress of any kind, and who is more likely to have a personality disorder from Cluster B of DSM-III-R (the borderline, narcissistic, histrionic group) rather than Cluster C (the sensitive, obsessional, perfection-istic, avoidant group) (Piran et al., 1988).

Individuals may, however, make transitions between AN and BN in both directions, although the path from food restricting AN to the AN bulimic subtype or BN at normal weight is the most common. Studying patients who have been ill for several decades allows the clinician to gain an appreciation of the potential for this two-way transition between AN and BN that may otherwise not be appreciated on a cross-sectional mental state examination or short-term follow-up. Chronically ill males with EDs not uncommonly go through multiple states along the spectrum of eating disorders illness by, at various times, restricting food, by binge-vomiting at various weights, and by using multiple additional methods to control weight, such as compulsive exercise, diet pills, abuse of Ipecac, or laxatives and diuretics.

Some principles and practical methods follow that we have found of use in the treatment of eating disorders based on this background conceptualization of the nature of the ED illnesses and an understanding of the relationship between AN and BN. More detailed descriptions are available elsewhere (Garfinkel et al., 1980; Mickalide & Andersen, 1985). Some results from the Johns Hopkins treatment program are described in Chapter 8 by Edwin and Andersen on psychological testing.

ASSESSMENT AND INITIAL MEDICAL STABILIZATION

Psychiatric History and Mental Status Examination

The first step of comprehensive treatment growing out of a detailed understanding of the ED illnesses is a thorough patient assessment that includes psychiatric history, mental status examination, and diagnostic formulation, along with initial medical stabilization. The psychiatric history of the male with an ED integrates the history of the eating disorder with a comprehensive general psychiatric history. We have found it very worthwhile to listen carefully to the patient's chief complaint on admission for inpatient or outpatient treatment and to record this statement verbatim. What he specifically seeks help for and desires from outpatient treatment or inpatient hospitalization may differ from what the family wishes or what the clinician may think needs to be accomplished. Often, patient complaints are phrased in terms of desiring improved self-esteem, improved mood, better ability to relate to others, and freedom from relentless thoughts and behaviors associated with the eating disorder, not necessarily a desire to gain weight. Attention paid to what the patient himself wishes from treatment will lead to more successful collaborative efforts and the perception by the patient that his needs and wishes are taken seriously.

In addition to a complete mental status examination, attention should be paid to eliciting the specific psychopathological motifs associated with the eating disorders—the morbid fear of fatness out of proportion to reality, the relentless pursuit of thinness, the distortion of body image, and the psychological triggers for binge episodes or bouts of starvation. The clinician's statement of diagnosis and formulation for the patient record will, of course, include an eating disorder diagnosis according to DSM-III-R criteria, but almost certainly will additionally include from one to several co-morbidities on Axes I and II, and sometimes Axis III of DSM-III-R.

There are very few eating disorders that appear diagnostically as "lone rangers"; most have psychiatric co-morbidities. In virtually all hospitalized ED patients and in the majority of ED outpatients, the eating disorder is associated with at least one psychiatric co-morbidity. Our studies (in preparation) have found that hospitalized restricting anorectics have, on the average, more than two psychiatric co-morbidities; anorectics with bulimic complications have almost four; and normal-weight bulimics have close to three additional psychiatric diagnoses. The most common co-morbidities include all the subtypes of mood disorder, especially bipolar II states (Simpson, et al., 1988), anxiety states, substance abuse, and personality disorders.

During the psychiatric assessment, the clinician has a chance to identify and ventilate the patient's fears and fantasies about treatment. Fears frequently include the terror of being made to be or allowed to become fat, as well as fears about future inability to cope with stress if binge episodes are no longer present. Fantasies, on the other hand, may include ideas of treatment being a vacation time or the belief that treatment will "cure" the patient. Some families think that their child can be dropped off like an automobile at a mechanic's shop to be passively fixed. We encourage the patient to understand that getting better takes hard collaborative work, a realistic amount of time, and the help of a team of multidisciplinary professionals. Even when these conditions are present, positive results cannot be guaranteed, although realistic optimism for a good deal of improvement is generally warranted.

We emphasize from the beginning of treatment that our goal is to work with the patient as a partner to help him become a happier, healthier, and more effective person. We specifically state that nobody is responsible for this illness and that there is no benefit in attempting to blame anybody for its origin. On the other hand we hope to understand more about the illness and give the patient an individual understanding of how his illness came into being as well as what keeps it going.

Family Assessment, Support, and Alliance

Families are very heterogeneous in their "structure," in their communication style, and in their attitude toward the patient's illness. They may feel conflicted, guilty, angry, "burned out," hopeful and optimistic, unrealistic, and/or demanding. A separate psychiatric history obtained from family members is essential, especially in regard to issues of the patient's pre-illness personality, the early developmental features of the patient, and their description of the origin and development of the eating disorder. Intertwined with the initial assessment of the family is the need for support, ventilation, instillation of realistic hope, and the removal of guilt and blame from the family's shoulders. We quickly express our interest in working with the whole family on a weekly basis. Sometimes, subgroups of the family need special attention; for example, the parents or the spouse may need a separate set of meetings for marital issues.

During the initial assessment period, as well as in subsequent meetings, the family will be evaluated in a variety of ways. Their communication pattern, their norms and expectations, their generational boundaries, how they handle the tasks of parenting or the spousal role, how they react to the patient's growth and development, as well as their own history of relationship with their parents, are all important. A number of ideas have been expressed in the psychiatric literature concerning the role of the family in the genesis and maintenance of the eating disorder. We believe the best approach is to take an empirical, nontheoretical view toward each family and to develop plans for treatment based on the needs of the individual family assessment rather than from a theoretical view of ED families.

Hedblom et al. (1982) described the results of an evaluation of 62 families of anorectic patients and found that while a large percentage of them did fit the role described by Minuchin et al. (1978) of being an enmeshed family, a substantial minority had, in contrast, almost abandoned their children, while a modest but important subgroup were balanced, normal, and healthy by all the usual indices. Our general guideline is that the more the distress comes from within the family, the better the prognosis for the patient because he will have a reasonable chance to grow and develop on his own once emancipated status apart from the family is achieved. The more the illness grows out of severely abnormal character traits within the patient, on the other hand, the worse the prognosis. The negative effect of very disturbed families on otherwise healthy offspring should not be underestimated, however.

Families often have partial information but not always sufficient or accurate information about the nature of the eating disorders. They will usually benefit both from a personal review by a team member of the nature of the EDs as well as from some appropriate reading material. In a polite way, we ask family members to function as family members and not as the professionals (doctors, lawyers, corporate executives) they may be in their vocations.

In summary, the guiding principles for the assessment phase of the family treatment are to rapidly initiate a comprehensive evaluation without attempting to fit the family into rigid theoretical formulations; offer a nonblaming, educational, and supportive stance toward the family; give realistic optimism based on hard collaborative work over sufficient time; plan a series of weekly family meetings. No two unhappy families are exactly alike, as Tolstoy said in the beginning of *Anna Karenina.* It is especially useful to ask the family what they would like to get out of the treatment process themselves and what specific issues and problems they would like to discuss and work on.

Standardized Tests for Psychological Assessment

The approach to standardized psychological testing ideally keeps a balance between general psychological tests and specific, valid, and reliable instruments for assessment of the eating disorders. Regarding the general psychological tests, the WAIS helps the clinician to understand the intellectual capacity of the patient and may offer insight into specific developmental difficulties in verbal and performance skills. We have found that, at times, the patient has become a "standard bearer" for his family's hopes and aspirations, and may be targeted by them for educational and vocational goals that are unrealistic in view of his intelligence. A number of our patients had been destined by their families for medical or legal careers despite average or below average intelligence.

The MMPI and SCL-90 are widely used and validated instruments to assess patterns of psychopathology and emotional distress. The MMPI, while not having demonstrated validity in all of its 10 subscales, has much usefulness in generating a profile that can be associated with specific patterns of psychological distress and behavior. It is not strictly a personality inventory but more a psychopathological inventory and has been used by Edwin et al. (1988) to accurately predict restricting vs. bulimic subtypes of AN.

The Affects Balance Scale (ABS) is an instrument that we feel should be more widely used because of its attempt not only to measure psychological distress but also to quantify the "positive," healthy emotions that a patient experiences, leading to a summary statement of the balance between his positive and negative feelings. The ability of the patient to work in therapy and make progress against the illness may at times be less related to the absolute level of psychological symptoms than to the ratio between his positive, adaptive, and healthy emotions compared to his painful and maladaptive mood states.

Finally, the NEO Personality Inventory (Costa & McCrae, 1985), a true test of dimensions of normal personality and not of psychopathology, will be helpful in assessing traits of personality. This relatively recently developed and multifaceted instrument (or the older Eysenck Personality Inventory) is useful for assessing dimensions of personality. At times, prognosis may be more related to the type and severity of personality traits than to the medical severity of the illness itself or the anorectic psychopathology.

The projective tests, while having a long and rich history in psychological testing, should be used selectively and only if there is reasonable belief that they may add something to the understanding of the patient or to his treatment plans that cannot be accomplished by in-depth interviews.

There are at least three standardized instruments for quantitative assessment of symptoms specific to the eating disorders. The Eating Attitudes Test (EAT: Garner et al., 1982) is essentially an epidemiological tool which has been demonstrated to have a high probability of identifying patients with eating disorders when they score more than 30 on this instrument. It is logically used to screen populations and should be followed by more specific symptom inventories such as the Eating Disorders Inventory (EDI: Garner et al., 1983). The EDI has eight subscales measuring a variety of clinical features characteristic of the eating disorders, as well as constructs theorized to lie behind the eating disorders (such as lack of interoceptive awareness and maturity fears). Finally, the Body Shape Questionnaire or BSQ has recently been developed to measure body image distortion and distress (Cooper et al., 1987).

Medical Stabilization

Prompt assessment of vital signs and the remainder of the full physical examination, along with determination of electrolytes and other appropriate laboratory studies, will all be used to document and stabilize the patient's initial medical status. The treating clinicians or medical consultants need to differentiate between starvation and/or binge-purge related symptoms that require immediate intervention (such as severe hypokalemia) and those that can be safely managed by gradual nutritional rehabilitation and sensible supportive care (feeling chilly without being seriously hypothermic; regular bradycardia with adequate perfusion). Accompanying, incidental, or ED-induced/exacerbated medical states (diabetes mellitus, seizures, asthma, etc.) need to be identified so that appropriate treatment can be given, which will then be modified by changes in body weight and organ functioning as the patient progresses. Recent helpful publications concerning medical aspects of treatment include: Harris (1983), Mitchell (1984), and Mitchell et al. (1987). Hyperalimentation, or even enteral feeding, is rarely indicated, and may be associated with multiple complications (Pertschuk et al., 1981).

BEGINNING DEFINITIVE TREATMENT

Nutritional Rehabilitation

Recognition of the need for prompt nutritional rehabilitation in a supportive environment was described a century ago by Gull, Lasègue, and more recently by other clinicians (Andersen, 1985). Nutritional rehabilitation is a necessary part of, but not by itself sufficient for, comprehensive treatment. It can be either overemphasized or underemphasized. Some medically oriented programs end when nutritional rehabilitation is accomplished and lead to premature discharge of the patient. Some entirely psychodynamic methods, on the other hand, attempt to deal with underlying issues but never get on to effectively reversing the self-starvation or to interrupting the binge/purge behavior.

Nutritional assessment by a trained dietitian usually precedes nutritional intervention. Anthropometric measurements, as well as selected lab tests (such as serum protein and albumin), are of value in determining extent of malnutrition, remaining body fat stores, and the presence of paradoxical hypercholesterolemia. Nutritional rehabilitation includes patient education during the entire course of treatment. Despite their ability to count calories, patients are usually lacking in sound concepts of what balanced nutrition involves. They overemphasize the importance of the exact caloric value of foods and develop abnormal patterns of eating behavior based on rigid concepts of "safe" and "dangerous" foods, and what is an acceptable body weight.

We usually start patients on 1200-1800 kilocalories "calories" per day, depending on their degree of starvation. Calories are increased gradually as medically tolerated in anorectic patients so that a restoration of about 3 lbs. per week of body weight is accomplished. Calories are increased by 300-500 per week until a maximum of between 3500 and 4500 calories per day is prescribed; some males tolerate 5000 calories per day (see Keys et al., 1950). Overweight bulimic patients may be placed on very gradual reducing programs, with stability of food intake emphasized over weight loss. They often desire lower final weights than the team is willing to set, some wanting to be frankly anorectic.

Initially, nutritional rehabilitation for anorectics prescribes foods that are low in fats and milk products because the enzymes responsible for lipid and lactose metabolism are thought to be inducible enzymes whose activity decreases in the bowel mucosa due to reduced substrate during self-starvation. Milk products and fats are gradually reintroduced. A minority of patients may have persisting lactose intolerance even when weight has been restored, which can be measured by a breath hydrogen assay after lactose challenge and may be also suggested by medical history.

The overall guide to nutritional rehabilitation is that a healthy range and amount of food should be eaten in a socially appropriate fashion. Food is initially treated like a medication. Patients have no initial role in selecting items of food (except for allergic foods and three dislikes) or in determination of level of calories eaten or choosing goals for body weight. These items are discussed when they are in their goal range for body weight. Other programs, of course, may use different nutritional techniques, including prescribing largely liquid nutrition or letting patients choose their daily amount and type of food intake in order to receive specific privileges. Empirical comparisons of the various type of nutritional rehabilitation programs have not been made.

As a result of a carefully thought-out program of nutritional rehabilitation, the patient can be promptly restored to the point where he is less cold, better able to mentally concentrate, more able to sit in a firm chair without physical discomfort, and can soon begin to develop some personal understanding of sound nutrition. He experiences gradual freedom from repetitive, intrusive thoughts about food.

Bulimic patients are initially treated like restricting anorectic patients if their weight is substantially lowered and if some weight restoration is required, even if they do not meet formal AN criteria in terms of weight loss. If weight is in the normal range on admission, a maintenance program of caloric intake is prescribed initially. Occasionally, a long-term program of weight reduction is prescribed for overweight BN patients. A major therapeutic task of the nutritional rehabilitation of bulimic patients is to identify psychologic triggers for binge episodes so that healthy alternatives may be chosen. Many bulimic patients have not had a normal meal in months, years, or decades. They have usually developed elaborate "approach-avoidance" patterns toward food in general or toward specific, feared foods, as well as toward places and times associated with binge eating.

Some of the concepts guiding the Overeaters Anonymous self-help groups are useful for ED treatment, but their concepts of some foods as addictive substances, while appearing plausible, cannot be uncritically applied to the treatment of patients with bulimia nervosa. Several months or, occasionally, years of treatment may be required before a healthy pattern of food intake has developed and a normal physiologic pattern of appropriate hunger before and moderate satiety after a meal is regularly present.

As outpatients, bulimic individuals need guidance in developing nutrition-ally balanced meals, eaten at regular times in a socially appropriate manner, so that each meal contains a healthy percentage of carbohydrates, proteins, and fats in the form of "exchanges." Outpatients often demonstrate greater accountability and responsibility for their nutritional intake when they are asked to record their daily food intake and their feelings associated with eating in an ongoing manner on 3 x 5 cards or other forms, noting especially feelings and events around the time of binge episodes. Outpatient sessions for all ED patients initially begin by looking together at the pattern of food intake during the week as recorded on their diary of foods.

Psychotherapy

The summary purpose of nutritional rehabilitation is to improve the patient's physical status so that, first, he is out of medical danger, and, secondly, he is able to engage in the central process of treatment: being persuaded to think and to act differently concerning food, body size and shape, and his overvalued beliefs about thinness. Effective psychological treatment has three principal characteristics: (1) it focuses on resolution of a central dynamic formulation; (2) it is multimodal in form; (3) it is sequential in its techniques according to the needs of the patient, not the training of the therapist.

1. Central Dynamic Formulation

Within a few weeks after treatment begins, the therapeutic team will have sufficient information about and experience with the patient in order to organize in a succinct statement the overarching purpose the eating disorder serves in his life. This statement is called the central dynamic formulation. It organizes the psychological information and experience concerning the patient into a conceptual unity and focuses the treatment program, in a coherent and understandable manner, on resolution of this conflict. We agree, in general, with Crisp's (1980) concept that anorexia nervosa is a maladaptive response to a crisis in development, but believe that this idea can be made more specific for each male with an eating disorder. Some of the central dynamic themes in males with eating disorders that we have found to be more likely to occur in them than in females are the following:

Past experience with obesity
In contrast to females who, in general, *felt* overweight before beginning their diets. The majority of males *were* overweight. The experience of being teased, criticized, or humiliated for obesity during crucial periods of development, coupled with a sensitive and vulnerable personality, leads to the young man's determination never to be exposed again to narcissistic injury. Actual obesity as a motivation for slimming overlaps, of course, with the experience of the subgroup of ED females who also were overweight before dieting, but is a much more common reason for dieting in males.

Defensive dieting—The fear of mortality
A dynamic formulation that we have seldom found to occur in women but have noted several times in men grows out of the decision to begin dieting to avoid the health hazards that were pointed out to parents who were obese.

Dieting related to sports
As discussed previously, men more often than women have, in our experience, dieted in order to perform better in sports or to avoid the consequences of anticipated weight gain after sports injury. As more women participate in competitive sports, this observation may change.

Other general dynamic formulations frequently made in males—but not exclusively in them—include the use of extreme thinness in order to gain the notice of parents who are paying more attention to an extroverted sibling; the use of the self-starvation to help hold together a failing parental marriage; the use of binge eating to operantly modify dysphoric moods; the use of excessive dieting to gain a greater sense of effectiveness and control when he is faced with a perfectionistic personality within and/or a demanding environment without.

2. Multimodal Format

A second characteristic of effective psychotherapy after organization of a central dynamic formulation is that it is *multimodal* in form, ideally integrating individual, group, and family therapy. Individual psychotherapy engages the patient in the process of mutually understanding and working through the central dynamic formulation, as well as carrying out the results of treatment through practical changes in his everyday life. Group therapy is useful both for reasons of economy of facilities and finances and for its unique ability to offer both confrontation and support from peers. The patient in a group of peers can be confronted about his distortions of body image in such a way that his facade of being healthy is broken down. Conversely, peers may be able to give support and encouragement that is accepted more quickly than when it comes from a therapist. While some programs strictly separate anorectic and bulimic patients into different groups, our experience at Hopkins, which began before the eating disorders were a common media topic (essentially, before the death of Karen Carpenter and the publication of DSM-III), has always emphasized the shared features of all patients with eating disorders, whether they were anorectic restrictors, anorectics of the bulimic subgroup, or bulimics at thin, normal, or above normal weight. Group process has been an integral part of treatment in most major medical centers treating and researching eating disorders. Pyle et al. (1984) have described intensive outpatient programs for bulimia nervosa. Lacey (1983) has integrated group therapy with psycho-dynamic work.

3. Meeting the Needs of the Patient

Thirdly, a characteristic of effective psychotherapy is that it is conducted with a *sequence* of methods that meets the needs of the patient rather than reflecting the training of the therapist. We find that the most helpful psychotherapy sequence begins with supportive and educational psycho-therapy, followed by cognitive-behavioral work, leading to psychodynamic psychotherapy, and finally to existential psychotherapy.

Supportive psychotherapy has been described by Bloch (1979) in a helpful way that defines it to be more than merely general encouragement. While an educational emphasis (see below) continues throughout treatment, it is especially emphasized in the beginning of psychotherapy when it helps the patient to understand the nature of his illness and the rationale for the comprehensive treatment program.

Cognitive-behavioral work, beginning with the pioneering efforts of Beck and Rush, has been advocated as effective in the treatment of both AN and BN. Garner and Bemis (1985) described concepts and methods of cognitive psychotherapy for anorexia nervosa, while Fairburn (1985) demonstrated cognitive-behavioral work to be effective in bulimia nervosa. The fundamental concept underlying cognitive psychotherapy is first to identify the abnormal patterns of thinking ("cognitive grids") that distort neutral information and lead to painful emotional consequences, and then to confront and change these abnormal thinking processes so that positive emotions and healthier behaviors will result. It integrates cognitive psychotherapy work with practical behavioral changes in daily life that will logically result from the changes in thinking. Some of the abnormal cognitive patterns characterizing many eating disorder patients are: overvaluing the benefits of thinness; using all-or-none reasoning; catastrophizing; employing the mechanisms of projection and intellectualization. Cognitive-behavioral psychotherapy work challenges the abnormal patterns of thinking and behavior of ED patients and helps bring about the long process of change by modifying the irrational, painful, and self-defeating patterns employed.

Psychodynamic psychotherapy, the third method in this sequence, helps the patient make connections between his symptoms and his vital life experiences, especially experiences in crucial relationships or with traumatic events. While several "schools" of dynamic therapy exist, they all help the patient make "meaningful connections" between psychological life and illness symptoms. Often they involve interpretation of the transference relationship between patient and therapist. Personality disorders from Cluster B of DSM-III-R, especially severe borderline states, are a relative contraindication for a primary emphasis on dynamic psychotherapy. These patients appear to benefit more from a here-and-now approach focused on personal stability and responsibility.

Existential psychotherapy, focusing on issues of identity and the meaning of suffering in life, becomes the logical concluding focus for this sequence of psychotherapy efforts. Frankl (1959) and others undergoing severe and aversive environments have found that the attempt to give meaning and purpose beyond and above their experience of suffering leads to some capacity to transcend these difficult circumstances. Using Hilde Bruch's ideas and especially the title of one of her books (*The Golden Cage*, 1978), we suggest to patients that they have put themselves in a golden prison by their dedication to the ideal of extreme slimness as the central theme guiding their life.

These overlapping emphases in method and content suggested for a logical sequence of psychotherapy experiences should not be taken to be inflexible or mutually exclusive. Supportive work is appropriate throughout treatment. Irrational thoughts may be probed and refuted at any time during therapy. In general, however, this sequence outlined above has been tried with many patients and in our experience makes sense, but often requires one to several years of treatment to be fully accomplished.

A limiting factor in psychotherapy may be the personality traits or the presence of a formal personality disorder in the patient. These issues of personality rather than the severity of the illness itself may at times prove the most difficult aspect of treatment. A recent study of Piran et al. (1988) has confirmed our clinical impression that anorectic patients most often have a personality disorder in cluster C, with avoidant, perfectionistic, anxious, and self-critical tendencies. Patients with bulimia nervosa more often have personality disorders from cluster B, including narcissistic, borderline, anti-social, and self-dramatizing traits. Patients with eating disorders, in addition to having some specificity of the type of personality disorder associated with their subgroup of eating disorder, have, in general, a higher than expected co-occurrence of an Axis II personality disorder.

Psychotherapy ideally balances a focus of decreasing illness symptomatology with an additional focus on increasing personal growth, self-understanding, and age-appropriate behaviors. It may be helpful in the course of psychological treatment to turn at times from a focus on a patient's *disabilities* to a focus on his *abilities and potential* for individual growth and development. Put in simple mathematical terms, even if the numerator representing unresolved symptoms remains the same, when this same numerator is put over a larger denominator representing a patient's total positive experiences and abilities, then the percentage of the individual's life, efforts, and consciousness occupied by the ED symptoms will decline to a smaller fraction in proportion to his increased capacity for healthy thinking and living. Adolf Meyer, more than a half century ago, emphasized the need for clinicians to identify what is working right in a patient's life (which is almost always greater than what is abnormal) so that these positive and healthy aspects of a patient can be fully employed to improve the unhealthy and maladaptive aspects.

The length of treatment in psychotherapy is variable and may range from months of inpatient treatment plus several years of subsequent outpatient work for the seriously ill to only a few outpatient sessions focusing on behavioral change and cognitive restructuring for the mildly ill and recently ill. In general, however, outpatients usually need a minimum of several months of work and often a year or two if significant ED symptoms are present.

Inpatient treatment can seldom be accomplished in less than three months for a classically starved anorectic and often requires at least six to eight weeks for a person with bulimia nervosa and several co-morbidities.

Pharmacotherapy

A general guide to the pharmacotherapy of patients with eating disorders is that treatment of most males with anorexia nervosa does not require psychopharmacological agents unless there is clear evidence of depressive illness in the patient. In contrast, a substantial minority or perhaps a slim majority of patients with bulimia nervosa may benefit from psychopharmacology, primarily with antidepressants. Other medications play a supplementary role at best, including the use of anti-anxiety agents to decrease the fear of eating in anorectics; lithium, carbamazepine, and verapamil to stabilize co-occurring bipolar disorders; and, rarely, fenfluramine to decrease urges to binge. A recent text (Garfinkel & Garner, 1987) has reviewed the subject of the psychopharmacology of AN and BN in detail.

Of increasing importance in psychopharmacological decisions on a particular patient is the family history of the individual patient. For example, when in doubt whether an anorectic male has a depressive illness or not, the presence of a strong family history of depression would generally sway the decision toward a clinical trial of an antidepressant for him.

Just what are antidepressant agents treating when used in patients with eating disorders? A lively controversy continues to exist whether they serve as anti-binge agents or rather, as we would suggest, they are acting, as their name implies, as an antidepressant for the affective co-morbidity that often triggers the binge behavior, namely depressive illness or depressive episodes. Medications used to stimulate appetite in anorexia nervosa are fundamentally flawed because, while there may be some decrease in appetite from severe starvation, the major problem for AN patients has to do with the changes in body size and shape that they fear will result from the caloric contents of food rather than having any intrinsic lack of appetite. To date, there is more convincing evidence for the view that cognitive-behavioral programs for BN without associated pharmacological agents are preferred for treatment of BN than there is for the reverse view that antidepressants are essential medications for the treatment of BN, but the debate is far from concluded.

Education

There are at least five areas where education is often needed for patients with eating disorders: (a) the signs and symptoms of illness, (b) nutrition, (c) social skills, (d) the work of psychotherapy, and (e) sex education. Many patients are benefited by an understanding of the signs and symptoms of their illness—whether it be self-starvation and/or binge-purge behavior. While education by itself rarely turns around the course of illness, it serves an important supplementary role when combined with psychotherapy, behavioral retraining, and psychopharmacology by engaging the healthy side of the person with knowledge and reasoning. The patient's preoccupation with thoughts of food can be explained to him, for example, as resulting from the natural response of a starved body to the motivated behavioral state of food deprivation, highlighting the role of hunger in focusing his consciousness on food.

A male with eating disorders will relate perhaps even more than women to the study by Keys et al. (1950) on experimental starvation in men. These volunteers underwent semi-starvation, losing about 23% of body weight with the goal of helping clinicians understand how refeeding and rehabilitation could best be accomplished. The men began to think incessantly about food and were preoccupied with food-related activities. They tended to either gulp their food or hoard it and eat it in small bites. They began to collect and swap recipes. Often they became asocial and sometimes quite reclusive. Helping patients separate out the nonspecific effects of starvation on mental life and behavior from the core psychopathology of the eating disorders helps them focus more clearly on the psychological basis of their illness and understand themselves better.

Patients are often "walking cash registers" in regard to constantly counting calories, but they have little sense of sound nutrition. A pretreatment nutrition quiz may be used formally or informally to help assess the patient's understanding of nutrition and plan educational efforts. By learning an exchange system to insure that each meal is balanced, men with eating disorders can first practice choosing types of food groups and then add choice of portion size of foods as they become healthier and are able to take over more and more responsibility for their own nutrition. By combining this knowledge of nutrition with the practical education of shopping for food, preparing meals, and serving and eating meals with friends and family, patients will acquire real-life skills that prepare them to cope nutritionally in today's world.

In addition, leaving hospital on passes to choose meals in fast food chains, in buffet cafeterias, and in sit-down restaurants will help prepare them to choose meals in a social context as a normal part of everyday life based on their nutritional education. Frequent brief leaves of absences for reasons of educational practice are essential during an inpatient program for eating disorders so that patients may experience multiple, increasingly difficult but usually successful attempts at healthy living, which can afterwards be reviewed with staff before the next step. The goal of these efforts is to make the transition from inpatient to outpatient status as small a step as possible.

Education and training in social skills helps patients overcome shyness and reverse a pattern many have of past unsuccessful efforts at socialization. Social skills teaching also takes the capacity for social interaction out of the category of being a magical or inborn ability and, instead, breaks it down into reasonable steps which can each be practiced until successful.

Education concerning the purposes and methods of psychotherapy, behavioral retraining, and psychopharmacology may help the patient to form a more fully collaborative therapeutic alliance. Clear explanations about transference and about how the development of a central dynamic formulation helps organize treatment may stimulate both the curiosity and cooperation of the patient so that he sees himself to be a partner in becoming well rather than the subject of a technical procedure.

Assigning a patient practical "homework" between sessions helps bridge the time between sessions and takes therapeutic work out of the context of being an academic activity which is forgotten once the session is over. For example, a patient may be asked to monitor his all-or-none thinking or his use of projection and to make note of these occurrences on 3 x 5 cards so that the next session can begin with mutual observation of these ineffective or painful ways of thinking. Sometimes, having a patient note his mood state every hour throughout the day may help document diurnal variations in mood or help him to discover and understand a rapidly cycling bipolarity of moods. Sometimes, a very reticent patient may be engaged in the process of self-disclosure only by being asked to write poetry or use creative art rather than through the usual open verbal exchange in psychotherapy (Woodall & Andersen, 1989).

Finally, education about human sexual development, about being comfortable with sexual feelings, and about acting responsibly in their sexual behaviors is helpful for many patients. Many young men are reluctant to admit they know little about sexuality. Some ANR males, as is the case with many anorectic female patients, may be uncomfortable even thinking about sexuality at all. Teenage males with eating disorders, more often than older males with a later onset of illness, may present issues in gender identity or sexual conflict that need to be explored. A sympathetic probing of the patient's sexual thoughts and feelings in the form of a developmental history will help place the role of sexuality in the patient's life within the perspective of his entire life story. Our approach in discussing sexuality has always been to work within the value system and norms of the patient. Although some information concerning biological sexuality and human reproduction is important for both male and female patients, sexuality is discussed in the context of feelings, relationships, and values rather than as an abstract or separate issue.

The return of sexual feelings and thoughts in a formerly starved male patient is usually associated with a return of normal levels of plasma testosterone (Andersen et al., 1982). Nurses often guess accurately when a male patient's testosterone is close to normal because the formerly starved male begins to be somewhat flirtatious; he may show interest in dating and report the return of nocturnal emissions. There is a great psychologic and behavioral difference between the young, sexually reticent, and perhaps sexuality-rejecting food-restricting anorectic male and the older, impulsive, "borderline" male with normal weight bulimia. These latter patients may be sexually very active and sometimes impulsive and irresponsible in their sexual behavior. In each of these extremes and in all the patients whose sexual life falls in between, the ED staff attempts to understand sexuality in the context of the development of the whole person, and in the context of responsible relationships. Men more than women tend to see sexuality as an activity apart from abiding relationships, separate from values, and distant from emotions.

CONSOLIDATION AND INTERNALIZATION OF TREATMENT

Step C of treatment represents the crucial transition from mere compliance with the program as an external force to the stage of choosing healthy behavior and less distorted thinking by personal choice through consolidating and internalizing the principles of treatment already described. The goal of this stage is to make a healthy way of life a well-practiced and clearly understood reality. During this stage, more and more controls are returned to the patient as he is engaged in behavioral tasks of gradually increasing difficulty. During this time he will shop for, prepare, and eat meals in a social context, as described above. He will buy "healthy" clothes and give or throw away former "unhealthy" (too small) clothes that triggered feelings of fatness. When an eating disorder patient attempts to get into clothes that are too small, his usual response, as with women, is to think that he is too large rather than that the clothes are too small. Role playing during this stage prepares him to act normally with family, with friends, or by himself, in the context of school, work, alone, or in public places, especially places previously associated with binge eating or food-restriction activity.

DISCHARGE PLANNING AND FOLLOW-UP

At the time of discharge from inpatient status, most patients are substantially improved but far from being completely well. Unfortunately, they are not "cured." They need to be sympathetically reminded that they remain vulnerable for some time to come and should participate in outpatient follow-up therapy for one to several years. A concept of "recovery" rather than "cure" is the practical and helpful way to convey this information to patients. The more seriously ill and the more chronically ill the patient, the more the need for a step-wise step-down program from inpatient status to outpatient follow-up.

Seriously ill patients may best be treated after discharge by use of Day Hospital for weeks to months. They may then be engaged in intensive psychotherapy several times a week, with the emphasis on integrated psychological, behavioral, and pharmacotherapeutic work as needed. Many families, therapists, or patients themselves underestimate the degree of effort and the length of time required by patients to achieve full freedom from the eating disorder. On the positive side, however, virtually every aspect of illness has the potential for substantial improvement or complete resolution.

EMPHASIS ON ASPECTS OF TREATMENT ESPECIALLY APPROPRIATE FOR MALES WITH EATING DISORDERS

In some past publications, males with eating disorders were considered to have a worse prognosis than females. No evidence has emerged that a pessimistic outlook is warranted for males on the basis of gender. In contrast, we have found in follow-up from six months to six years after inpatient treatment that the average male with an eating disorder was still in a thin-normal range of weight (92% Ideal Body Weight) and maintaining considerable overall improvement in functioning (Andersen & Mickalide, 1983). Realistic optimism is, therefore, very appropriate for males with eating disorders.

The special features of eating disorders that are unique to males as well as the shared features that are common to all patients with eating disorders need to be understood and treated. For example, the general medical consequences of starvation and the demoralizing and physically dangerous effects of purging behavior are not unique to either sex. On the other hand, the gradual, curvilinear return of plasma testosterone in the starved male, leading to increased thoughts of sexuality and the gradual return of sexual functioning, contrasts with the stepwise return of menses and reproductive hormone functioning in a woman who regains healthy weight.

Males, in general, need assistance in coping with a different kind of cultural pressure and stereotype than that faced by women with eating disorders. More often, men feel subtly or overtly under cultural pressure to achieve a classical male body shape, the inverted, triangular upper body. They become very self-critical when they perceive lack of adequate muscular definition or the presence of any "flab." They may be subjected to the demands of a "macho" culture in which they are expected not to show emotions, to be always strong, and to enjoy traditional male activities, such as working on cars and playing contact sports. Many males with eating disorders are uncomfortable with this stereotyped role but find it hard to evolve another more comfortable or acceptable role without feeling unmasculine or vulnerable to ridicule.

SUMMARY

In closing, it may be helpful to remember again that there are few "lone rangers" diagnostically amongst the eating disorders—they most often occur along with other co-morbidities on Axis I and II of DSM-III. The use of a detailed interview technique such as the SADS-L (Schedule for Affective Disorders and Schizophrenia) or the DIS (Diagnostic Interview Schedule) for DSM-III-R will help the clinician identify these co-morbidities.

We try to convey to patients the idea that getting over the eating disorder is the beginning of being well rather than a stopping point. Additionally, having an eating disorder, if it is comprehensively treated, may leave the patient in better overall health and maturity than if he had never had this disorder. The principle here is to encourage the patient to accept the illness, to treat it fully, and to move on in his personal development, using as a guide Erikson's understanding of the tasks associated with these stages of development (Erikson, 1950). Eating disorders place a tremendous physical and psychosocial burden on the individual patient, his family, and society in general. They often result in an arrest or regression of individual development, but, if adequately treated, they may be followed by greater maturity than if he had not experienced the eating disorder.

Comprehensive treatment strives to achieve a balance between symptom reduction and personal psychosocial growth. When the work of diminishing symptoms, for example decreasing the persisting fear of fatness or body image distortion, appears to slow down and become unproductive, it is time to focus therapeutic effort on areas of normal growth and development, the practice of skills and attitudes that lead to success in daily living, and appropriate risk taking. The principle here is that if there is some remaining chronic symptomatology, it can be used helpfully as a kind of "smoke detector" for undetected stress instead of the patient's becoming discouraged by its persistence. For example, if a young man suddenly feels very fat when, in fact, he knows his weight has not changed, then this is a clue that there is a significant emotional distress present somewhere in his life that needs to be identified and relieved.

Gradually, patients using this concept make connections between transient increases in symptomatology and underlying issues and stresses, such as, anxiety before a test, anger at a family member, demoralization over ineffective efforts at socialization, etc. They can use the waxing and waning symptomatology to monitor their success in these real-life areas. This theme could be summarized the visually provocative phrases: "Grow flowers in addition to pulling up weeds"; "If symptoms persist, put a leash on them and give them a healthy function in your life." For example, obessional thinking can be redirected when it cannot be eliminated.

Lastly, clinicians will benefit from a renewed appreciation of the secondary mechanisms by which these disorders are perpetuated, so that treatment will include vigorous efforts to correct the multiple abnormalities that perpetuate the eating disorder. Issues of illness-related identity, the acquired social benefits of the "sick role," the overvalued beliefs about thinness, the excessive anticipatory anxiety about wellness, all need to be explored and treated as the patient gets better.

There may be surprising resistance to letting go of apparently unhealthy, uncomfortable, and sometimes dangerous medical symptoms related to AN or BN, but this resistance or reluctance becomes less surprising when the therapist helps the patient understand the stabilizing role his illness has played in crucial areas of development and functioning. When there is present a fear that "nothingness" will result from giving up his identity as an anorectic or a bulimic, when there is the fear of having to be perfect if he is at normal weight, when he fears he will never be allowed to say "no" to requests from others because he is well, when he feels incapable of diminishing intolerable emotional distress by other means, then the stance of continued anorectic or bulimic symptomatology becomes more understandable to the therapist and patient. We convey our belief to patients that the purposes originating and sustaining the eating disorder in his life are all good and normal purposes, but the methods he has chosen to achieve these purposes are ones that are painful, only partially effective, and dangerous. We urge him to "trade in and trade up" for more adaptive, more effective, age-appropriate ways of thinking and acting.

In conclusion, treatment of males with eating disorders remains an exciting, hopeful clinical challenge but a somewhat neglected area of research in psychiatry. Certain similarities to the treatment of females with eating disorders are appropriate, but there exist also unique and special aspects of diagnosis and treatment pertinent to males with eating disorders. As more clinical and research information are gathered, more scientific as well as empathic efforts can be directed toward prevention, toward early identification, and toward effective treatment of males with eating disorders. In the meantime, even with currently available methods and knowledge, a comprehensive treatment effort can be implemented that deals with both the shared and unique features of males with eating disorders, emphasizing balanced efforts at symptom reduction as well as growth enhancement, and which warrants realistic optimism for immediate and long-term psychiatric improvement of males with anorexia nervosa or bulimia nervosa.

REFERENCES

American Psychiatric Association. (1987). *Diagnostic and Statistical Manual of Mental Disorders (3rd ed. rev.).* (pp. 67, 68–69). Washington, D.C.: Author.

Andersen, A. E. (1985). *Practical Comprehensive Treatment of Anorexia Nervosa and Bulimia.* Baltimore: Johns Hopkins University Press.

Andersen, A. E. & Mickalide, A. D. (1983). Anorexia nervosa in the male: An underdiagnosed disorder. *Psychosomatics, 24,* 1066–1075.

Andersen, A. E., Wirth, J. B., & Strahlman, E. R. (1982). Reversible weight-related increase in plasma testosterone during treatment of male and female patients with anorexia nervosa. *International Journal of Eating Disorders, 1,* 74-83.

Bloch, S. (1979). Supportive psychotherapy. In S. Bloch (Ed.), *An Introduction to the Psychotherapies* (pp. 196-220). New York: Oxford University Press.

Bruch, H. (1978). *The Golden Cage: The Enigma of Anorexia Nervosa.* New York: Random House.

Cooper, P.J., Taylor, M. J., Cooper, Z., & Fairburn, C. G. (1987). The development and validation of the body shape questionnaire. *International Journal of Eating Disorders, 6* (4), 485-494.

Costa, P. T., Jr. & McCrae, R. R. (1985). *Neo Personality Inventory Manual.* Florida: Psychological Resources.

Crisp, A. H. (1980). *Anorexia Nervosa: Let Me Be.* New York: Grune and Stratton.

Edwin, D., Andersen, A. E., & Rosell, F. (1988). Outcome prediction by MMPI in subtypes of anorexia nervosa. *Psychosomatics, 29*(3), 273-282.

Erikson, E. H. (1950). *Childhood and Society.* New York: W. W. Norton and Company, Inc.

Fairburn, C. G. (1985). Cognitive-behavioral treatment for bulimia. In D. M. Garner & P. E. Garfinkel (Eds.), *Handbook of Psychotherapy for Anorexia Nervosa and Bulimia* (pp. 160-192). New York: The Guilford Press.

Frankl, V. E. (1959). *Man's Search for Meaning*. New York: Pocket Books.

Garfinkel, P. E. & Garner, D. M. (Eds.). (1987). *The Role of Drug Treatments for Eating Disorders*. New York: Brunner/Mazel.

Garfinkel, P. E., Moldofsky, H., & Garner, D. M. (1980). The heterogeneity of anorexia nervosa. *Archives of General Psychiatry, 37*, 1036-1040.

Garner, D. M. & Bemis, K. M. (1985). Cognitive therapy for anorexia nervosa. In D. M. Garner & P. E. Garfinkel (Eds.), *Handbook of Psychotherapy for Anorexia Nervosa and Bulimia* (pp. 107-146). New York: The Guilford Press.

Garner, D. M. & Garfinkel, P. E. (1980). Socio-cultural factors in the development of anorexia nervosa. *Psychological Medicine, 10*, 647-656.

Garner, D. M., Olmsted, M. P., Bohr, Y., & Garfinkel, P. E. (1982). The eating attitudes test: Psychometric features and clinical correlates. *Psychological Medicine, 12*, 871-878.

Garner, D. M., Olmsted, M. P., & Polivy, J. (1983). The eating disorder inventory: A measure of cognitive-behavioral dimensions of anorexia nervosa and bulimia. In P. L. Darby, P. E. Garfinkel, D. M. Garner, & D. V. Coscina (Eds)., *Anorexia Nervosa: Recent Developments in Research* (pp. 173-184). New York: Alan R. Liss, Inc.

Harris, R. T. (1983). Bulimarexia and related serious eating disorders with medical complications. *Annals of Internal Medicine, 99*, 800-807.

Hedblom, J. E., Hubbard, F. A., & Andersen, A. E. (1982). Anorexia nervosa: A multidisciplinary treatment program for patient and family. *Social Work in Health Care, 7*(1), 67-86.

Keys, A., Brozek, J., Henschel, A., Mickelsen, O., & Taylor, H. L. (1950). *The Biology of Human Starvation*, Vol. II. Minneapolis: University of Minnesota Press.

Lacey, J. H. (1983). An outpatient treatment program for bulimia nervosa. *International Journal of Eating Disorders, 2*(4), 209-214.

Mickalide, A. E. & Andersen, A. E. (1985). Subgroups of anorexia nervosa and bulimia: Validity and utility. *Journal of Psychiatric Research, 19*(2/3), 121-128.

Minuchin, S., Rosman, B.L., & Baker, L. (1978). The anorectic family. In *Psychosomatic Families*, (pp. 51-73). Massachusetts: Harvard University Press.

Mitchell, J. E. (1984). Medical complications of anorexia nervosa and bulimia. *Psychiatric Medicine, 1*, 229-255.

Mitchell, J. E., Seim, H. C., Colon, E., & Pomeroy, C. (1987). Medical complications and medical management of bulimia. *Annals of Internal Medicine, 107*(1), 71-77.

Morgan, H. G. & Russell, G. F. M. (1975). Value of family background and clinical features as predictors of long-term outcome in anorexia nervosa: Four-year follow-up study of 41 patients. *Psychological Medicine, 5*, 355-371.

Pertschuk, M. J., Forster, J., Buzby, G., & Mullen, J. L. (1981). The treatment of anorexia nervosa with total parenteral nutrition. *Biological Psychiatry, 16*, 539-550.

Piran, N., Lerner, P., Garfinkel, P. E., Kennedy, S. H., & Brouilette, C. (1988). Personality disorders in anorexic patients. *International Journal of Eating Disorders*, 7(5), 589-599.

Pyle, R. L., Mitchell, J. E., Eckert, E. D., Hatsukami, D. K., & Goff, G. (1984). The interruption of bulimia behaviors. *Psychiatric Clinics of North America*, 7(2), 275-286.

Simpson, S. G., DePaulo, J. R., & Andersen, A. E. (1988). Bipolar II Affective Disorder and Eating Disorders. Presented at *Society of Biological Psychiatry*, 43rd Annual Meeting, Montreal Canada, May 4-8.

Woodall, C. & Andersen, A. E. (1989). The use of metaphor/poetry therapy in the treatment of the reticent subgroup of anorectic patients. In E. K. Baker & L. Hornyak (Eds.), *Experimental Techniques in the Treatment of Eating Disorders*. New York: Guilford Press.

Woodall, C., DiDomenico, & Andersen, A. E. (Submitted for publication). Professional anorexia nervosa: Identity and existential issues.

10

Outcome of Anorexia Nervosa in Males

Thomas Burns and Arthur H. Crisp

Studies of anorexia nervosa in the male indicate that the psychosocial and clinical characteristics are essentially indistinguishable from the female (Crisp & Burns, 1983; Hsu, 1980). This finding would be unremarkable, indeed expected, in many disorders. That anorexia nervosa is predominantly a female disorder, thought at times to be exclusively so (Cobb, 1943; Nemiah, 1950; Selvini, 1965), has given rise to a body of theory about its aetiology which, in varying degrees, stresses the central significance of conflicts surrounding femininity and feminine appearance.

Much of this postwar emphasis on the emotional development of the female has generated speculation about what would lead a male patient to develop a "female disorder." Such speculation has centered around issues of gender identity problems, massive obesity, and more profound development disorders (Bruch, 1973; Crisp & Toms, 1972). The unity of a syndrome is not based entirely on its features at presentation but also on common features of course and prognosis (Russell, 1970). Before concluding, therefore, that anorexia nervosa is an identical disorder in both sexes, it is necessary to examine its natural history and, if possible, its response to accepted treatments.

A study of the outcome in anorexia nervosa in the male is necessary to illuminate a number of questions. If the course and outcome were found to be dramatically different from that in the female, it would encourage reconsideration of the earlier suggestions (Cobb, 1943; Nemiah, 1950; Selvini, 1965) that they are different disorders and that the apparently similar presentations are only the common-end pathway of quite separate processes.

If, however, the course is substantially similar to that in the female, then a search for markers of good and poor prognosis needs to be undertaken to guide clinical practice. Lastly, it can be hoped that any variations in course and outcome between the sexes may highlight factors which contribute to the development and maintenance of the disorder. This may in turn yield clues to more effective therapies.

Clinical reporting of male anorectics is hampered by the relative rarity of the condition. Follow-up studies are affected in the same manner, only more so. In addition, most researchers have been reluctant to include males in common studies because of the problems of assessing outcome in a uniform manner, as return of menstruation has been relied upon so heavily as a measure. The lower percentage of body weight comprising fat in the male (Crisp, 1980) also poses problems of interpreting outcome data: Is the return to within 15% of normal weight, accepted in female studies, too generous for men? Perhaps they need to be much closer to their standard weight to be considered recovered. These factors have led to the remarkable discrepancy between the frequency of males being reported in the literature and their being included in follow-up studies. Hsu's (1980) review of the outcome literature demonstrates this dramatically. In 16 series there were only 23 male cases out of a total of 787 patients (2.9%). This compares to Bliss and Branch's (1960) 51 males out of 473 cases in 18 presentation studies (11%).

Table 1 lists the published studies of Anorexia Nervosa in the Male. Only three attempts to follow up males and assess their outcome have been made (Burns & Crisp, 1984, 1985; Dally & Gomez, 1979; Hasan & Tibbets, 1977). On the basis of case histories and the earlier descriptive studies, the outcome in the male has been thought to be better (Dally & Gomez, 1979; Hasan & Tibbets, 1977) and worse (Crisp & Toms, 1972) than the female.

The outcome of anorexia nervosa has been shown to depend substantially on the history and clinical features of the patients studied (Hsu, 1980; Hsu et al., 1979; Theander, 1970). Physicians treating mild brief episodes were convinced that it was a benign disorder, whereas psychiatrists dealing with patients who had graduated to mental hospitals were deeply pessimistic (Beck & Brochner-Mortensen, 1954). For a meaningful comparison of outcome, a male population must be compared with a female population where the severity and duration of the illness are at least fairly similar. It would be no use comparing a group of females with mild early anorexia nervosa seen in a Pediatric Clinic with, say, a group of male tertiary referral patients with many years of illness. Not only do the two populations need to be fairly comparable, but they also need to be described fully and reliably so that the inevitable differences between the two groups can be properly accounted for.

TABLE 1

Published Studies of Anorexia Nervosa in the Male

Author	Date	No. Patients
Falstein et al.	1956	4
Bruch	1973	9 (5 primary A/N, 4 atypical)
Crisp & Toms	1972	13
Beumont et al.	1972	6 (+ 25 in literature review)
Hasan & Tibbets	1977	10
Sreenivasan	1978	3
Hay & Leonard	1979	5
Dally & Gomez	1979	12 (8 primary, 4 atypical)
Sheppard et al.	1984	9
Kiecolt-Glaser & Dixon	1984	4
Ziesat & Ferguson	1984	3
Anderson & Micalide	1985	9 (plus 7 bulimic)

To date, the only published study which conforms to these requirements is that carried out by the authors at St. George's Hospital in London (Burns & Crisp, 1984, 1985). This will be reported on in detail here and drawn upon for discussion of the outcome in males. Two major studies of outcome in the female, one conducted at the Maudsley Hospital on 38 female patients (Morgan & Russell, 1975) and one at St. George's on 100 female patients (Hsu et al., 1979) will be used as comparisons for the males. All three studies have used substantially the same methods and assessments, thereby facilitating comparison. As yet, there doesn't exist any other published study of follow-up in the male which is large enough or detailed enough for any statistical comparisons to be made with the present reported series.

STUDY SAMPLE AND METHODS

Twenty-eight male patients were identified by a search of the case notes of over 400 anorectics treated at the St. George's Clinic or earlier under the consultant care of the second author. A minimum of two years had elapsed since assessment. They were traced and, after consultation with their family doctors, approached directly. One patient was excluded from the study because of increasing doubt about the diagnosis. Of the 27 remaining, 23 were interviewed; in 15 cases this interview was complemented by an interview with both parents and in two cases with the mother alone. Three interviewed patients refused permission for their families to be contacted. Four patients were not interviewed (three refused and one was living abroad). Two of these completed questionnaires and information was available from the family practitioner on all four, supplemented by parents on two. The range of the follow-up was two to 20 years, with a mean of eight years (S.D. 8.7 years).

As mentioned above, much of the disagreement over the outcome in anorexia nervosa has stemmed from the different clinical features of the patient populations studied. The clinical features of this study population are dealt with in detail in Chapter 9 in this volume. A similar female population (Hsu et al., 1979) will be used as the main reference population for comparison. Both these groups were composed of patients with severe chronic anorexia nervosa, as was the Maudsley reference series.

ASSESSMENT OF OUTCOME

Outcome was measured by using clearly defined scales developed and used in the Maudsley study. The patients functioning in the six months preceding the interview were assessed. Assessment was not only in terms of eating habits and weight (the "Nutritional Scale") but also sexual functioning (the "Pychosexual Scale"), employment, accommodation, emancipation from family and general mixing (the "Socioeconomic Scale"), and disturbances in the patients mental state other than features of anorexia nervosa ("The Mental State"). The menstrual outcome used in the female studies obviously had to be omitted for the male. Higher scores represent better functioning and an average outcome score (ranging from 4 to 16) was constructed by adding the scores.

Both of the reference studies divide outcome into general outcome categories of good, intermediate, and poor. These correspond to clinicians' needs. A good outcome denotes both physical and psychological recovery. Poor indicates that the condition has persisted essentially unchanged or is even worse. Patients with an intermediate outcome are those who show a degree of recovery, having made some progress but with clear evidence of the disorder's continuing impact upon them, usually in terms of their ability to hold the normal weight and maintain a normal dietary regime.

GENERAL OUTCOME CATEGORIES

The absence of menstrual disturbance as a marker makes dividing outcome in male patients into three such groups difficult. Allocating all the men with normal body weight (> 85% MPMW) to good outcome as Morgan and Russell (1975) did results in a good outcome in 59% (cf. 34% in their females). It would then be argued that the "intermediate" outcome groups identified in the Maudsley and St. George's female studies (those with normal weight but disturbed menstruation plus a smaller number with unstable weight but regular menstruation) have been lumped in with the good outcome group. In order to make comparisons with these two studies meaningful and also to do justice to the range of clinical outcome, a third, intermediate, category needed to be constructed.

Menstruation, along with weight, were taken as the most objective indicators of recovery in both studies. The three outcome categories were constructed by weight restoration (with a threshold of 85% MPMW) and menstrual function. Russell suggested that decreased potency in the male is equivalent to amenorrhea in the female as an outer sign of the hormonal disturbance which constitutes one component of the diagnostic triad for anorexia nervosa. Careful questioning of the patients about their sexual habits at follow-up met with surprisingly little resistance. Sexual activity (intercourse or masturbation) was taken as an indicator of potency. Patients who had experienced a reduction of sexual drive often remarked upon it spontaneously and had little difficulty in identifying it as part of their illness.

The three General Outcome Categories were thus defined for the male by weight and sexual activity.

1. **Good Outcome** indicated weight restoration to 85% MPMW and regular sexual activity.
2. **Intermediate Outcome** indicated weight restoration to 85% MPMW but with absent or irregular sexual activity, or weight restoration to 80-85% MPMW with regular sexual activity.
3. **Poor Outcome** indicated weight below 85% MPMW with absent or irregular sexual activity.

Not surprisingly, the general outcome categories and the average outcome score are highly correlated (Pearsons R = 0.893, p < 0.001).

Good Outcome: 12 Patients, 44%

All the 12 patients in the Good Outcome group had a stable body weight over 85% MPMW at follow-up (mean 94.9%). Seven had no problems at all with diet. Four (33%) were worried about their weight still and two had periods when occasionally they restricted their food intake. Six were married at follow-up. All reported regular sexual intercourse, apart from one who masturbated regularly. One was in a period of reduced sexual activity in his marriage after his wife had found out about an affair he had been having.

As a group, they had a high average outcome score (14.7). All except one were in full employment and only three has failed to establish themselves independently from their families. These three lived with their parents, but were optimistic about eventually moving out. The degree of social contact varied within the group, although all had some activities and contact outside their families. Relationships with fathers at follow-up were predominantly distant and unremarkable. Two described this relationship as good. While one patient described his relationship with his mother as "enmeshed," the others were equally divided between distant, unremarkable, and good. None of these patients were rated as abnormal in their mental state assessment.

A third of the cases had experienced psychiatric disorders (virtually all anxiety, though tinged with alcohol abuse in two cases) during the follow-up period. This rate of psychiatric disorder is higher than in the Intermediate and Poor Outcome patients. It probably represents the stresses of adapting to a life without the defensive posture of anorexia nervosa. As a group, they had remained in contact with the psychiatric services for just over eight months after discharge and this is remarkably more than the mean of just over three months for those who did not recover fully. Return to normal weight, therefore, seems well reflected in the patients' general adaption.

Good Outcome Case History

Initial Assessment: Age 17 Years, MPMW 83%

Alan came to England with his family at the age of 11 from Southern Italy. His parents ran a couple of restaurants and obesity was the rule on both sides of his family. Soon after his arrival in this country, he began to overeat and gain weight. Three years previously this became compulsive and his weight increased to 80 kg. He then eliminated carbohydrates from his diet and began to lose weight. His regime deteriorated into one of severe abstinence and, latterly, vomiting, with overeating at meal times.

His family had been in turmoil for the last four years as the relationship between his parents deteriorated. His father had a mistress and two years previously had left his wife to live with her. Apparently, philandering was a well-established activity in his father's family. He remarked, "All the men are the same in my dad's family—they've all got women on the side—it's terrible." During the last year, the patient's obvious success with women (he had intercourse on a fairly casual basis) had incurred his mother's censure: "Just like his father." He had been close to his father and missed him considerably. He had younger twin sisters and felt his obligations as the man of the family.

After a two-week admission for investigations, he was seen for four sessions as an outpatient. He recognized his dread of following in his father's footsteps and understood his anorexia as an avoidance of this fate. He remained, however, very guilty about his eating bouts and keen to keep his weight down to 45 kg. He stopped attending.

Follow-Up: Age 32 Years, MPMW 100%

He had now been married for eight years and was the father of a 15-month-old daughter. His weight had gradually increased to normal about two years after his contact with the hospital. He had returned to an active sporting life. During the last two years, his weight had gone up about 3-4 kg to 63 kg because of "nervous eating." He had opened his own restaurant and was working excessively. His marriage had suffered because of an affair during his wife's pregnancy, but they felt that things were on the mend. He had no particular anxieties about food and weight, apart from feeling that he had got a bit paunchy of late (which he had). The patient takes his family obligations very seriously and employs both his mother and two sisters in his restaurant.

Intermediate Outcome: 7 Patients (26%)

Four of the patients with an intermediate outcome had a MPMW over 85% at follow-up and 3 had fallen to between 80-85%. Two patients actively restricted their intake and one patient used purgatives on occasions when he thought he had eaten too much. All but one expressed concern about body weight to some degree. The men complained of abdominal fatness and occasionally about their buttocks. None in this series mentioned their faces or thighs as areas of concern, as would have been expected with female patients. The only two bulimic patients and one of the three vomiting patients were in this group. Neither of the bulimic patients was vomiting more than once or twice a day and rarely on every day. Neither described a central preoccupation with his vomiting. Only one was married at follow-up, although two were divorced. Two had a regular sexual relationship, but two experienced no sexual impulses whatsoever.

Five still lived at home despite a mean age at follow-up of 30 years. One thought he would never be able to establish his independence from home. All were in full employment and had at least some social contacts. The ability of anorectics to remain in employment despite having to deal with severe and protracted personal problems has been remarked upon by many authors. It was very noticeable in this group, many of whom seemed to be triumphing over considerable adversity to maintain their social functioning. They reported less happy relationships with their families. On the whole this was more one of distance and lack of support rather than of continuing conflict.

Three of the patients were rated as mildly disturbed on their mental state assessment. None were rated as markedly disturbed. A mild disturbance is one which while distressing the patient does not prevent his from carrying out any significant activities. The disturbance noted was one of minor affective states, usually a mixture of anxiety and depression, with some mild obsessional features in one of the cases. Only one had had a defined psychiatric disorder (alcohol abuse) since discharge. This group had a mean average outcome score of 11.8 and a mean body weight of 89% MPMW.

Intermediate Outcome Case History

Initial Assessment: Age 33 Years, MPMW 81.6%

This 33-year-old man presented with a 12-year history of anorexia nervosa. He had dieted from 85 kg down to about 60 kg where he had remained with minor fluctuations. He practiced abstinence, with carbo-hydrate avoidance punctuated by occasional binges followed by vomiting and remorse. His weight loss seemed to have been sparked off by his relationship with his wife-to-be.

His father was a rather quiet, conscientious civil servant who was under his wife's thumb. Mother was a puritanical woman with "a mania against sex." She was very close to her son, who had been school phobic. He rebelled in adolescence. He stayed out at parties, drank, and had brief, promiscuous relationships. The only important one was with a divorcée 10 years his senior who had two children.

During his military service, he began to drink heavily and on discharge had difficulty settling in a steady job. Around this time, he met a respectable, local girl of whom his mother approved. He was unable to contemplate any sexual relationship with her, although remaining potent with casual encounters. These he considered "lust" and not "love." At this time, he was sensitive about his fitness and "maleness" and saw his weight loss as making him less masculine. His marriage to her was unconsummated and annulled after eight years.

At assessment, he was very regular and obsessional in his eating and daily routine. During his admission, with restoration of his weight, he became rebellious towards his parents again and struck up impulsive relationships with female patients. He lost weight just before being discharged to an outpatient anorectic group, but failed to attend after the second meeting.

Follow-Up: Age 43 Years, MPMW 88.4%

For about two years after discharge his weight had remained low. He was now steady at 67 kg. His eating was, however, rigorously controlled. He has Muesli with milk for breakfast, or just milk alone. For lunch, he had yoghurt, cottage cheese, and an apple. He had the same for dinner. This diet was the same every day except for his day off when he had a cooked meal in a restaurant in the evening. The thought of bread or potatoes was still quite abhorrent to him. He thought that his drinking kept his weight up—he drank 2-3 pints of beer most days. His life was rigidly obsessional, his room spartan, with his few possessions carefully in their places. He bathed twice a day and spent half an hour shaving and washing each morning. He was working as a swimming baths attendant and swam most days. He also did regular weight lifting and was heavily muscled. He saw his mother one week a year and allowed her to "feed him up" for that period. He was a social recluse and had no contact with women. He tended to blame this on his alopecia totalis which had developed four years previously.

Poor Outcome: 8 Patients (30%)

These eight patients has a mean MPMW of 72.6%, with three below 75%, the other five weighing between 75 and 85% MPMW. They all exhibited active, chronic anorexia nervosa, often admitting to keeping their weight just above the level which would activate psychiatric involvement. All practiced regular abstinence and were continuously worried about their weight. None of them binged or vomited. One was married and one divorced. None had any sexual feelings or activity apart from occasional masturbation.

Two were independently established away from their parents though neither considered their present functioning adequate. Four considered independence impossible and two were occasionally optimistic about achieving it. None was socially adequate but all, apart from one, had at least one friend. Three were unemployed and one was in occasional employment. All of those living with their parents found the relationship difficult and complicated although open conflict was extremely rare. Often the family had adapted to the patient's strict routines and efforts to encourage weight gain had been long abandoned. Apart from one who had a remarkably good (if impoverished) social facade and complained of nothing other than his anorexia, all had abnormal mental states. Four were rated as markedly disturbed, and three mildly. These patients had a mean average outcome score of 7.8. None had died or were in institutions at follow-up. These patients show, therefore, a picture of continuing anorexia nervosa combined with severe handicaps in both personal relationships and social adjustment.

Poor Outcome Case History

Initial Assessment: Age 23 Years, MPMW 88%

This patient developed anorexia, characterized by bulimia, vomiting, abstinence, and purging, while on a historical "grand tour" of Europe at the age of 18 aimed to "outclass" his siblings. He was treated at another hospital on and off during the next four years, but progress was not made and he developed pulmonary tuberculosis.

He is the youngest of triplets born to an elderly couple. He felt unwanted and found being a triplet embarrassing. He did poorly academically compared to his brothers. He had an enormous appetite and weighed around 105 kg in his late teens. He probably bullied his brothers and was his father's favorite. On his 18th birthday he was hit by a van and knocked unconscious for four days. On recovery, he was irritable and aggressive and was sent to his aunt to stay. Soon after this, his mother died of carcinoma of the stomach and he came back to take her place in the home—cooking, cleaning, organizing Christmas, etc. He visited her grave daily and became so difficult that his brothers had to leave six months after her death. It was then he gave up his job and went off on his grand tour.

His father had been a P.O.W. in Burma and had retained an aversion towards food. Mother had been married previously and led a vigorous social life, but, with the birth of the triplets, she rarely went out without her husband.

After admission he had a very stormy course with many rows. After one, he discharged himself, took an overdose, and requested readmission. The last two months of his stay were uneventful. He had intensive individual psychotherapy, which was extended into his 16th outpatient follow-up visit, and considerable efforts were expended in family therapy to no avail before being abandoned. One year after contact ceased he was working regularly, his weight 3 kg below target, and going to night classes. His relations with his family were conflict-ridden and devoid of warmth.

Follow-up: Age 28, MPMW 72.6%

He was still living at home with his father and their relationship remained stormy. He weighed 57 kg and was losing weight slowly. Although he had gained control of his anorexia to some extent in the last few months, he had been vomiting daily only five months ago. He had put a brake on his decline by excessive work. He went to his office at 5 a.m. and worked furiously till 7 p.m. He was still attending night classes. He had no contact with the opposite sex and no real hope of emancipating himself from his aggressive-dependent relationship with his father. He was very concerned with his health and worried that he would develop tuberculosis again; it was fear of this illness, he said, which had motivated him to gain weight originally at St. George's.

The distribution of patients according to outcome measures is shown in Table 2.

NUTRITIONAL OUTCOME

Overall, body weight had been normal (>85% MPMW) in just over half of the patients at follow-up and this rises to three-quarters if minor, short-lived deviations are allowed. This compares very closely with the outcome in female patients with similar illnesses. The 37% who were totally free of preoccupations about weight and diet is also in the upper range of outcome for female patients. While not all patients with normal weight were free of worries, it is clear that only those who have sustained weight gain normalize their dietary behavior and preoccupations.

Difficulties in eating with others were reported less often by the men—26% compared to figures in the 30 to 35% range for females. Similarly, vomiting and purgative abuse was much less in the men—about one in 10 compared to respectively a fifth and a third in the females. A possible explanation of this

TABLE 2

Distribution of the Patients According to Outcome Measures**

Category	No. patients (%)	Nutritional outcome			Sexual activity		Adjustment ratings (12 point scale, 12 optimal)			Average outcome score (16 points)
		Weight %MPMW	Disturbed* food intake	Concern* over weight/ shape	Regular active/ married stable relationship	Rare/ Absent	Mental	Sexual	Socio-economic	
Good	12 (44%)	94.5	0	1: 8%	12†: 100%	0	12	11	10.2	14.7
Intermediate	7 (26%)	89	2: 29%	2: 29%	3 : 43%	4: 57%	10.3	7.3	9.1	11.8
Poor	8 (30%)	72.5	8: 100%	8: 100%	0	8: 100%	7.9	4.8	6.2	7.8
Total	27	86.6	10: 37%	11: 41%	15 : 56%	12: 44%	10.3	8.2	8.7	11.9

* = more than half the time.

† = only one patient (a schoolboy) not having regular sexual intercourse in a stable relationship or marriage. Eight patients married at follow-up.

**Reprinted with permission from Burns & Crisp (1984), "The Outcome of Anorexia Nervosa in Males," *British Journal of Psychiatry*, *145*, 319–325.

difference may lie in the higher proportion of men reporting excessive activity—over half of the men, with a quarter consciously using it to control weight.

PSYCHIATRIC OUTCOME

The higher proportion reported as psychiatrically "normal" at follow-up— 63% compared to 40% for the Maudsley and 47% for the St. George's female studies—may be due to the longer follow-up period. The males were followed up, on average, eight years after presentation compared to five and six years respectively for the females studies. Morgan and Russell (1975) commented that mental state was more often normal as follow-up time increased. The three British studies have generally lower recorded levels of psychiatric abnormality than most other studies. This may be due to somewhat artificial separation out of anorectic symptoms from the estimation of mental state. It may also reflect the traditionally higher threshold for psychiatric disorders associated with British psychiatry.

Notwithstanding these reservations, it is important to note that none of these patients had developed psychosis at any time. None of the disturbed patients had normal body weight and the most prominent symptom at follow-up was anxiety and not depression as so often reported in other studies.

That anorexia nervosa "breeds true" receives further support from this study. Only one recorded patient had developed a durable disorder (a spider phobia). The other disturbances in the recovered group were transient crises associated with relinquishing the disorder. Patients with poorer outcomes exhibited persistent problems in impulse control which had developed parallel to their isolation. Only one patient had substituted a severe psychiatric disorder for his anorexia nervosa compared to the 20% and 16% in the female studies.

PSYCHOSOCIAL OUTCOME

Two-thirds of the whole sample had poor relations with their fathers and half with their mothers. Only a fifth were fully satisfied with their parental relationships. These figures are very similar to those in the female studies and are difficult to interpret in the absence of adequate control groups. The commonest cause of dissatisfaction was a feeling of distance and coldness in the relationship.

Only a third of the men were living in their own homes and a further quarter were away at University at follow-up. Despite the longer follow-up, this is less than for the female studies where 60% and 68% respectively were independently established from their parents. Assessments of "social ease" and friendships is notoriously difficult. About a third of the men complained of social awkwardness and difficulties in acquiring friends. This is similar to that reported in the Maudsley series, but higher than in the St. George's female series. Meaningful comparisons will have to await more formalized measures of such features. As with females, these patients were able to keep in employment—80% in full employment. To simply say that anorexia nervosa selectively spares work capacity in these patients fails to convey the frenetic quality of their need to work. Excessive application to work and its routines stemmed both from the need to hold thoughts of food (and the attendant risk of overeating) at bay and from a puritanical, almost ascetic, drive to deny personal needs and comfort.

PSYCHOSEXUAL OUTCOME

A third were married at follow-up, of whom only one was married at presentation. All who had subsequently married were recovered, whereas the patient who was married at the onset had a poor outcome. One whose marriage was annulled had an intermediate outcome (see case history). These findings are similar to the St. George's females.

Half of the patients considered their sexual activities as an important source of pleasure and had a stable partner. A higher proportion of men, however, actively avoided sexual contacts—37% compared to 23% and 17% in females. This higher figure may represent the ability of sexually disinterested females to accept a sexual relationship for its social comfort, whereas social anxiety in men may contribute towards shyness and sexual avoidance. Just under a third of the men had no sexual feelings whatsoever and all of these men were underweight. Interestingly, as with females, a small number of nutritionally recovered patients persisted with psychosexual problems. Results in the male are, therefore, compatible with the suggestion that the psychosexual problems in anorexia nervosa are not purely a result of weight loss but may be part of a more pervasive disturbance in interpersonal functioning.

Whether the low birth rate in these men (five children to three patients) is a consequence of time "lost" to their illness or a reflection of a more enduring disturbance remains an open question.

TABLE 3

Body Weight Over Time in the Male Series

Body Weight	1 Year	2 Years	4 Years
85% − 115% MPMW	14 (54%)	16 (59%)	14 (67%)
75% − 85% MPMW	5 (19%)	8 (30%)	5 (24%)
Below 75% MPMW	7 (27%)	3 (11%)	2 (9%)
Total	26 (100%)	27 (100%)	21 (100%)

COMPARISON WITH OUTCOME IN THE FEMALE

Both the studies used as female reference points for this comparison use a minimum of 4 years for follow-up, while this study has a minimum of 2 years. This is an important consideration as Crisp (1980) has suggested that the natural history of established anorexia nervosa which remits is characterized by a mean duration of illness of 4.6 years (2.5 years standard SD). Indeed, investigation of follow-up notes of these male patients shows that there is a marked, early weight loss which is gradually reversed with time. Table 3 shows the increase in weight over time in the male group.

No significant differences between the two-year and four-year follow-up groups was demonstrated, so the total two year follow-up group was used for all comparisons. To insist on restricting the sample to the four-year follow-up for comparison would be artificially precise as both the mean duration and range of follow-up are markedly greater in the male series. Despite these imponderables, the table is suggestive of an improved outcome with greater length of follow-up.

Table 4 shows the general outcome in the male and the two female studies broken down for both the total group and the inpatient samples. The St. George's female study included patients who had been treated with outpatient psychotherapy (generally considered to have a better prognosis).

The removal of the outpatient group in the female series worsens the outcome, but there is no impact in the males. This is because the seven males who were not admitted were a heterogenous self-selected group rather than those judged clinically less severe.

While none of the differences are statistically significant, the trend (whichever of the three sets of figures is chosen) is consistently towards a marginally better prognosis in the male. To some extent, this better outcome in men may be an artifact of the criteria of recovery used. The greater proportion of good-to-intermediate outcomes recorded in the male (as

TABLE 4

Distribution of Outcome in Males and St. George's and Maudsley Female Series of Anorexia Nervosa**

Categories	Present Series		Hsu et al.		Morgan & Russell*
	Total	I.P.	Total	I.P.	Total
Good	12 (44%)	9 (45%)	48 (48%)	22 (45%)	13 (34%)
Intermediate	7 (26%)	5 (25%)	31 (30%)	18 (37%)	12 (32%)
Poor	8 (30%)	6 (30%)	21 (20%)	8 (16%)	11 (29%)
Dead	0	0	2 (2%)	1 (2%)	2 (5%)
Untraced	0	3	0	0	0
Total	27	20	105	49	38

*Morgan & Russell's series contained 3 male patients whose results have been removed for the purpose of comparison.
**Reprinted with permission from Burns & Crisp (1984), "The Outcome of Anorexia Nervosa in Males," *British Journal of Psychiatry, 145,* 319–325.

opposed to the equal distribution between these two categories in the female in patient studies) is the most noticeable difference in the pattern of outcome.

Three possible explanations present themselves for this discrepancy. As already mentioned, the proportion of body fat on the male is less than that in the female and thus the cut-off point of 85% MPMW may be too low. Had it been placed at 90% MPMW two patients with regular sexual activity but weight between 85 and 90% MPMW would have been reclassified as intermediate outcome, more closely paralleling the outcome in the female.* A MPMW of 90% may, therefore, be of more suitable limit for weight restoration in male patients for use in future studies.

A second possibility is that sexual function is not an adequate equivalent for menstrual function in the assessment of outcome. Studies of testosterone levels in recovering anorectics (Andersen et al., 1982; Beumont et al., 1972; Crisp et al., 1982) indicate a rapid rise in testosterone production parallel with weight gain, and presumably a rapid return of sexual potency in the male. This is in contrast to the situation in females where the return of menstrual function can be considerably delayed, even when weight restoration is maintained. Menstrual function, therefore, may be a better indicator of a stable, established weight restoration than is sexual functioning in the male. It may be that the

---

*The detailed comparison of the St. George's male and female series in Chapter 6 is based on these altered weight thresholds where the rationale is further discussed.

information on sexual function is less accurate than that for menstrual functioning, although there is no reason to believe that this is so.

The third possibility is that the outcome profile in males is genuinely different from that in females, that once recovery is initiated in males it is more often, or more rapidly, achieved. This could stem from one of the likely causes for the original discrepancy in the rates of anorexia nervosa in males and females—namely, society's unequal concern with weight in the two sexes. The ideal of slimness for women as a major factor in the incidence of anorexia nervosa has been commented upon by virtually all major authorities. This "ideal" is no doubt a significant factor in Nylander's (1971) findings that the majority of adolescent girls want to lose weight, whereas their male peers do not. It is not inconceivable, therefore, that recovery in the male is less complicated due to the absence of this incessant social pressure to be slim to which the recovering female is exposed.

PREDICTORS OF OUTCOME

Predictors of poor outcome were sought in the characteristics of the illness at presentation, the history of the illness, early and family history, and outcome at one year. Table 5 displays those features which were associated with poor outcome at follow-up. The St. George's female series significances for these variables is given for reference. Not surprisingly, given the sample sizes, much weaker correlations were found in the male.

Severity of disorder was assessed in terms of longer duration of illness and degree of weight loss. Both were positively related to poor outcome in the males. Long duration of illness was related to poor outcome in the St. George's female study but not shown in the Maudsley series. A later onset of disorder, found in other series to be related to poor outcome, was only weakly associated in the males. Greater loss of weight and low body weight were correlated with poor outcome in all the studies.

Unfortunately, no specific dietary habits emerge as strong indicators of outcome. While there is a suggestion in the males that use of laxatives and anxiety in eating with others are associated with a poorer outcome, it is difficult to be sure that this is not simply an expression of longer duration of illness with which they were both related. Interestingly, bulimia, which is associated with a poor outcome in the female literature, shows a weak reverse trend in the men. This is probably an artifact of the concentration of rigid abstaining men in the poorest outcome group and should be treated with caution.

The poor outcome in these passive abstaining men is borne out further by the observation that a lack of sporting interest during illness is also associated with poor outcome. This finding is in the context of the much commoner use of exercise to control weight in men (see Chapter 6).

Disturbed relationships with parents in childhood were associated with poor outcome, as in the female studies. Poor social adjustment shows only a weak association, but a good social adjustment is significantly associated with a good outcome. As with the St. George's females, we failed to demonstrate the association with childhood neuroticism shown in the Maudsley study. This cluster of results does, however, support the clinical notion of the shy, compliant child doing relatively badly (Bruch, 1973; Crisp, 1977).

As can be seen in Table 5, the most powerful indicators of outcome are aspects of premorbid psychosexual development. Sexual activity, including sexual fantasy and masturbation, was strongly associated with a good outcome and its absence with a poor outcome. This is not an artifact of the age of onset. Possible circularity with sexual functioning used as a component of the outcome measure needs to be borne in mind. It is difficult to make direct comparisons with psychosexual development in the female. Early reporting in the female tends to be oblique; direct, specific questioning seems not to have been undertaken. This is undoubtedly due to the preponderance of male researchers in the early studies and the prevailing cultural views of female sexuality. With the increased openness about women's sexuality, it is likely that comparable information will soon be available.

CONCLUSIONS

While the study on which most of this chapter is based was carefully structured to test specific hypotheses, a number of impressions emerged which deserve mention. The men distinguished more clearly between issues of sexuality and "self" than did women when describing their recovery from anorexia nervosa. Sexual functioning returned early in the men and its return (often preceding social self-confidence and, therefore, as unwelcome as its departure had been welcome) was described in a much more circumscribed, almost external manner than was the return of menstruation in the female. It seemed to have less central or symbolic role for men. They associated their recovery more with improving social competence and mastery.

Along with this slightly distant attitude to returned sexuality, the men displayed an absence of concern about what appears to be either delayed or lowered fertility. Despite an average age at follow-up of 29 years, only three of the 27 men were fathers. None expressed any concern about this or voiced

TABLE 5

Data From Presentation Associated With Poor Outcome at Follow-Up*

Factor	Test of Significance	Average Outcome or General Outcome Score	p	p in Hsu et al. (1979) Study
Long duration of illness	Kendalls Tau	Average	<0.05	<0.00
Higher age of presentation	Kendalls Tau	Average	<0.09	<0.00
Onset after 20 years	X^2	General	<0.09	<0.05
Previous treatment	X^2	General	<0.05	<0.00
Weight features				
Low minimum weight during illness	F Test	General	<0.01	<0.01
High percentage body weight loss during illness	F Test	General	<0.05	
Low body weight at presentation	F Test	General	<0.07	<0.05
Symptoms				
Absence of bulimia	X^2	General	<0.08	
Purging	U Test	Average	<0.08	
Inability to eat in company	U Test	Average	<0.07	<0.00
Lack of sporting interest during illness	X^2	General	<0.01	
Disturbed childhood relationship				
with father	X^2	General	<0.02	
with mother	X^2	General	<0.05	<0.0
Poor social adjustment as child	X^2	General	0.008	<0.01
Absence of premorbid				
sexual activity	X^2	General	<0.05	
masturbation	X^2	General	<0.01	
sexual fantasy	X^2	General	0.001	

*Reprinted with permission from Burns & Crisp (1984), "The Outcome of Anorexia Nervosa in Males," *British Journal of Psychiatry, 145,* 319–325.

any anxieties that they might have damaged themselves permanently (a common anxiety in females).

Another feature reported in this sample was a subjective impression of a delayed impact of treatment. A number of men spontaneously reported how experiences, while an inpatient, had felt more powerfully therapeutic when recalled many months after discharge. For example, one man had been unable to make use of his psychotherapy while he was an inpatient and had lost weight rapidly after discharge. He brought stability to his chaotic, impulsive life by converting to a fundamentalist Christian faith. Within this strict and rather concrete moral environment, he soon found himself preoccupied with reevaluating his inpatient psychotherapy experiences. Over the course of about a year, he relinquished both his anorexia and his religious conversion.

In summary, this study of long-term follow-up of 27 men suffering from anorexia nervosa has indicated that the course and outcome of this disorder and those identified factors associated with outcome in the male are remarkably similar to those in the female. There has been nothing in this study to support any suggestion of increased durable gender identity problems in male anorexics, nor that markedly more severe or abnormal psychopathology is required to develop the disorder in men. Therefore, it substantiates the growing evidence that the disorder is probably identical in both sexes and that the difference in incidence is a reflection of the fact that most adolescent girls diet where as few adolescent boys do rather than of any specific psychosexual significance for fat deposition in girls. The gateway for many boys is undoubtedly through excessive exercise combined with weight control. Therefore, in our present culture this is likely to increase.

A number of these men at follow-up commented on how embarrassing it had been for them to be suffering from what was perceived by their fellow patients as a "girls' " disorder. Their need to express their precarious masculine identity in this situation may have led to much of the impulsive, acting-out behavior reported in males. It is clearly important and humane to be able to reassure such a struggling patient that his disorder is just as "normal" (if not as common) for males as it is for females.

APPENDIX: OUTCOME MEASURES

A. NUTRITIONAL OUTCOME

Scale A.1. Body Weight

1. Always much deviation, sufficient to cause concern.
2. Always deviation, but only at times sufficient to cause concern.
3. Usually near average but occasional deviation, sufficient to cause concern.
4. Near average all the time.

Scale A.2. Dietary Restriction

1. All the time.
2. More than half the time.
3. Less than half the time.
4. Normal all times.

Scale A.3. Worry About Body Weight or Appearance

1. All the time.
2. More than half the time.
3. Less than half the time.
4. No worry.

B. SOCIOECONOMIC OUTCOME

Scale B.1. Relationship with Nuclear Family

1. Enmeshed/stormy.
2. Distant.
3. Unremarkable.
4. Satisfactory/good.

Scale B.2. Emancipation from Family

1. Many difficulties, sees no prospect of becoming independent to a satisfactory degree.
2. As for 1, but at times feels difficulties can be surmounted.
3. Some difficulties but they are surmountable.
4. No difficulties.

Scale B.3. Personal Contacts (Apart from Family)

1. None.
2. Few and superficial.
3. Many and superficial.
4. Many both close and superficial

Scale B.4. Social Activities

1. None outside family.
2. Solitary pursuits outside family.
3. Variable. Mainly solitary but some group activities outside family.
4. Adequate group activities. Mixes well outside family.

Scale B.5. Employment

1. No paid employment.
2. Up to 50% of last six months in paid (or unpaid) employment.
3. More than 50% of time in regular paid employment, but not 100%.
4. Regular full-time paid employment without major absences.

C. PSYCHOSEXUAL OUTCOME

Scale C.1 Attitude Towards Sexual Matters

1. Active disgust/revulsion.
2. Avoidance (dislike).
3. Disinterest.
4. Pleasurable.

Scale C.2. Professed Aim in Sexual Relationships

1. To remain single.
2. Would marry but afraid to do so.
3. Would marry appropriate person but would not have children.
4. Definitely wants to marry and have children or has done so.

Scale C.3. Overt Sexual Behavior

1. None/avoided sexual contact.
2. Intermittent, no durable relationship.
3. Regular, but no durable relationship.
4. Pleasurable sexual activity with durable relationship (including marriage).

D. MENTAL STATE
(as observed at interview and reported abnormalities during preceding six months)

1. Grossly abnormal or psychotic.
2. Marked disturbance but not psychotic, e.g., anxiety/depression.
3. Mild disturbance.
4. Normal.

REFERENCES

Andersen, A. & Mickalide, A. (1985). Anorexia nervosa and bulimia: Their differential diagnoses in 24 males referred to an eating and weight disorders clinic. *Bulletin of the Menninger Clinic, 49* (3), 227–235.
Andersen, A. E., Wirth, J. B., & Strahlman, E. R. (1982). Reversible weight-related increase in plasma testosterone during treatment of male and female patients

with anorexia nervosa. *International Journal of Eating Disorders, 1* (2), 74–83.

Beck, J. C. & Brochner-Mortensen, K. (1954). Observations on the prognosis in anorexia nervosa. *Acta Medica Scandinavica, 149,* 409–430.

Beumont, P. J. V., Beardwood, C. J., & Russell, G. F. M. (1972). The occurrence of the syndrome of anorexia nervosa in male subjects. *Psychology of Medicine, 2,* 216–231.

Bliss, E. L. & Branch, C.H.H. (1960). *Anorexia Nervosa: Its History, Psychology and Biology.* New York: Paul B. Hoeber.

Bruch, H. (1973). *Eating Disorders.* New York: Basic Books.

Burns T. & Crisp, A. H. (1984). The outcome of anorexia nervosa in males. *Brit. J. Psych, 145,* 319–325.

Burns, T. & Crisp, A. (1985). Factors affecting prognosis in male anorexics. *Journal of Psychiatric Research, 19* (2–3), 323–283.

Cobb, S. (1943). *Borderlands of Psychiatry.* Cambridge, Mass.: Harvard University Press.

Crisp, A. H. (1977). The differential diagnosis of anorexia nervosa. *Proceedings of the Royal Society of Medicine, 70,* 686–690.

Crisp, A. H. (1980). *Anorexia Nervosa: Let Me Be.* London: Academic Press.

Crisp, A. & Burns, T. (1983). The clinical presentation of anorexia nervosa in males. *International Journal of Eating Disorders, 2* (4), 5–10.

Crisp, A. H., Hsu, L. K. G., Chen, C. N., & Wheeler, M. (1982). Reproductive hormone profiles in male anorexia nervosa before, during, and after restoration of body weight to normal: A study of twelve patients. *International Journal of Eating Disorders, 1* (3), 3–9.

Crisp, A. H. & Toms, D. A. (1972). Primary anorexia nervosa or weight phobia in the male. *British Medical Journal, 1, 334*–338.

Dally, P. J. & Gomez, J., with Isaacs, A. J. (1979). *Anorexia Nervosa.* London: Heinemann Medical.

Falstein, E. I., Feinstein, S. C., & Judas, I. (1956). Anorexia nervosa in the male child. *American Journal of Orthopsychiatry, 26,* 751–772.

Halmi, K. A. (1974). Anorexia nervosa: Demographic and clinical features in 94 cases. *Psychometrical Medicine, 36,* 18–26.

Hasan, M. K. & Tibbets, R. W. (1977). Primary anorexia nervosa (weight phobia) in males. *Postgraduate Medical Journal, 53,* 146–151.

Hay, G. G. & Leonard, J.C. (1979). Anorexia nervosa in males. *Lancet,* 574–576.

Hsu L. K. G. (1978). *Anorexia Nervosa—A* Prognostic Study. Unpublished MD dissertation, University of Hong Kong.

Hsu L. K. G. (1980). Outcome of anorexia nervosa: A review of the literature (1954 to 1978). *Archives of General Psychiatry, 37,* 1041–1046.

Hsu L. K. G., Crisp, A. H., & Harding, B. (1979). Outcome of anorexia nervosa. *Lancet 1,* 61–65.

Kiecolt-Glaser, J. & Dixon, K. (1984). Postadolescent onset male anorexia, *Journal of Psychosocial Nursing, 22* (1).

Morgan, H. G. & Russell, G. F. M. (1975). Value of family background and clinical features as predictors of long-term outcome in anorexia nervosa: Four-year follow-up study of 41 patients. *Psychological Medicine, 5,* 335–371.

Nemiah, J. C. (1950). Anorexia nervosa. *Medicine, 29,* 225–268.

Nylander, I. (1971). The feeling of being fat and dieting in a school population: An epidemiology interview investigation. *Acta Sociologica Medica Scandinavica, 1,* 17–26.

Russell, G. F. M. (1970). Anorexia nervosa—Its identity as an illness and its treatment. In J. H. Price (Ed.), *Modern Trends in Psychological Medicine,* Vol. 2. London: Butterworths.

Selvini, M. P. (1965). Interpretation of mental anorexia. In J. E. Meyer, & H. Feldmann, (Eds.), *Symposium on Anorexia Nervosa. Göttingen.* Stuttgart: Thieme Verlag.

Selvini, M. P. (1974). *Self Starvation.* Trans. Arnold Pomerans. London: Human Context Books.

Sheppard, N. P., Malone, J. P., & Jackson, A. (1984). Male anorexia nervosa: A review of nine patients. *Irish Medical Journal, 77 (1)* 4–8.

Sreenivasan, U. (1978). Anorexia nervosa in boys. *Canadian Psychiatric Association Journal, 23,* 159–162.

Theander, S. (1970). Anorexia nervosa: A psychiatric investigation of 94 female patients. *Acta Psychiatrica Scandinavica,* Supplement 214.

Ziesat, H. A. & Ferguson, J. M. (1984). Outpatient treatment of primary anorexia nervosa in adult males. *Journal of Clinical Psychology, 40 (3),* 680–690.

11

A Professionally Led Support Group for Males with Eating Disorders

Michael P. Levine, Trent A. Petrie, Jerome Gotthardt, and Todd D. Sevig

Most experienced clinicians believe the goals of therapy for eating disorders would include: (1) restoration and maintenance of set-point weight; (2) development of normal eating patterns; (3) overcoming pathological attitudes about the body, the self, and relationships; (4) strengthening coping skills; and (5) helping the individual discover and use social resources which can facilitate both recovery and future development (Andersen, 1985; Fairburn, 1985; Garfinkel & Garner, 1982; S.C. Wooley & O.W. Wooley, 1985). This chapter focuses on professionally led support groups as a potentially important component of this multidimensional approach (Enright, Butterfield, & Berkowitz, 1985; Enright & Tootell, 1986; Rubel, 1984). We describe the development of a professionally led support group for males, including the unique problems and benefits attributable to the all male composition. This chapter also contrasts the characteristic features of such groups with formal group therapy on the one hand and self-help groups on the other.

Special thanks are extended to Amy Baker Dennis (Executive Director) and Arline Iannicello of the National Anorexic Aid Society, Inc. We also wish to express our appreciation to the Pittsburgh Educational Network for Eating Disorders (Anita M. Sinicrope, Director) and to Carol Marshall of the Kenyon College Library.

Mutual aid groups have been formed to help patients and their families deal with virtually every known physical and psychological disorder (A. Gartner & Riessman, 1984; A. Katz, 1981). However, as of this writing there are few controlled investigations of self-help/support groups in general (Gottlieb, 1985) and no controlled studies of their role in recovery from eating disorders. Evidence for the usefulness of these groups is based on the undeniable success of Alcoholics Anonymous in helping thousands of alcoholics stay sober (Ray, 1983), the widespread establishment of eating disorder groups (Enright et al., 1985), professional testimonials (e.g., Edmands, 1986; Kinoy, 1985), and uncontrolled assessments of small samples participating in support groups for women with eating disorders (e.g., Franko, 1987) or for spouses and parents (e.g., Goodwin & Mickalide, 1985; Leichner, Harper, & Johnson, 1985).

In addition, Huon (1985) found that, relative to no treatment and bibliotherapy only conditions, a self-administered treatment for bulimia was more effective at post-treatment and 6-month follow-up when the women had contact with another woman who portrayed herself as a recovered-recovering bulimic. Although hardly definitive, these various reports do suggest that self-help/support groups merit the serious attention of professionals involved in the treatment of males with eating disorders.

A WORKING DEFINITION OF SOCIAL SUPPORT

Social support refers to the resources which people obtain from their attachment and commitment to other people (A. Katz, 1981). With respect to the potential role of mutual aid groups in recovery from eating disorders, these resources can be usefully divided into six categories (Silver & Wortman, 1980; Wills, 1985):

1. *Emotional support.* The opportunity to share and express feelings, coupled with empathic feedback concerning the authenticity and appropriateness of pressing emotional experiences.
2. *Esteem support.* The experience of being accepted and valued by people who are willing to listen reflectively and empathetically instead of judgmentally.
3. *Informational support.* The opportunity to collaborate with people whose information, advice, and guidance are potentially helpful in clarifying problems, generating options, and developing workable solutions.
4. *Companionship.* Enjoyment of the friendships which emerge in the course of pleasurable social activities.

5. *Motivational support.* The availability of encouragement and reassurance, offered in an atmosphere of hope. This enables the recipient to endure frustrations and to persist in the solution of complex, long-term problems.
6. *Status support.* Some mutual aid groups may produce positive changes in self-perception and social recognition by offering the individual a meaningful role and a valued identity within the larger community.

THE NEED FOR SOCIAL SUPPORT

The close relationship between mental health and social support is evident in the fact that modern definitions of psychological abnormality emphasize the criteria of social maladaptiveness, role inefficiency, and alienation (American Psychiatric Association, 1987; Levine, 1987; Rosenhan & Seligman, 1984). Indeed, an extremely pernicious consequence of severe psychological or physical disorders is their tendency to disrupt meaningful relationships, leaving the individual feeling disconnected, insecure, and vulnerable (Roback, 1984a).

Many women with eating disorders lead lives characterized by withdrawal, profound loneliness, sustained interpersonal conflict, and other indices of social maladjustment (Johnson & Berndt, 1983; Norman & Herzog, 1984, 1986; Thompson & Schwartz, 1982). In other words, they have low levels of support precisely at a time when added social support might be most helpful in engaging and benefiting from multidimensional treatment.

From the perspective of support group facilitators, the most salient reasons for severe interpersonal problems and concomitant lack of social support are: the emotional lability created by short-term restrictive dieting and long-term starvation (Garner, Rockert, Olmsted, Johnson, & Coscina, 1985); the fierce rigidity of the drive for thinness (Garfinkel & Garner, 1982); preoccupation with dieting, weight, and calories (Garfinkel & Garner, 1982); the secretive nature of binge-eating and purging (Abraham & Beumont, 1982); the large amount of time spent planning, carrying out, and reacting to binges and purges (Andersen & Mickalide, 1985); and the frequent co-occurrence of eating disorders with substance abuse, depression, personality disorder, sexual abuse, and a chaotic family environment (Humphrey, 1986; Mitchell, Hatsukami, Eckert, & Pyle, 1985; Pope & Hudson, 1984; Root, Fallon, & Friedrich, 1986).

There is also the mistrust and hypersensitivity experienced by the sizeable minority of people with eating disorders who have endured the full force of our culture's prejudice against overweight (Andersen, 1986; Garner, Rockert, et al., 1985; O. W. Wooley & S. C. Wooley, 1982). Weight restoration will alleviate some aspects of severe social maladjustment in some clients (Garner, 1987), but recent reports indicate that in many cases alienation and lack of support will persist despite clear improvements in eating behavior (Hall, 1985; Norman & Herzog, 1986).

Given the many parallels between eating disorders in males and females (Andersen, 1986; Andersen & Mickalide, 1985), it is hardly surprising that Mitchell and Goff (1985) report that all 12 of their males bulimic patients "were experiencing significant social disruption from the eating disorder" (p. 912). As discussed later in this chapter, many men with eating disorders are also depressed and/or demoralized (see also Andersen, 1986). Thus, they may suffer the added stigma of violating cultural norms which encourage masculine inhibition of both emotional expression and intimate disclosure (Belle, 1987; Hammen & Peters, 1978). This stigma might be intensified when the man suffers from a disorder inaccurately perceived as a "woman's problem" (Mitchell & Goff, 1985).

STRATEGIES FOR INCREASING SOCIAL SUPPORT

At first glance it would seem that a multimodal approach to treatment—individual, group, psychoeducational, and marital-family therapy—is sufficient to create a level of social support necessary for the sustained hard work of eliminating the eating disorder and reorienting toward health instead of illness (Andersen, 1985). However, in our experience many males seeking treatment for eating disorders are simply unable to participate fully in this ideal program, which is usually carried out on an inpatient basis. Some have an insurance plan that precludes anything more than biweekly individual sessions. Many men, by virtue of their stubborn refusal to eat and/or their chronic pattern of binge-eating, purging, substance abuse, and emotional lability (cf. Garner, Garfinkel, & O'Shaughnessy, 1985), have alienated their families to a point where these "natural" sources of support refuse to get involved. Last, but hardly least, are two sad facts. First, many cities and towns do not have the professional resources for a multidimensional approach. Second, some males with eating disorders are reluctant to enter an eating disorders "program" because they have suffered at the hands of unprepared physicians and psychologists (Garner, 1985).

These limitations strongly suggest that males with eating disorders need lowcost, nonthreatening opportunities for social support in conjunction with, or as an entry into, specialized professional treatment. However, the viability of support groups is not based solely on the deficits of clients or institutions. Self-help/support groups deserve a place in the multimodal approach to treatment because they also offer the possibility of immediate and lasting benefits which are not easily derived from any other form of therapy (Enright et al., 1985; Enright & Tootell, 1986; Kinoy, 1985; Rubel, 1984).

MUTUAL AID GROUPS: SOME GENERAL THEMES

"Support groups should be thought of as surrogate support systems for persons who have experienced support loss or whose existing support systems are inalterably deficient vis-à-vis their support needs" (Pearson, 1983, p. 364). Although this definition seems straightforward enough, the topic of "mutual aid groups" can be very confusing for professionals and consumers alike. Within the category are, at a minimum, "hospital-based disease management groups" (Roback, 1984a), "self-help groups" (Meehan, Wilkes, & Howard, 1984), "support groups," and "professionally led support groups" (Enright & Tootell, 1986). Theoretically, each has a different structure, a different set of goals and procedures, and different policies concerning the role of professionals and professional organizations (Enright et al., 1985; Levy, 1982). In practice there is considerable overlap. Consequently, we believe it is important to acknowledge some general themes before delineating the significant distinctions.

The Essence of Mutual Aid Groups

Rubel (1984) characterizes self-help/support groups as "small, voluntary groups designed to provide their members with support, encouragement, and a nonjudgmental, safe atmosphere in which to voice problems and concerns as well as joys and triumphs" (p. 382). The organizers may be either professionals or patients whose needs are not being fully met by existing mental health organizations. In either case, the mutual aid group seeks to mobilize small groups of patients (or family members) at various stages of recovery around the following conviction: Face-to-face interactions and a sense of mutual responsibility for each other can empower people to recover from (cope with) an eating disorder and to reorient themselves to health instead of illness (Enright et al., 1985; A. J. Gartner & Riessman, 1982; A. Katz, 1981; Pearson, 1983).

Mutual Aid Groups vs. Group Therapy

Group Therapy

Mutual aid groups are "therapeutic" groups, yet they should not be confused with "group therapy" (Brotman, Alonso, & Herzog, 1985; Enright et al., 1985; Roback, 1984b). Participants in group therapy pay a fee for what is clearly understood to be regular attendance at a specific number of treatment sessions conducted by a qualified mental health professional in a clinical setting. In most instances the group therapist carefully screens potential members to ensure a manageable group size and to recruit people who are insightful, socially oriented, tolerant of emotional expression, and capable of implementing group exercises and homework assignments. Contact between participants outside of the group is discouraged to avoid alliances which might lessen the ability of each group member to receive, withstand, and integrate feedback from the other members (Brotman et al., 1985).

The diversity of approaches falling under the rubric of "group therapy for eating disorders" works against a succinct statement of its goals and objectives (see Brotman et al., 1985, for a review). In general, group therapy uses specific "techniques" to eliminate maladaptive behaviors and attitudes, to replace them with skills for continued development, and to build self-esteem (Brotman et al., 1985; MacKenzie, Liversley, Coleman, Harper, & Park, 1986).

Mutual aid groups

The prototypical self-help/support group is free of charge and open to anyone who identifies himself or herself as having an eating disorder and who does not pose a blatant threat to the support atmosphere (Brotman et al., 1985; Enright et al., 1985). Some programs (e.g., Enright & Tootell, 1986) conduct one group for individuals with restricting anorexia nervosa and another for people with bulimia nervosa, based on the observation that differences in impulsivity and psychosexual maturity sometimes make it very difficult for these subgroups to relate. Other programs (e.g., Kinoy, 1985) conduct "mixed" groups because the organizers emphasize the many common features of restricting anorexia nervosa and bulimia nervosa.

In most mutual aid programs, participants are encouraged, but not required, to seek treatment from a physician and a psychotherapist. Attendance is voluntary and unrecorded, and therefore group composition usually varies from session to session. In contrast to the principles of group therapy, members of mutual aid groups are encouraged to develop relationships with each other outside of the weekly or biweekly sessions. In many self-help/support groups, there is no limit to the number of sessions a person may attend, i.e., the group "is there for people" as long as they deem it valuable (Kinoy, 1985).

Some mutual aid groups revolve around specific presentations on eating disorders (e.g., alternatives to bingeing) and related topics (e.g., intimate relationships). In other groups the participants determine the content. Regardless of structure, mutual aid groups differ from process-oriented therapy groups in that they encourage participants to discuss past experiences and current living circumstances, even if these reflections do not contribute to the illumination of interpersonal processes within the group (Brotman et al., 1985; Enright et al., 1985).

The Goals of Mutual Aid Groups

The ultimate goals of both naturally occurring and contrived support systems are the same as those of professional treatment: amelioration of deficiency and promotion of healthy development (Andersen, 1985; Pearson, 1983). However, with the exception of some "self-help" groups (e.g., Meehan et al., 1984), most mutual aid groups do not use "techniques" designed to produce immediate symptom reduction, structural personality change, and/or corrective emotional experiences in the realm of interpersonal interactions (Enright et al., 1985). Instead, the overriding goal of self-help/support groups is to teach members to provide themselves with the six major benefits of social support. More specifically, all mutual aid groups for people with eating disorders seek to (Enright et al., 1985; Kinoy, 1985; Meehan et al., 1984; Roback, 1984b; Rubel, 1984):

1. Help participants overcome the withering effects of isolation induced by the disorder itself and by its negative impact on interpersonal relationships (**companionship, emotional support,** and **status support**);
2. Provide a safe and caring atmosphere in which participants can experience, identify, express, and validate their feelings about the disorder, treatment, and recovery (**emotional support**);
3. Foster within the group a spirit of accurate empathy, unconditional positive regard, and authenticity (Rogers, 1951) so that members can increase their self-esteem as they learn to be more flexible in their expectations of themselves and others (**esteem, emotional,** and **motivational support**);
4. Help members understand and participate in the reciprocal relationship

between personal empowerment and reaching out to others (**esteem, motivational**, and **informational support**);

5. Help clients understand and adjust to the demands of "therapy" and improved health (**motivational, informational,** and **esteem support**);

6. Educate participants about the nature, causes, and treatment of eating disorders (**informational support**);

7. Emphasize that restrictive dieting, binge-eating, purging, and/or excessive physical activity are self-defeating and self-perpetuating "solutions" to personal problems (**informational** and **emotional support**).

8. Provide some form of therapeutic support in the broadest sense for persons who have been harmed by inept physicians and therapists (see Garner, 1985), or for whom individual and specialized treatment is too expensive or too far away (**emotional, esteem,** and **motivational support**).

The Beneficial Processes in Mutual Aid Groups for Eating Disorders

Although it is very important to distinguish between group therapy and group support, some of the "component processes" of group therapy (Yalom, 1975) are also active in self-help/support groups for eating disorders and for other psychological problems (Franko, 1987; Goodwin & Mickalide, 1985; Knight, Wollert, Levy, Frame, & Padgett, 1980; Leichner et al., 1985). Yalom (1975) refers to these processes as "curative factors," but we prefer to recognize their applicability to mutual aid groups as well as to therapy groups by calling them "beneficial group processes." Table 1 portrays the connection between each of the beneficial group processes and the components of social support to which they contribute.

Instillation of hope

Mutual aid groups typically consist of people at various stages of recovery from anorexia nervosa and bulimia nervosa, including some who have "been all the way through it." The presence of both "mastery and coping models" (Meichenbaum, 1972), coupled with factual information that eating disorders can be treated successfully, offers the encouragement and future-oriented perspective which constitute the experience of "hope."

Universality

Many people with eating disorders come to their first support group meeting "with the disquieting thought that they are unique in their

TABLE 1

The Relationship Between Beneficial Group Processes and the Components of Social Support to Which They Contribute

Beneficial Group Process[b]	Components of Social Support[a]					
	Emotional	Esteem	Informational	Companionship	Motivational	Status
Universality	X	X	X	—	X	X
Imparting information	—	—	X	—	X	—
Altruism	—	X	—	—	X	X
Instilling hope	—	—	—	—	X	—
Imitation[c]	X	—	X	—	X	—
Corrective emotional experience	X	X	—	X	—	X
Group cohesion	X	X	—	X	X	X

Note. X = process contributes to that component; — = process does not contribute.
[a] After Wills (1985).
[b] After Yalom (1975).
[c] Includes vicarious classical conditioning and vicarious instrumental conditioning.

wretchedness" (Yalom, 1975, p. 7). This is particularly true of men. Some have been the only male "case" at a hospital (Andersen & Mickalide, 1983), whereas others are acutely embarrassed by their perception that they have a "woman's disorder" (Mitchell & Goff, 1985). A male's discovery that he is not alone in his struggle with anorexia nervosa and/or bulimia nervosa is often his initiation into the corrective emotional value of "support." For those few males who are transparently proud of their unique abnormality, the presence of other males with eating disorders serves as a source of healthy dissonance (Kinoy, 1985).

Imparting of information

Group members receive a good deal of information, either as formal instruction or as advice. Through any number of cognitive social learning methods (Bandura, 1977)—lectures, readings, role plays, modeling by group leaders—participants learn about the tremendous variety of topics related to eating disorders.

If the group is functioning effectively, members will also be gently advising each other in a manner reminiscent of current "cognitive" approaches to therapy: (1) how to recognize distorted attitudes; (2) how to recognize the relationship between distorted attitudes, unhealthy self-statements, and self-defeating emotions; (3) how to gather and examine the evidence for these beliefs; and (4) how to generate and evaluate alternative thoughts and/or behaviors (Beck, Rush, Shaw, & Emery, 1979).

Altruism

Experts (e.g., A Gartner & Riessman, 1984; Rodolfa & Hungerford, 1982; Rubel, 1984) believe one of the most beneficial aspects of mutual groups is the opportunity to "receive through giving, not only as part of the reciprocal giving-receiving sequence but also from the intrinsic act of giving" (Yalom, 1975, p. 13). Learning to provide support to people who appreciate your presence in the group can held erode the layers of shame, despondency, and continuous self-consciousness which envelop so many people with eating disorders.

Imitation (observational learning)

Group members will likely observe, encode, and practice many types of adaptive "behavior" during their exposure to the actions and verbalization of other members. In the ideal group the modeled (and, hopefully, reinforced) "sequences" would include (1) faithful attendance of support group meetings, even if they are sometimes emotionally demanding; (2) effective selection and utilization of treatment (as opposed to support) resources; (3) encouragement of family and friends to make use of treatment and support services; (4) assuming responsibility for making needed changes in one's life, whether it be something specific, such as eliminating binge-eating or something more general such as being more accepting of oneself; and (5) procedures for identifying, challenging, and replacing distorted attitudes about eating, weight, and self.

Corrective emotional experiences

The support group is expressly designed to be a safe arena for consensual validation of feelings and for practice in healthy emotional expression (Levy, 1976; Rubel, 1984). The opportunity for authentic emotional expression is likely to be particularly crucial in the success of groups for males, given their conditioned deficits in emotionality (Brannon, 1985). At the basic level participants can share the pain and other turmoil of their struggles, secure in the knowledge that feelings will not be dismissed or devalued by those who cannot see beyond externals—slenderness, masculinity, success, a sharp sense of humor, etc. (S. Katz, 1985). If the group is guided by principles of respect and unconditional positive regard for each member, then participants can begin to use the understanding and experience of other group members to acknowledge personal feelings and experiment with their significance for evaluating experience.

Group cohesiveness

Cohesiveness, defined as both an individual's attraction to the group and the sum of the group members' commitment to each other, sets the stage for many of the other "beneficial processes." In addition, a solid sense of "we-ness" will empower some members to experiment with support—to take the chance of telephoning between sessions, to go out for coffee (not "diet" soft drinks!) after the group meeting, and to use peer pressure within the group to promote healthy attitudes about body weight and eating.

SUPPORT GROUPS VERSUS SELF-HELP GROUPS

Self-Help Groups

There are two major types of mutual aid groups: self-help and support (Enright et al., 1985; Enright & Tootell, 1986). In general, "self-help" groups are organized and led ("facilitated") by people with eating disorders; mental health professionals are not permitted to be facilitators unless they have had an eating disorder. Many "self-help" groups began at a time when expert treatment for eating disorders was very hard to find (Enright et al., 1985). Consequently, some group leaders are both committed to the "pure" power of peer interaction and vociferous in their distrust of the mental health professions. Based on the survey research of Enright et al. (1985) and on descriptions of several influential self-help programs (Meehan et al., 1984; Rubel, 1984), it is our impression that "curing" eating disorders is an explicit goal of many self-help groups. Some of these groups seek to eliminate symptoms by employing highly structured programs reminiscent of cognitive-behavioral group therapy (e.g., Meehan et al., 1984).

Support Groups

Support groups are not designed to "cure" eating disorders. Thus, *most* "support" groups, as contrasted with *some* "self-help" groups, do not attack bingeing, purging, dieting, or life skills in a step-by-step fashion. Rather, the "beneficial processes" of support groups are intended to reinforce and extend the "curative factors" operative in the various modes of treatment offered by mental health and medical professionals (Enright et al., 1985). The foundation of this effort is the client's need to be a valued person with meaningful interpersonal relationships, not just an "anorexic" or "bulimic" in need of treatment. Support groups are led by either mental health professionals or recovered lay persons, and in some programs both (Enright et al., 1985).

Professionally Led Support Groups

Some support groups are led by mental health professionals who receive training *and* ongoing supervision in both the "facilitation" of supportive relationships and the provision of accurate information about eating disorders and treatment services. Effective leaders need not be certified therapists who specialize in the treatment of eating disorders. The more crucial qualities are maturity, a commitment to helping people with eating disorders, a solid knowledge of eating disorders and local treatment services, the ability and willingness to listen nonjudgmentally, some experience with group processes, and an openness to various life-styles and paths to recovery (Enright & Tootell, 1986; Iannicello & Tootell, 1985; Kinoy, 1985).

Facilitator's role
Most clients come to a support group with a strong need for the "three E's": encouragement, empathy, and education. The two principal functions of the

facilitator are (1) helping clients to identify and express these needs and (2) gradually transferring the responsibility for meeting these needs from the "expert" facilitator to other members of the group. As noted by Enright and Tootell (1986), "to avoid the possibility of the support group becoming a therapy group, facilitators must continually remind themselves that the goal of the group is to assist members in developing a support system through peer interaction" (p. 240). In this regard, Larocca (1983, cited in Enright et al., 1985) observes that a support group is effective to the extent that the role of the facilitator undergoes a series of predictable transformations from "expert" to "facilitator" to inconspicuous executive.

Advantages

There would seem to be at least four advantages to using professionals as group facilitators (for a fuller discussion of advantages and disadvantages, see Enright et al., 1985; Enright & Tootell, 1986; Rubel, 1984). First , their advanced (and, hopefully, ongoing) education increases the probability that group discussions will counteract, and not reinforce, myths about nutrition, body weight, self-control, and eating disorders, all of which are prevalent and pathogenic in people with anorexia nervosa and bulimia nervosa (see Garner, 1985; Garner, Rockert, et al., 1985). Second, professionals are better prepared to identify and refer persons whose psychological condition (e.g., major affective disorder) or physical status (severe emaciation) threatens the supportive atmosphere of the group.

Third, many mental health professionals have received specific training in promoting the development of healthy relationships within a group. This orchestrating function is very important. Facilitators must be able "to direct requests for information, feedback, and support to other group members as much as possible, emphasizing the value of everyone's knowledge and experience" (Enright et al., 1985, p. 506).

Finally, professional facilitators can provide stability and continuity. One of the goals of our support group is helping men with eating disorders to understand and participate effectively in multidimensional treatment. If a man has made substantial progress in treatment, or even if he has just made maximal use of an effective support group, it is expected that his renewed familial ties and new relationships will supercede the relatively infrequent group meetings as a healthy source of support. In this regard, we hope there will come a point, validated by the individual's therapist and by the support group, where the man decides he is no longer "recovering," but now "recovered." Thus, in the course of "open" support group meetings, the recovering men will eventually move on, while the attendance of new and continuing participants will vary somewhat from session to session. In this shifting environment, the professional facilitator(s) can be the source of continuity for the group.

DEVELOPING THE NATIONAL ANOREXIC AID SOCIETY'S SUPPORT GROUP FOR MALES

Historical Rationale

The National Anorexic Aid Society, Inc. (NAAS), located in Columbus, Ohio, provides support, education, and referral for the wide variety of lay persons and professionals affected by eating disorders. During the past 12 years, NAAS has offered independent and professionally led support groups for people with restricting anorexia nervosa, for people with bulimia nervosa, and for families and friends. These groups have always welcomed males with eating disorders, but only a handful have ever attended. On those rare occasions when a male did attend, he would usually remain silent, leave early, and never return. One man in our group said that, although he was aware of the NAAS support groups, he chose not to attend "because I would have felt terribly uncomfortable and embarrassed being the only male in the group."

It appears that approximately 10% of referrals to eating disorders clinics are male (Andersen, 1985), and that perhaps 0.3 - 1.0% of college males are bulimic (Gray & Ford, 1985; Pyle, Halvorson, Neuman, & Mitchell, 1986). Our growing recognition of eating disorders in males (Mitchell & Goff, 1985; Scott, 1986), coupled with the absence of males in NAAS's thriving support group program, led to the development of a professionally led support group exclusively for men.

Initial Structure

Group meetings were held for 90 minutes on the first and third Tuesday of each month. This arrangement was designed to provide sufficient contact without creating a quasi-therapeutic environment which might dissuade participants from pursuing professional treatment. The group was open and free of charge. The only requirements were (1) a desire to overcome anorexia nervosa and/or bulimia nervosa; (2) a willingness to respect the members' confidentiality; and (3) an openness to the possibility of receiving and providing support.

Facilitators

Based on NAAS's model of support groups (Enright et al., 1985; Iannicello & Tootell, 1985), we had hoped to develop separate support groups for males with restricting anorexia nervosa and males with bulimia nervosa (regardless of body weight). Consequently, four facilitators (the authors) were recruited and trained: a college professor (M.L.), a licensed clinical psychologist (J.G.), and two graduate students in counseling psychology (T.P. & T.S.). One of the graduate students (T.P.) is a recovered bulimic; both had experience directing therapy groups.

Publicity

Letters describing the male support group (and other NAAS services) were sent to all Columbus area organizations which might serve men at risk for eating disorders. Recipients included: mental health centers; dance studios; inpatient programs for treatment of compulsive disorders and/or substance abuse; the Residence Life program at Ohio State University; two organizations providing support and services for gays; and the Central Ohio Men's Network.

Columbus area newspapers, radio stations, and television stations also aided greatly in our publicity efforts. An unexpected benefit of competitive media interest in the novel topic of males with eating disorders was the frequent opportunity for public education about the prevention and treatment of eating disorders in females as well.

PHASE 1: BUILDING A GROUP

Attendance and Group Composition

For the first several months attendance varied from five to nine: two to five males with eating disorders and three to four facilitators (the authors). Such low and inconsistent attendance was disappointing but predictable, given the combination of a relatively rare disorder and the well-documented reluctance of males to acknowledge psychological problems and seek help (McMullen & Gross, 1983). Each man was asked to complete and return a modified form of the Diagnostic Survey for Eating Disorders (Johnson, 1985) and a complete EDI (Garner, Olmsted, & Polivy, 1983). Between November 1986 and June 1987, 12 men participated at one time or another, and six (50%) returned completed questionnaires. The completion rate for the nine men who attended two or more sessions was 67%.

In order to expand our sample, we distributed our questionnaires to the participants in a male support group sponsored by the Pittsburgh Educational Network for Eating Disorders (PENED). The demographic and self-reported diagnostic data for 17 men in the two groups are shown in Tables 2 and 3. Although the less than ideal return rate in our sample cannot be overlooked, these data coincide with our notes in suggesting that the modal support group participant is a fairly well-educated man in his mid-30s who has a very long history of bulimic behavior and significant problems with body dissatisfaction, depression, perfectionism, and interpersonal distrust (see Table 4).

Assessment of Beneficial Group Processes

Fifteen men who had participated in four or more sessions also completed anther two-part questionnaire (available upon request from the first author) concerning the six components of social support (see Table 5). The individual items were statements generated by the authors (e.g., "I feel more hopeful about the future") plus statements taken from the 12 categories of Q-sort items used by Yalom (1975, pp. 78–81) to represent the 12 "curative factors" of group therapy.

Group Interactions

During the first few months, group sessions provided informational and motivational support, with some instances of emotional ventilation and empathic support. A striking discovery for the men was that each had previously believed himself to be the only man with "this woman's disorder." As predicted by Yalom's (1975) curative factor of "universality," each man reported considerable relief from the simple opportunity to "tell his story" and have it affirmed by the other men (see Table 5, Esteem and Status).

Helplessness and hopelessness are omnipresent issues for this "chronic population" (see Table 2). In accordance with the motivational function of social support, several men said a group designed especially for them was instrumental in forging a new commitment to recovery following a period of unsuccessful involvement with self-treatment, no treatment, and/or treatment by physicians and mental health professionals. The data in Table 5 (Motivational and Status) suggest that membership in a group of men who are acting on their "commitment to recovery" is an important component of the support group as an antidote to hopelessness.

Discussions of hope and hopelessness led to detailed consideration of new advances in the multidimensional treatment of eating disorders (Andersen,

TABLE 2

Demographic Data for Males in Two Eating Disorder Support Groups

Age (Years)			Religion	
Range	19–61		Catholic	7
Median	36		Protestant	6
Mean	37		Jewish	2
			Other	2
Marital Status			Current Living Situation	
Single	7		Partnered	7
Married	6		Alone	6
Divorced	3		Family	2
Separated	1		Other	2

Education	
Graduate degree	5
Some graduate training	3
College degree	2
Some college	4
High school degree	3

Note: All 17 respondents were Caucasian.

TABLE 3

**Self-Reported Diagnostic and Treatment Status for Males
in Two Eating Disorder Support Groups**

Diagnosis		Currently Receiving Professional Treatment
Bulimia Nervosa	9	Yes = 9
Anorexia Nervosa	2	No = 8
Anorexia Nervosa, Bulimia Subgroup	2	
Atypical ED	1	
Other	3	

Age of Onset and Duration

	Range	Median	Mean	S.D.
Age of eating disorder onset (yrs.)	9–33	20	20	7.6
Duration of eating disorder (yrs.)[a]	2–30	17	16	8.9

Areas of Life in Which Eating Disorder Interferes

Area	Percentage of Sample Indicating Often or Always
Thoughts	88
Feelings about self	88
Personal relationships	60
Daily activities other than work	50
Work or school	35

Note: Unless otherwise noted, N = 17 for all entries.
[a]N = 15

TABLE 4

Mean EDI Subscale Scores for Males in Two Eating Disorder Support Groups

	Self-Reported Diagnosis							
	Bulimia Nervosa (N = 9)		Anorexia Nervosa (N = 3)[a]		Anorexia Nervosa Bulimic Subgroup (N = 2)		Other[b] (N = 4)	
Subscale	Mean	SD	Mean	SD	Mean	SD	Mean	SD
Drive for thinness	11.7*	6.2	0*	0	11.0	11.0	8.0	3.2
Bulimia	7.4*	5.7	0.7	0.9	8.5	8.5	3.8	2.7
Body dis-satisfaction	13.9	8.8	10.7	1.7	19.5	6.5	22.3	4.9
Ineffectiveness	9.0	8.5	7.3	0.9	17.0	4.0	8.3	6.3
Perfectionism	10.0	4.2	6.0	2.2	10.0	4.0	5.0	2.5
Interpersonal distrust	3.8	2.6	6.0	0.8	9.5	6.5	7.8	5.1
Interoceptive awareness	8.9	8.5	2.3*	3.3	11.5	0.6	8.8	3.5
Maturity fears	2.3	2.0	1.0*	0.8	0.5*	0.6	5.0	2.5

Note: Sample sizes do not permit between-group comparisons. Thus, the focus is the general comparability of male and female scores. Within the first three columns, entries marked by an * are not significantly less than the means reported for groups of females (*N*'s = 49, 40, and 45) with comparable diagnoses (Garner, Garfinkel, & O'Shaughnessy, 1985, p. 585). This was determined by application of the conservative *z*-score method using Tchebycheff's inequality for distributions of unknown shape (Hays, 1973, p. 303) and an alpha level = .01, one-tail.
[a]One individual in this group completed the EDI, but did not complete the other questionnaires.
[b]Two "compulsive overeaters," one "binge eater," and one "chronic overeater."

1985; Garner & Garfinkel, 1985). In the spirit of cognitive therapy (Garner & Bemis, 1985), the men were encouraged to test their convictions of hopelessness by seeking treatment from experts in the area of eating disorders.

The men had a great need for information about eating disorders (see Table 5, Informational). Some literature was distributed (e.g., Garner, Rockert, et al., 1985; Levine, 1986), but we also devoted a large portion of the initial group meetings to presentation of factual information. Topics included the physical and emotional consequences of starvation-binge-purge cycles; hard-driving exercising as a form of purging; set-point theory; the relationship between dieting and bingeing; body dissatisfaction and body image distortion

TABLE 5

The Effect of Professionally Led Support Groups for Males with Eating Disorders on Six Components of Social Support

Component of Social Support	Percentage Describing It as Very Helpful or Very Important
Emotional	
Learning to identify and express feelings	80
Receiving open, honest feedback from the group	80
Esteem	
Being understood and accepted by the group	100
Group acceptance and understanding of personal and potentially embarrassing revelations	87
Informational	
Written information about eating disorders	80
Opportunity to clarify the nature of their own eating disorder	66
Advice of facilitators	66
Companionship	
Trusting and being trusted by group members	80
Practice in discussing their eating disorder with other people	80
Motivational	
Seeing other group members take risks with revelations or new patterns of thought/behavior	80
Opportunity to interact with group members who are farther along the path to recovery	80
Opportunity to interact with a recovered co-facilitator	50
Status as Group Member	
Helping, and being helped by, other members	94
Being in a group that was like an understanding and accepting family	66
Just knowing other males with eating disorders	60

(see Table 4); and dichotomous thinking about self-control. These discussions illustrated the tremendous overlap between eating disorders in men and women (Andersen, 1986; Mitchell & Goff, 1985; Scott, 1986).

As facilitators, we initially attempted to divert questions from ourselves to group members (Enright et al., 1985). However, we usually ended up providing the answers, because even the best educated of the men held tight to distorted beliefs and attitudes about food, weight, shape, and exercise (Garfinkel & Garner, 1982). An exception was the ability of men receiving specialized treatment to discuss its benefits in a straightforward and persuasive manner (see Table 5, Motivational).

Clinical Issues

Emotional expression

As shown in Table 3, nearly 90% of the men reported that their eating disorder frequently had a negative effect on their feelings about themselves. Nonetheless, despite their professed desire to get beyond an exchange of facts and similar personal histories, the men had a very hard time expressing and examining feelings of any type. Shame, habitual secrecy, alexithymia, perfectionism, and interpersonal distrust (see Table 4), and a "macho" performance orientation all made intimacy within or outside the group very difficult. What little emotional expression occurred tended to devolve rapidly into a safer intellectualization. Facilitators of men's groups (e.g., Rodkin, Hunt, & Cowan, 1982) have found it takes considerable effort and patience to develop an ambience in which men will allow themselves to share and explore intense feelings. In our case, the sociocultural obstacles to intimacy were magnified by the presence of a shifting constituency, many of whom presented with deficits in interoceptive awareness (see Table 4), depression, and/or character disorder.

Fear of fat

Andersen (1986) reports that, in contrast to his female patients, many of his male patients have actually been overweight or obese prior to the onset of their eating disorders. This suggests that males will have a particularly difficult time assimilating one very important implication of set-point theory: For many people with eating disorders ("normal weight" bulimia included), eventual acceptance of a culturally disapproved body weight is a crucial aspect of both enhanced self-acceptance and a focus upon the quality of life instead of upon eating or not eating (Garner, Rockert, et al., 1985; S. C. Wooley & O. W. Wooley, 1985).

Prejudice against overweight (O. W. Wooley & S. C. Wooley, 1982), coupled with high body dissatisfaction (see Table 4), was indeed a highly emotional topic in our support group and in the PENED group (R. Wilps, personal communication, October 15, 1987). On the edge of tears, several men recalled being teased (e.g., call "lard ass"), publicly humiliated (e.g., criticized for their appearance by a parent or supervisor), rejected (e.g., by a potential lover), or even physically assaulted as a result of being overweight. These vicious memories invariably gave way to the angry and telling proclamation: "I will never be fat again, even if it kills me."

In retrospect it is clear that the emotional foundation of this high drive for thinness (see Table 4) was not responsive to our demonstrations of the relationship between set-point, starvation, and bingeing, as well as to our interest in the men as men trying to gain control over their lives, and not as men who are successful or unsuccessful dieters. Facilitators of support groups for males with eating disorders should make it a point to explore and work through the relationship between body dissatisfaction and the various forms of intimidation and abuse experienced by participants who are or were overweight (Andersen, 1986; R. Wilps, personal communication, October 15, 1987).

Sexual orientation

During our sixth meeting, a newcomer stated that his drive for thinness and fear of obesity were due in part to the "blatant pressure" on unpartnered gay men to be slender: "Body shape and how you look are three-fourths of the gay game in the bars." He then openly, and not a little aggressively, questioned whether the heterosexual men in the group would "understand." After a moment of uncomfortable silence, another gay man said he understood, and then several of the heterosexual men expressed a supportive willingness to listen further.

We observed no apparent conflict between heterosexual and homosexual men. Given that competitive pressure for slenderness increases the risk of eating disorders (Garfinkel & Garner, 1982), and given the homophobic tendencies of many males in our society (Brannon, 1985), facilitators of support groups for males should anticipate the presence of gay members (Andersen, 1986; Wilps, cited in PENED Newsletter, 1987) and be prepared to deal with the entangled issues of male sexual orientation and masculine sex role(s).

Characterological deficits

We believe well over half of the men attending our group exhibited significant characterological deficits. Had we screened out these individuals, as is done routinely in establishment of therapy groups (Brotman et al., 1985), we simply would not have had enough men for a group.

As noted earlier, under the best of circumstances it is very difficult to move a group of males with eating disorders beyond information al and motivation- al support and towards the more interpersonal goals of emotional and es- teem support plus companionship. The task of identifying and experiencing powerful emotions was rendered almost impossible at times by the unwitting actions of the men with character disorders—expansive monologues about themselves, lack of empathy and insight, overt insensitivity to others, short attention span, and irresponsible attendance despite dramatic public pronouncements of commitment to complete recovery. Eventually, we were able to "manage" these behaviors through a combination of consistent limit-setting within the group and "coaching" of appropriate group behavior during private counseling sessions (by J.G.) outside the group. Yet, in the final analysis, working with men who have both an eating disorder and a character disorder was a frustrating reminder that one important function of a support group is simply motivating people with pronounced developmental deficits to enter and remain in long-term psychotherapy.

PHASE 2: DEVELOPING COHESIVENESS AND FRIENDSHIPS

Reevaluating the Need for Support

During the first few months of the program, when meetings were held every two weeks, there was little cohesion and closeness among the members. Consequently, they requested weekly meetings.

The men readily accepted and much appreciated the change to weekly meetings. Within a week, several had established contacts with each other outside the group. A week later, one man proudly recounted to the group how he had telephoned another member to enlist his help in preventing a binge. Several weeks later the men began going out for coffee after the support group meeting.

Group Interactions

The change to weekly meetings produced more consistent attendance and greater cohesiveness. With a little urging from the facilitators, the men became more active in asserting their needs for support and in developing a weekly agenda which incorporated each participant.

In this context of heightened "group awareness," the men began to admit and explore their needs for one another in regard to companionship, emotional expression, and self-esteem (see Table 5). Interactions now revolved around such topics as (1) the loneliness and hopelessness associated with chronic starvation and/or bulimia; (2) cognitive schema which mitigate assertiveness by confusing like-dislike with agree-disagree; (3) trust in one's body and emotions as a source of evaluative feedback; (4) the paradox of developing greater self-control by relinquishing some control to a therapist; (5) self-defeating but self-perpetuating behavior (e.g., working so hard to ensure short-term harmony in relationships that the final and inevitable result is a state of ubiquitous threat and vulnerability); and (6) the relationship between low self-esteem, interpersonal mistrust, and the protective strategies of moving over or towards people (Horney, 1950). Perhaps most important, group interactions were no longer "about" eating disorders. They were opportunities for the men to *help each other* by sharing ways in which the aforementioned issues really affected them and by discussing effective coping (see Table 5, Motivational and Status).

Clinical Issues

Abstinence versus non-abstinence models of recovery

From the outset the men spoke frequently about being "in control" and "out of control." The subject was usually their eating disorders, but sometimes it was drugs or anger or a general sense of ineffectiveness in life (see Table 4). When group interactions in Phase II evoked strong and potentially uncontrollable feelings, the topic of "control" became even more salient. All but one of the men insisted on explaining "lack of control" in terms of the equivalence between bulimia and chemical dependency. Two of the men with bulimia nervosa had already embraced the disease theory of alcoholism, one as a "recovering" alcoholic, the other as a certified drug counselor whose father is an alcoholic. A third bulimic man said: "All my life I've been addicted to something. Now it's food, because drugs and sex aren't safe anymore."

Although there are no research data with which to evaluate its relative merits (Bemis, 1987), we encouraged the men to *consider* our serious reservations about the application of the addiction-abstinence model of chemical dependency to the treatment and support of people with eating disorders (Bemis, 1985, 1987; Enright et al., 1985; Garner, 1985, 1986; Rubel, 1984). It is important to note here that our intent was not conversion through confrontation. Rather, we hoped to foster personal choice based on awareness of alternatives and their implications. Thus, we made it clear that, despite our misgivings, the addiction-abstinence approach might be helpful for some individuals with bulimia nervosa (Bemis, 1985; Mitchell, Hatsukami, Goff, Pyle, Eckert, & Davis, 1985). We also acknowledged the many parallels between the *experience* of bulimia nervosa and the addiction-abstinence *model* of chemical dependency (Bemis, 1985).

Proponents of the addiction-abstinence model maintain that bulimia nervosa is an incurable lifelong disease from which one is never recovered, but always recovering (Bemis, 1987). We asked the men to consider whether this perspective creates unnecessary pessimism and encourages conversion of eating disorders into "therapy/support group disorders" (Rubel, 1984). We also advocated that the men think of food "cravings" and "obsessions" as reversible "symptoms" of restrictive dieting and suboptimal body weight, not evidence of a disease whose only antidotes are personal willpower and/or submission to unrelenting peer pressure (Garner, 1985, 1986).

The addiction-abstinence model rests upon the principle that treatment and support will be ineffective until clients (1) decide to abstain completely from bingeing and purging, and (2) acknowledge abstinence as the sole and ultimate goal of recovery (Bemis, 1985). In contrast we believe that support groups for men (or women) should increase their unconditional positive self-regard (Rogers, 1951) and their willingness to collaborate with peer or professional helpers in experimenting with change, even if change is gradual (Enright et al., 1985; Garner & Bemis, 1985).

In our experience, insistence on "complete abstinence" as the only acceptable status of a support group member sets the stage for excessive and debilitating shame in response to inevitable relapse (Enright et al., 1985). Similarly, a harsh division between abstinence and illness reinforces the dichotomous and intolerant style of thinking which often forms the foundation of bulimia and concomitant problems with stress and coping (Garner & Bemis, 1985). Dividing foods into "diet" (= controllable = good = safe) vs. "binge" (= uncontrollable = bad = dangerous) gives food a magical quality which legitimizes a transfer of control from the person to various external sources, be they food, support groups, or some "Higher Power" (Rubel, 1984). Our support group program is oriented toward empowering the person to move beyond an obsession with food, beyond participation in the support group, and toward a more meaningful life in light of whatever his spiritual values are (Bemis, 1987; Enright & Tootell, 1986).

PHASE III: GRADUATION AND DESEGREGATION

Eight months after the first support group meeting, one influential participant, who had been feeling much better for some time, decided he was ready to leave the group. This caused the remaining three men to spend a long time examining and discussing the paths of their own recovery. A few weeks later, another man returned to his full-time law studies, leaving only two regulars to sustain the group. Two new men appeared in the succeeding weeks, but did not return.

After consulting with the two remaining men and the staff of NAAS, we decided to experiment with a bulimia support group consisting of males and females who had considerable support group experience. Men and women with bulimia have much in common (Andersen & Mickalide, 1985; Mitchell & Goff, 1985), including the need to improve relationships (not necessarily sexual) with the opposite sex. In addition, men and women whose bulimia is not accompanied by anorexia tend to have low levels of interpersonal distrust (see Table 4; Garner, Garfinkel, & O'Shaughnessy, 1985).

This coed group, facilitated by a male-female team, has been very well received by all participants despite some initial nervousness on everybody's part. In fact, we have come to perceive the transfer of our men from a same-sex group to a coed group as a developmental "graduation" of sorts.

OVERALL EVALUATION

Previous investigations of support groups (e.g., Leichner et al., 1985) had led us to believe that systematic evaluation of an open support group for males with eating disorders would be very difficult. In some respects, our worst fears were realized. Low and inconsistent attendance, coupled with moderate compliance by "regulars" and dropouts, produced only a moderate-sized sample of completed questionnaires. Even with the addition of men from the PENED group, it is clear that our evaluative data need to be interpreted with caution.

We began our support group "experiment" with two general hypotheses. First, men who gave the group a chance would find it beneficial. Second, the beneficial impact would be manifest in the six areas of social support discussed previously: Emotions, self-esteem, provision of information, opportunity for companionship, motivation for recovery, and status as a member of a group devoted to overcoming eating disorders (Silver & Wortman, 1980; Wills, 1985).

The responses from the 15 men who returned the questionnaire are consistent with both hypotheses. A solid majority (80%) reported that their eating disorder had improved during support group participation, and that they felt more hopeful about the future as a result of their group experiences (87%). Table 5 reveals that each of the six components of support had a distinctly positive effect on a clear majority of the participants who attended four or more sessions. These data reinforce Enright et al.'s (1985) contention that the key features of a professionally led support group are (1) the opportunity to be understood and accepted by a group of people "in the same boat"; (2) observing and interacting with a variety of people, some of whom, although not recovered, are coping more successfully with their disorder; (3) learning to help and be helped by other men. In other words, the important components of ongoing support group participation are primarily a function of direct interaction with the men, not advice from the facilitators (Enright et al., 1985; Rubel, 1984). However, the data also suggest that professional leadership may play an important role facilitating emotional expression and in meeting the demand for accurate information about eating disorders (Enright et al., 1985).

CONCLUSIONS

There are five general lessons to be drawn from our experience in facilitating a support group for males with eating disorders. First, a professionally led support group can have a variety of positive effects on men who give it a chance. For some men, the support group will serve as a safe but temporary transition into professional therapy. For others the group will be a valuable adjunct to ongoing therapy by providing the education, the motivation, and the long-term perspective necessary to make maximal use of various forms of professional treatment.

Second, it is likely that men with eating disorders are in greater need of social support than are women with eating disorders. After some hesitation, the men in our group came to acknowledge that the obsession with control inherent in the masculine sex-role, as well as their embarrassment at having a "woman's" disorder, intensified the secrecy and isolation classically associated with eating disorders. The implication of this finding is simple, but very important: Support groups for men with eating disorders need to meet often. In addition, extra effort by the leader and, eventually, the participants will be required to (1) publicize the group to males who currently have an eating disorder; (2) reach out to high-risk populations (e.g., gays, dancers, athletes); and (3) train mental health professionals as facilitators (not group therapists).

Third, men with eating disorders (and men in general) find it difficult to perceive psychophysical problems in terms of mental health and to admit the need for help of any kind. Perhaps most important, men are much less likely than women to recognize the specific utility of social support in coping with emotional distress (McMullen & Gross, 1983). Consequently, facilitators must pay much more attention than we did to working with therapists who are in a position to make referrals and to otherwise "support" the support group. In addition, facilitators should consider rituals or exercises which foster immediate development of group cohesion, thereby setting the stage foremotional support. In this regard, we probably waited too long before having the men themselves assume the major responsibility for sustaining the group.

Fourth, facilitating an open support group for males with eating disorders is likely to be challenging and frustrating, particularly for professionals with experience in group therapy. Ongoing supervision and, yes, "support" are necessary to help facilitators cope with low attendance, personality disorders, frequent repetition of material for new members, and the need to focus on support provided by the membership instead of treatment directed by the therapist (Enright et at., 1985; Rubel, 1984).

Finally, our attempts to evaluate the impact of the support group for men highlight more than just the methodological challenges which await research-minded organizations. As is the case for the treatment of eating disorders, the processes and outcomes of support group participation have been the subject of considerable controversy and very little research (Garner, 1987). Therefore, our theoretical biases (e.g., an addiction-abstinence model is inappropriate) and experiential background (e.g., some men and many women benefit from professionally led support groups with open membership), whatever they may be at the moment, should not preclude a willingness to test our ideas empirically or to experiment with other strategies for providing support.

REFERENCES

Abraham, S. F. & Beumont, P. J. V. (1982). How patients describe bulimia or binge-eating. *Psychological Medicine, 12,* 625–635.

American Psychiatric Association. (1987). *Diagnostic and Statistical Manual of Mental Disorders* (3rd ed. rev.) (DSM-III-R). Washington, D.C.: Author.

Andersen, A. E. (1985). *Practical Comprehensive Treatment of Anorexia Nervosa and Bulimia.* Baltimore: The Johns Hopkins University Press.

Andersen, A. E. (1986). *Anorexia Nervosa and Bulimia in Males.* Unpublished manuscript.

Andersen, A. E., & Mickalide, A. D. (1983). Anorexia nervosa in the male: An underdiagnosed disorder. *Psychosomatics, 12,* 1066–1075.

Andersen, A. E. & Mickalide, A. D. (1985). Anorexia nervosa and bulimia: Their differential diagnoses in 24 males referred to an eating and weight disorders clinic. *Bulletin of the Menninger Clinic, 49,* 227–235.

Bandura, A. (1977). *Social Learning Theory.* Englewood Cliffs, N.J.: Prentice-Hall.

Beck, A. T., Rush, A. J., Shaw, B. F., & Emery, G. (1979). *Cognitive Therapy for Depression.* New York: Guilford.

Belle, D. (1987). Gender differences in the social moderators of stress. In R. C. Barnett, L. Biener, & G. K. Baruch (Eds.), *Gender and Stress* (pp. 257–277). New York: Free Press.

Bemis, K. M. (1985). "Abstinence" and "nonabstinence" models for treatment of bulimia. *International Journal of Eating Disorders, 4,* 407–437.

Bemis, K. M. (1987). *Abstinence and nonabstinence approaches to bulimia nervosa: Must bulimia stop before treatment can begin?* Paper presented at The Sixth National Conference on Eating Disorders of the National Anorexic Aid Society/Center for the Treatment of Eating Disorders, Columbus, Ohio, October.

Brannon, R. (1985). Dimensions of the male sex role in America. In A. G. Sargent (Ed.), *Beyond Sex Roles* (2nd ed., pp. 296–316). St. Paul: West Publishing.

Brotman, A.W., Alonso, A., & Herzog, D. B. (1985). Group therapy for bulimia: Clinical experience and practical recommendations. *Group, 9,* 15–23.

Edmands, M. S. (1986). Overcoming eating disorders: A group experience. *Journal of Psychosocial Nursing, 24,* 19–25.

Enright, A. B., Butterfield, P., & Berkowitz, B. (1985). Self-help and support groups in the management of eating disorders. In D. M. Garner & P. E. Garfinkel (Eds.), *Handbook of Psychotherapy for Anorexia Nervosa and Bulimia* (pp. 491–512). New York: Guilford.

Enright, A. B. & Tootell, C. (1986). The role of support groups in the treatment of eating disorders. *American Mental Health Counselors Association Journal, 8,* 237–245.

Fairburn, C. G. (1985). Cognitive-behavioral treatment for bulimia. In D. M. Garner & P. E. Garfinkel (Eds.), *Handbook of Psychotherapy for Anorexia Nervosa and Bulimia* (pp. 160–192). New York: The Guilford Press.

Franko, D. L. (1987). Anorexia nervosa and bulimia: A self-help group. *Small Group Behavior. 18,* 398–407.

Garfinkel, P. E. & Garner, D. M. (1982). *Anorexia Nervosa: A Multi-dimensional Perspective.* New York: Brunner/Mazel.

Garner, D. M. (1985). Iatrogenesis in anorexia nervosa and bulimia nervosa. *International Journal of Eating Disorders, 4,* 701–726.

Garner, D. M. (1986). Problems with the Overeaters Anonymous model in the treatment of bulimia. *National Anorexic Aid Society Newsletter, 9* (1), 1–2.

Garner, D. M. (1987). *Recent advances in the treatment of eating disorders.* Paper presented at The Sixth National Conference on Eating Disorders of the National Anorexic Aid Society/Center for the Treatment of Eating Disorders, Columbus, Ohio, October.

Garner, D. M. & Bemis, K. M.(1985). Cognitive therapy for anorexia nervosa. In D. M. Garner & P. E. Garfinkel (Eds.), *Handbook of Psychotherapy for Anorexia Nervosa and Bulimia* (pp. 107–146). New York: Guilford.

Garner, D. M., Garfinkel, P. E., & O'Shaughnessy, M. (1985). The validity of the distinction between bulimia with and without anorexia nervosa. *American Journal of Psychiatry, 142,* 581–587.

Garner, D. M., Olmsted, M. P., & Polivy, J. (1983). The Eating Disorders Inventory: A measure of cognitive–behavioral dimensions of anorexia nervosa and bulimia,

In P. L. Darby et al. (Eds.), *Anorexia Nervosa: Recent Developments in Research* (pp. 173–184). New York: A. R. Liss.

Garner, D.M., Rockert, W., Olmsted, M. P., Johnson C., & Coscina, D. V. (1985). Psychoeducational principles in the treatment of bulimia and anorexia nervosa. In D. M. Garner & P. E. Garfinkel (Eds.), *Handbook of Psychotherapy for Anorexia Nervosa and Bulimia* (pp. 513–572). New York: Guilford.

Gartner, A. & Riessman, F. (Eds.). (1984). *The Self-help Revolution.* New York: Human Sciences Press.

Gartner, A. J. & Riessman, F. (1982). Self-help and mental health. *Hospital & Community Psychiatry, 33,* 631–635.

Goodwin, R. A. & Mickalide, A. D. (1985). Parent-to-parent support in anorexia nervosa and bulimia. *Children's Health Care, 14,* 32–37.

Gottlieb, B. H. (1985). Social support and community mental health. In S. Cohen & S. L. Syme (Eds.), *Social Support and Health* (pp. 303–326). New York: Academic Press.

Gray, J. & Ford, K. (1985). The incidence of bulimia in a college sample. *International Journal of Eating Disorders, 4,* 201–210.

Hall, A. (1985). Group psychotherapy for anorexia nervosa. In D. M. Garner & P. E. Garfinkel (Eds.), *Handbook of Psychotherapy for Anorexia Nervosa and Bulimia* (pp. 213–239). New York: Guilford.

Hammen, C. L. & Peters. S. (1978). Interpersonal consequences of depression: Reponses to men and women enacting a depressed role. *Journal of Abnormal Psychology, 87,* 322–332.

Hays, W. L. (1973). *Statistics for the Social Sciences* (2nd ed.). New York: Holt, Rinehart and Winston.

Horney, K. (1950). *Neurosis and Human Growth.* New York: Norton.

Humphrey, L. L. (1986). Family dynamics in bulimia. In S. C. Feinstein (Ed.), *Adolescent Psychiatry: Developmental and Clinical Studies* (vol. 13, pp. 315–332). Chicago: University of Chicago Press.

Huon, G.F. (1985). An initial validation of a self-help program for bulimia. *International Journal of Eating Disorders, 4,* 573–588.

Iannicello, A. & Tootell, C. (1985). *Support Group Packet of the National Anorexic Aid Society.* Columbus, Ohio: National Anorexic Aid Society.

Johnson, C. (1985). Initial consultation for patients with bulimia and anorexia nervosa. In D. M. Garner & P. E. Garfinkel (Eds.), *Handbook of Psychotherapy for Anorexia Nervosa and Bulimia* (pp. 19–51). New York: Guilford.

Johnson C. & Berndt, D. J. (1983). Preliminary investigation of bulimia and life adjustment. *American Journal of Psychiatry, 140,* 744–777.

Katz, A. H. (1981). Self-help and mutual aid: An emerging social movement. *Annual Review of Sociology, 7,* 129–155.

Katz, S. (1985). Anorexia and bulimia support group helping victims' families. *Canadian Medical Association Journal, 132,* 1077–1079.

Kinoy, B. P. (1985). Self-help groups in the management of anorexia nervosa and bulimia: A theoretical base. *Transactional Analysis Journal, 15,* 73–78.

Knight, B., Wollert, R. W., Levy, L. H., Frame, C. L., & Padgett, V. P. (1980). Self-help groups: The members' perspectives. *American Journal of Community Psychology, 8,* 53–65.

Leichner, P. P., Harper, D. W., & Johnson, D. M. (1985). Adjunctive group support for spouses of women with anorexia nervosa and/or bulimia. *International Journal of Eating Disorders, 4,* 227–235.

Levine, M. P. (1986). Eating disorders: Focus on males. *National Anorexia Aid Society Newsletters, 9* (4), 1–4.

Levine, M.P. (1987). *Student Eating Disorders: Anorexia Nervosa and Bulimia.* Washington, D.C.: National Education Association.

Levy, L. (1976). Self-help groups: Types and psychological processes. *Journal of Applied Behavioral Science, 12,* 310–322.

Levy, L. (1982). Mutual support groups in Great Britain. *Social Science in Medicine, 16,* 1265–1275.

MacKenzie, K. R., Liversley, W. J., Coleman, M., Harper, H., & Park, J. (1986). Short-term group psychotherapy for bulimia nervosa. *Psychiatric Annals, 16,* 699–707.

McMullen, P.A. & Gross, A. E. (1983). Sex differences, sex roles, and health-related help-seeking. In B. M. Depaulo, A. Nadler, & J. D. Fisher (Eds.), *New Directions in Helping: Volume 2—Help-Seeking* (pp. 233–263). New York: Academic Press.

Meehan, V., Wilkes, N. J., & Howard, H. L. (1984). *ANAD: Applying New Attitudes and Directions.* Highland Park, Illinois: National Association of Anorexia Nervosa and Associated Disorders, Inc. – ANAD.

Meichenbaum, D. H. (1972). Examination of model characteristics in reducing avoidance behavior. *Journal Behavior Therapy and Experimental Psychiatry, 3,* 225–227.

Mitchell, J. E. & Goff, G. (1985). Bulimia in male patients. *Psychosomatics, 25,* 909–913.

Mitchell, J. E., Hatsukami, D., Eckert, E. D., & Pyle, R. L. (1985). Characteristics of 275 patients with bulimia. *American Journal of Psychiatry, 142,* 482–485.

Mitchell, J. E., Hatsukami, D., Goff, G., Pyle, R. L., Eckert, E. D., & Davis, L. E. (1985). Intensive outpatient group treatment for bulimia. In D. M. Garner & P. E. Garfinkel (Eds.), *Handbook of Psychotherapy for Anorexia Nervosa and Bulimia* (pp. 240–253). New York: Guilford.

Norman, D. K. & Herzog, D. B. (1984). Persistent social maladjustment in bulimia: A 1-year follow-up. *American Journal of Psychiatry, 141,* 444–446.

Norman, D. K. & Herzog, D. B. (1986). A 3-year outcome study of normal-weight bulimia: Assessment of psychosocial functioning and eating attitudes. *Psychiatry Research, 19,* 199–205.

Pearson, R. E. (1983). Support groups: A conceptualization. *The Personnel and Guidance Journal, 61,* 361–364.

Pittsburgh Educational Network for Eating Disorders (PENED), (1987). Males and eating disorders. *PENED Newsletter, 3* (5), 4–5.

Pope, H. G., Jr. & Hudson, J. I. (1984). *New Hope for Binge-eaters: Advances in the*

Understanding and Treatment of Bulimia. New York: Harper & Row.

Pyle, R. L., Halvorson, P. A., Neuman, P. A., & Mitchell, J. E. (1986). The increasing prevalence of bulimia in freshman college students. *International Journal of Eating Disorders, 5,* 631–647.

Ray, O. (1983). *Drugs, Society, and Human Behavior* (3rd ed.). St. Louis: Mosby.

Roback, H. B. (1984a). Introduction: The emergence of disease-management groups. In H. B. Roback (Ed.), *Helping Patients and Their Families Cope With Medical Problems* (pp. 1–33). San Francisco: Jossey- Bass.

Roback, H. B. (1984b). Conclusion: Critical issues in group approaches to disease management. In H. B. Roback (Ed.), *Helping Patients and Their Families Cope with Medical Problems* (pp. 527–543). San Francisco: Jossey-Bass.

Rodkin, L. I., Hunt, E. J., & Cowan, S. D. (1982). A mens's support group for significant others of rape victims. *Journal of Marital and Family, 8,* 91–97.

Rodolfa, E. R. & Hungerford, L. (1982). Self-help groups: A referral resource for professional therapists. *Professional Psychology, 13,* 345–353.

Rogers, C. R. (1951). *Client-centered Therapy.* Boston: Houghton Mifflin.

Root, M. P. P., Fallon, P., & Friedrich, W. N. (1986). *Bulimia: A Systems Approach to Treatment.* New York: Norton.

Rosenhan, D. L. & Seligman, M. E. P. (1984). *Abnormal Psychology.* New York: W. W. Norton.

Rubel, J. A. (1984). The function of self-help groups in recovery from anorexia nervosa and bulimia. *Psychiatric Clinics of North America, 7,* 381–394.

Scott, D. W. (1986). Anorexia nervosa in the male: A review of clinical, epidemiological and biological findings. *International Journal of Eating Disorders, 5,* 799–819.

Silver, R. L., & Wortman, C. B. (1980). Coping with undesirable life events. In J. Garber & M. E. P. Seligman (Eds.), *Human Helplessness: Theory and Applications* (pp. 279–340). New York: Academic Press.

Thompson, M. G. & Schwartz, D. M. (1982). Life adjustment of women with anorexia nervosa and anorexic-like behavior. *International Journal of Eating Disorders, 1,* 47–60.

Wills, T. A. (1985). Supportive functions of interpersonal relationships. In S. Cohen & S. L. Syme (Eds.), *Social Support and Health* (pp. 61–82). New York: Academic Press.

Wooley, O. W. & Wooley, S. C. (1982). The Beverly Hills Eating Disorder: The mass marketing of anorexia nervosa (Editorial). *International Journal of Eating Disorders, 1,* 57–69.

Wooley, S. C. & Wooley, O. W. (1985). Intensive outpatient and residential treatment for bulimia. In D. M. Garner & P. E. Garfinkel (Eds.), *Handbook of Psychotherapy for Anorexia Nervosa and Bulimia* (pp. 391–430). New York: Guilford.

Yalom, I. D. (1975). *The Theory and Practice of Group Psychotherapy* (2nd ed.). New York: Basic Books.

SECTION IV

Integration

12

A *Proposed Mechanism Underlying Eating Disorders and Other Disorders of Motivated Behavior*

Arnold E. Andersen

In the history of science, description of a phenomenon generally precedes elucidation of the underlying mechanism. Anorexia nervosa (AN) as a clinical phenomenon has been well described for at least three centuries (Morton, 1694). Bulimia nervosa (BN), although more recent in its formal recognition as a separate psychiatric syndrome, has also been thoroughly documented (Garfinkel, Moldofsky, & Garner, 1980; Russell, 1979). There is general agreement concerning the clinical description of these syndromes in regard to their diagnostic criteria, natural history, and their medical and social consequences.

Treatment approaches for the eating disorders (EDs), however, have varied considerably, reflecting the lack of agreement concerning the etiology and mechanism of these clinically well described syndromes. When a disorder is more fundamentally understood in regard to underlying mechanism, treat-

---

The author is very grateful for comments and suggestions by Drs. Joseph Brady, Joseph Coyle, Paul McHugh, and Robert Robinson in preparation of this manuscript.

ments flow rationally from this knowledge of the essential nature and mechanism of the disorder, even if treatments are not always immediately successful.

In past and present times during which convincing evidence for a specific mechanism and etiology of AN and BN has been lacking, a clinician's choice of treatment methods for those syndromes has generally been guided by what he or she personally believed, explicitly or implicitly, to be the probable origin and mechanism involved. For example, when AN was theorized in the early part of this century to be caused by an abnormality in pituitary functioning, proposed treatments logically involved medical methods. Only after some time did AN come to be distinguished from Sheehan's syndrome of postpartum pituitary necrosis.

The hypothesized link of AN to other primary underlying medical disorders has not been quickly put aside. The medical textbook edited by the Johns Hopkins Medical School faculty only recently relocated the discussion of AN from the section on endocrinology to the section on psychiatry. Other more recent attempts have been made to understand AN as a condition originating from abnormal functioning of the brain, with logical, albeit unproved, implications for treatment. Frequent references have been made to putative abnormalities of hypothalamic functioning in the recently published literature concerning AN, sometimes modified by the qualification that these abnormalities may be secondary or functional in nature. More subtle and complex variations on this theme of abnormal brain functioning as the etiology of AN have included suggestions that dysregulation of the corticosteroid pathways or disorders of integrative neurophysiological functioning may be involved (Gold et al., 1986; Leibowitz, 1983).

A completely different approach, the psychodynamic approach to understanding the essential nature and mechanism of AN, also began during the first decades of the 20th century. This approach proposed the view that AN sprang from something very different than abnormal brain functioning, suggesting instead its origin to be a psychologically understandable defense against unacceptable sexual thoughts and conflicts (Deutsch, 1981; Szyrynski, 1973). Psychoanalytic formulations led to sustained and energetic psychotherapeutic efforts, but produced relatively little documented improvement in the clinical condition of patients with AN.

In the past two decades, multiple additional psychodynamic hypotheses concerning the etiology of AN have been proposed, including the view that AN represents an illness of the entire family system, with the ill person being not the real patient but instead only the overt symptomatic expression of an underlying family disorder (Root, Fallon, & Friedrich, 1986; Rosman et al,

1977). Other recent psychodynamic efforts at describing AN have evolved, leading to enthusiastic but equally unproven concepts of etiology, such as the theories of object relations (Sours, 1980), self-psychology (Goodsitt, 1985), and feminist psychoanalytic concepts (Orbach, 1985).

These multiple, unreconcilable hypotheses concerning the origin of AN have led to no convincing description of a specific central mechanism underlying the eating disorders that would explain all the available data. Such a state of knowledge—good clinical description, multiple conflicting hypotheses about etiology, and no single convincing mechanistic explanation that encompasses all the available date—is characteristic of a field that is in a relatively primitive stage of scientific understanding.

The following hypothesis attempts to describe a mechanism underlying the eating disorders which will encompass all the empirical data currently available concerning AN and BN. If correct, it may lead to more rational concepts of treatment. The hypothesis may be stated as follows:

> Anorexia nervosa and bulimia nervosa are examples of behavioral disorders, specifically disorders of motivated behavior, all of which have as their uniting feature a common, underlying mechanism of operant (instrumental) behavioral conditioning which underlies the stepwise progression of these illnesses through a characteristic and predictable set of stages. This mechanism is not further reducible to a more basic abnormality of biochemistry or neural structure, and is not understandable, on the other hand, by reference to more complex systems of integration, such as the family unit or society in general. All behavioral disorders may be best understood by reference to a specific, unifying, non-reducible, behavioral mechanism described by Skinner (1953).

More detailed discussion of operant conditioning in the context of the history and development of learning theory is provided by Bachrach (1975).

This chapter attempts to specify the defining features shared by all disorders of motivated behavior; it describes the implications for treatment of the eating disorders growing out of the hypothesis of a common operant mechanism; it attempts to refute challenges to this proposed mechanism; finally, it applies the concept of an underlying operant conditioning mechanism to other abnormalities of motivated behaviors (both innate and acquired), including sexual disorders and alcohol and drug abuse. It suggests as well a potential application of the hypothesis to acquired disorders of other, non-motivated behaviors, such as compulsive gambling and overspending.

Science evolves by both continuous and discontinuous means. Kuhn (1962) has outlined the process of new paradigm formation. Existing paradigms guide "normal science" in a continuous fashion until phenomena are found which cannot be understood by the existing paradigm. Then, in a discontinuous manner, the reigning paradigm falls and, after a period of chaos, a new organizing and integrating hypothesis emerges. In complementary fashion, Popper (1959) has suggested the method by which scientific hypotheses may be tested, namely by the process of falsifiability, rather than by absolute confirmation. No hypothesis can be proven to be absolutely true; its strength comes from the absence of falsifiability. The methods of both Kuhn and of Popper will be used in this discussion.

COMMON DEFINING FEATURES OF DISORDERS OF MOTIVATED BEHAVIORS

1. *A motivated behavioral disorder (MBD) may be defined as a psychiatric syndrome in which the primary and essential abnormality is an abnormality of motivated behavior (in contrast to syndromes in which the primary abnormality is in mood, such as manic-depressive illness, or thought, as in schizophrenia). It develops by stages, in predisposed individuals, from a preceding, normal, and voluntary behavior. The behavioral abnormality is not causally understandable by reference to a preceding primary change in the neurophysiology, neurochemistry, or social organization of the individual.*

AN and BN both begin by voluntary changes in the eating behavior of the individual—specifically, by food restriction. There may be a variety of antecedent conditions that increase the probability that dieting behavior will take place in a given individual, including the sociocultural norms of our society regarding thinness, beliefs within the person's family, critical attitudes toward self, distressing events during development, and painful alterations in mood. These antecedents, however, do not lead to the behavior of dieting in a causally stereotyped manner. Voluntary dieting behavior is the primary alteration that initiates the development of either AN or BN, and voluntary behavior (emitted behavior) initiates the development of other MBDs.

In contrast, for example, seizure behavior is also an abnormal behavior, but clearly springs from a preceding, nonvoluntary abnormality of electrical activity in the brain, which stereotypically leads to the observed abnormal movements. Huntington's Disease, as well, is clinically manifested by abnormalities of behavior, but these abnormal behaviors result from preceding causal alterations in brain chemistry and structure which are secondary to an inherited dominant genetic disorder.

2. *A motivated behavioral disorder may be additionally defined as a disorder in which the primary underlying mechanism responsible for the stepwise development of the disorder is operant (instrumental, voluntary) conditioning, which modulates the eating behavior thorough operantly understandable alteration of a variety of antecedent states.* To be a primary behavioral disorder, in sum, a disorder must be primarily governed in its stepwise development by a mechanism of operant conditioning.

There is a strong tendency in medical research to employ what essentially is a process of reductionism, because reducing disease phenomena to primary alterations in biochemistry and neurophysiology has proven to be very successful in elucidating the etiology and mechanism of many medical disorders, such as Huntington's Disease or seizure disorder. The reason for the misapplication of reductionistic methods to areas in which they do not validly apply may be illustrated by the humorous anecdote of the drunkard who was asked why he was looking for his car keys under the street light when, in fact, he had lost them in the dark further down the street. His answer was: "Because the light is better here."

Analytic methods of biochemistry and electrophysiology are extraordinarily powerful and useful, but there is a tendency in medical research to overuse or misuse them by attempting to reduce all human disorder into more fundamental biochemical and/or electrophysiological types of knowledge. The pendulum appears to have swung in some sectors of psychiatry from decades of nonempirical (and usually unprovable) dogmatic psychodynamic theorizing to a time of equally dogmatic insistence that all psychiatric disorders are understandable as abnormalities of brain functioning.

3. *Normal motivated behavior develops into a motivated behavioral disorder when it is no longer under personal control and/or has significant adverse psychological, social, or physical consequence.* Deciding to skip a meal because a deadline must be met at work or choosing to eat an extra serving of food at Thanksgiving dinner do not, of course, by themselves constitute eating disorders or abnormal behaviors. In contrast, repeated refusal of adequate amounts of food, leading directly to a state of starvation or indirectly to binge eating, not understandable as a consequence of reasonable, personal, or vocational goals, imprisonment, or involuntary deprivation, or resulting from a primary medical or psychiatric illness, defines the behavior to be psychiatrically abnormal. When dieting is taken to the point where menses cease, when other weight-related indices of abnormal body functioning are present, when the food restricting individual always feels cold, when there is relentless mental preoccupation with thoughts of food, then it is reasonable to classify the behavior as a behavioral disorder.

Parenthetically, the term "behavioral disorder" does not constitute a moral or legal indictment of the individual, but is a practical clinical judgment, derived in a manner that is similar to the way a personality disorder is defined. A diagnostic term (diagnosis means, literally, "through knowing") has three fundamental purposes: to provide a shorthand word for a complex phenomenon; to give prognostic information; and to lead to treatment. Most alterations in behavior occur along a line of continuous variation, with no clear point being reached to announce when abnormality occurs and normality ceases. It is on the basis of an admittedly changing and somewhat arbitrary, but nonetheless useful, consensus process that a point is defined when these behaviors may be said to constitute a disorder.

At their extremes, there are few disagreements when a behavior or personality trait is abnormal. There is some intrinsic imprecision, however, regarding just when a normal behavior or a trait of personality become a disorder. To the experienced clinician, this problem is less significant than to the theoretician or to the student of the history of science, if one keeps in mind the functional requirement that to be a behavioral disorder the behavior in question must no longer be under personal control and/or must cause significant changes in psychological, social, or physical functioning. Each of these defining characteristics can be empirically studied and described.

In some ways, the process whereby a behavior becomes a disorder may be seen as being analogous to the process of an individual getting into a canoe some distance above Niagara Falls and then proceeding downstream. Initially, the behavior of the individual in the canoe is voluntary, but after a time of variable duration, it clearly becomes no longer voluntary. This analogy suggests, incidentally, that additional, later, secondary, supplemental mechanisms may be associated with perpetuating the behavior in question and should be examined separately from the primary operant causal mechanism.

4. *Behavioral disorders usually grow out of behaviors which are either universal in the population, such as the innate (motivated) behavior of eating, or acquired behaviors related closely to the motivated behaviors, such as alcohol consumption, or to non-innate but frequently acquired behaviors such as gambling.* The fact that serious behavioral disorders may evolve from normal, innate, adaptive behaviors may account for their persistence once established, and their resistance to treatment. The persistence of behaviors related to the maintenance of body weight, to reproduction, or to defense would, not surprisingly, be well-defended behaviors because they have great survival value for the organism and its entire species under normal circumstances.

These motivated behaviors integrate internal, regulatory responses (endo crine, biochemical, and neurological) with sensory inputs from and motor responses to events in the external world, all related to meeting the specific deprivation state of the organism. (Parenthetically, some behaviorists are unhappy with the terms "need" or "deprivation state" or any terms that imply knowledge not directly observable or countable. There is linguistic disagreement between these behaviorists and phenomenologically oriented clinicians. The strict behaviorists endorse only terms that can be scientifically observed, such as "verbal behavior," while the latter freely use terms reflecting the patient's reported perception of inner, nonobservable but phenomenologically understandable states. This philological and philosophical disagreement has long roots and will not be soon solved).

The amount of attention and effort the organism devotes to a particular motivated behavior at a given time is roughly proportional to the amount of "deprivation" or "need" for that particular behavior. Potentially competing behaviors are arranged in a kind of hierarchy, with pressing needs coming first. Up to a certain point, the more food-deprived an organism is, the hungrier it is, and the more attention and effort are given to searching for, acquiring, and then consuming, food. But if the organism is attacked while feeding, it will usually stop its feeding behavior (whether in the searching or consuming phase) and defend itself instead, returning to feeding behavior once the competing behavior is no longer required.

There are additional, frequently occurring behaviors, not related to biological survival, which may be behaviorally reenforced on a similar operant basis—for example, gambling behavior and impulsive spending. These behaviors, when out of control, also can be stated to constitute clinically significant behavioral disorders if they meet the criteria for behavioral disorders. They may be understood as developing into clinically significant disorders through the effects of an operant mechanism on antecedent conditions, increasing the subsequent frequency of the emitted problem behavior in question.

APPLICATION OF OPERANT HYPOTHESIS TO ANOREXIA NERVOSA AND BULIMIA NERVOSA

1. *Eating disorders usually begin (approximately 95% of the time) by voluntary attempts at weight reduction through dieting behavior.* As required by the definition for all abnormalities of motivated behavior, AN and BN usually begin by voluntary restriction of food intake such that caloric energy ingested is less than total energy expended, resulting in net weight loss.

2. *In approximately 5% or less of cases, initial weight loss may be due to inadvertent or iatrogenic causes, but subsequent weight loss becomes voluntary.* This fact does not falsify the hypothesis because, after some initial decrease in weight from these other causes, the individual who begins involuntarily then goes on to develop an eating disorder by voluntarily continuing the food restriction on his or her own. After the initial weight loss, the process, thereafter, continues much as when voluntary dieting behavior is the cause of the initial weight loss. (See Chapter 9 on treatment for further discussion of inadvertent or iatrogenic origins.)

3. *The most common antecedent conditions whose operant alteration by dieting behavior lead to an increase in dieting behavior are the following: perceiving oneself to be out of control or ineffective in dealing with some aspect of life; feeling depressed or demoralized; fearing the social, psychological, and physical changes that accompany personal development; wishing to stabilize a family structure that is changing in an undesired way; not receiving adequate attention from the family; belonging to a social, recreational, or vocational group that rewards weight loss.* Each of these antecedent conditions has been described, either anecdotally or empirically.

4. *Anorexia nervosa which begins by normal voluntary dieting behavior changes into a behavioral disorder by a process of behavioral shaping, passing through a set of predictable, step-wise stages.*

Stage 1 of AN is characterized by voluntary dieting to decrease body weight or improve body shape and is sometimes combined with exercise. At this stage there is no behavioral disorder necessarily present, and it is not possible to predict confidently which specific, dieting individuals will go on to develop clinical AN, although, as a class, certain groups of individuals will have a higher probability of developing AN.

Stage 2 is present when the dieting behavior is no longer under personal control and/or has produced significant abnormality in social, psychological, or physical functioning. At this stage, there is not only the pursuit of thinness of Stage 1, but also the development of a morbid fear of fatness. Now the dieting behavior has become linked, in an operantly understandable manner, to stabilizing or improving a variety of antecedent states, as noted above, including fears associated with development, painfully critical views of self, abnormal moods, and unstable or undesired family situations. Clinical AN is now present and meets DSM-III-R criteria for AN, or for an atypical eating disorder, if some but not all features for full DSM-III-R AN are present.

Stage 3A occurs when dieting behavior is autonomous and the individual cannot voluntarily interrupt it for any significant period of times. A person with AN in Stage 3A is no longer able to change his eating behavior even when there is resolution or improvement of the antecedent condition which was initially stabilized or improved by the operant consequences of the dieting behavior. The abnormal behavior now has a life of its own.

Other mechanisms may now additionally stabilize the abnormal eating behavior, and it may become disassociated from the primary stimulus condition: for example, if the family situation improves sufficiently so that the starved state of the patient no longer is necessary to regulate its structure and functioning (perhaps to keep mom and dad from divorcing); or if a crisis in personal development has been resolved, but the individual is unable to relinquish self-starvation, then Stage 3A is present. The additional (secondary) mechanisms that may contribute to perpetuating Stage 3A include the development of medical symptoms such that attempts at normal eating now lead to other uncomfortable, frightening physical symptoms, including refeeding edema and abdominal pain.

Stage 3B is present when the starved anorectic's physical state and whole anorectic way of life are necessary to the individual's sense of identity. The mechanism here, we would suggest, is an existential one, with some operant aspects involved as well. The individual fears the state of nothingness associated with giving up the illness more than the consequences of continued illness. The individual no longer *has* AN, but *is* AN (Woodall & Andersen, submitted for publication). The mechanisms underlying the equating of personal identity with clinical AN appear to involve, from one viewpoint, simply another example of operant conditioning.

But even operant instrumental behavioral conditioning does not fully explain the complex process of identity formation. In parallel with the previously stated principle, that operant mechanisms may not be adequately explained by the analysis of the operant mechanism into more basic biochemical or neurophysiological components, so existential mechanisms could be said to be not completely understandable by resolution into a more basic operant behavioral mechanism. Identity formation and existential development may be understandable only as unique levels of human organization, even though there are multiple factors subserving the process. The three stages of AN are summarized in Table 1.

5. *Bulimia nervosa represents the inadvertent outcome of a failed attempt to become thinner by weight loss, which in predisposed individuals leads to BN instead of AN. It too progresses by stages.* Dieting behavior leads, in a subgroup of predisposed individuals, to the forceful expression of hunger by bouts of binge eating against one's will, characteristic of BN, instead of developing into the continued self-starvation that characterizes classical AN. Clinical and research data suggest that individuals in whom dieting leads to

TABLE 1

Stages of Development of Anorexia Nervosa

STAGE 1: A NORMAL BEHAVIOR
Normal, voluntary dieting behavior.

STAGE 2: A DIAGNOSABLE DISORDER
Dieting not under personal control and/or dieting has serious medical, social, psychological consequences. Characterized by morbid fear of fatness. DSM-III-R criteria met.

STAGE 3A: AUTONOMOUS BEHAVIOR.
The disorder does not resolve even if conditions stimulating its origin have resolved. Behavior not susceptible to any degree of personal control. Secondary mechanisms frequently present.

STAGE 3B: ILLNESS BECOMES AN IDENTITY
The patient identifies with being the illness, not only having the illness (I *am* anorectic). Prospect of loss of illness leads to existential fears of nothingness.

binge behavior at various weights rather than to self-starvation alone are individuals who are characterized by one or more of the following compared to patients with restricting AN: more impulsivity; more self-dramatization; more likely to have borderline personality features or other Cluster B personality disorders by DSM-III-R (Piran et al., 1988). They usually have had, on the average, a higher body weight preceding dieting, compared to those who develop AN, restricting subtype. They also appear to be more likely to have a preexisting mood disorder, especially the recently described bipolar II condition (Simpson, DePaulo, & Andersen, 1988). They seem more sensitive to and less tolerant of dysphoric mood states, and are more likely to perceive hunger as being intolerable.

In analogous fashion to AN, the following stages characterize the evolution of BN:

Stage 1A is characterized by apparently normal dieting behavior which occurs in approximately 75% of young, middle class women sometime during their teenage years or early 20s (Nylander, 1971). Stage 1A of BN is identical to Stage 1 of AN.

Stage 1B of BN begins when binge behavior occurs as a result of the dieting behavior (with or without increased exercise) of Stage 1A. The onset of binge eating begins initially in BN because of the normal effect of increased hunger on feeding behavior in the presence of abundant food. The initial binge behavior, therefore, may be seen as an *involuntary, physiologically understandable consequence* of voluntary dieting. Self-induced vomiting and other means of avoiding weight gain resulting from the binge may, in contrast, be understood as being (at least initially) *voluntary, psychologically understandable behaviors* resulting from fear of weight gain that could result from the binge eating.

Some initial binge eating after food deprivation is, by itself, a normal response to food of persons who have been involuntarily starved. In these non-dieting involuntarily starved individuals, compensatory binge eating does not lead to the cyclic binge-purge behavior of BN because of the absence of the characteristic central psychological motif of a morbid fear of fatness. In the BN person, however, the compensatory binge provokes great fear and leads to a vicious circle of bingeing, purging or fasting, increased hunger, and more bingeing.

Stage 2 of BN is present when the binge behavior generalizes through operant conditioning to become a means of improving a variety of painful, antecedent mood states, the most common being depression; it no longer serves to alleviate hunger alone. Other dysphoric states improved by binge-eating include anger, anxiety, and feeling bored or "stuck." Stage 2 of BN represents a significant clinical progression from Stage 1B because the binge behavior now operantly alters a greatly expanded range of antecedent mood states in contrast to Stage 1B where bingeing improves only a physiologically derived perception, hunger. The behavior can now be defined to be part of a clinical disorder. It is under only partial personal control. The patient can almost always identify the emotional triggers which lead to the binge behavior characteristic of Stage 2, even if hunger continues to sometimes initiate the eating.

In Stage 2, hunger becomes much less important as an antecedent state modified operantly by binge behavior. In fact, many individuals say they no longer know what hunger feels like because of their chaotic eating style. For others, however, hunger, especially hunger occurring from early daytime calorie restriction (skipping breakfast and lunch), may still play a role in producing binges. Exquisite sensitivity to and decreased tolerance of any kind of uncomfortable mood state develop. The binge appears to alter as a consequence of this heightened dysphoria in a manner somewhat similar to the way a "drug fix" alters dysphoria, although an exact analogy would be misleading. There are significant social, physical, and psychological consequences for the bulimic behavior in this stage.

Stage 3A represents the stage of autonomous binge behavior (similar to autonomous food restriction in 3A of AN) in which the individual feels incapable of interrupting the binge behavior even for logical reasons such as avoiding medical complications, avoiding social unpleasantness, or sparing

TABLE 2

Stages of Development of Bulimia Nervosa

STAGE 1A:	NORMAL DIETING BEHAVIOR takes place. Similar to AN, Stage 1.
STAGE 1B:	Dieting behavior and weight loss lead to INVOLUNTARY BINGE BEHAVIOR, based on response to hunger.
STAGE 2:	A DIAGNOSABLE DISORDER. The trigger for binge behavior generalizes from hunger to a variety of painful mood states. Marked fear of fatness is present. Meets DSM-III-R criteria. May have serious medical, social, psychological consequences.
STAGE 3A:	AUTONOMOUS BEHAVIOR. Binges autonomous, frequent, large. SECONDARY MECHANISMS often present.
STAGE 3B:	ILLNESS BECOMES AN IDENTITY. The thought of living without bulimic behavior provokes great fear, leading to an existential lack of identity and fear of inability to cope.

himself psychological distress after the binge. Here, as in Stage 3A of AN, there may be additional biological mechanisms which help to perpetuate the illness. The frequency of binge behavior in Stage 3A may be truly astounding—for example, 20-30 binges per day. Binges may be fewer in number but last for hours. The individual usually will continue to respond to the binge behavior with some compensatory behavioral means of avoiding weight gain, such as by inducing vomiting, by taking laxatives and diuretics, by exercising strenuously, or by fasting. At times, however, the patient may be thoroughly demoralized, not attempt to compensate for binge-eating, and become obese.

Stage 3B is defined as being present when there is such personal identification between the individual's sense of self and the bulimic behavior that the individual cannot imagine an existence in which binge behavior is not present. Here the mechanism of stabilization (as in Stage 3B of AN) is not well understood presently, but may be conceptualized as involving an "existential" level of organization not reducible to more basic biological or social behavioral mechanisms. The consolidated stage of identity formation based on bulimic symptoms usually results from long experience with the illness, especially when the BN occurs throughout the critical stages of adolescent and preadolescent social and psychological development. Characteristic of Stage 3B is that the thought of abandoning the binge behavior leads to feelings of extreme loss, fear of nothingness, and a sense of anomie. Table 2 summarizes the stages of natural progression of bulimia nervosa.

6. *Later, supplemental mechanisms that perpetuate the eating disorders during Stages 2 and 3A include:*

Biochemical/physiological mechanisms. Once a person has been starved for an extended period of time, eating normal amounts and kinds of food may produce bloating, nausea, and other physical discomforts. Specific supplemental secondary mechanisms causing medical symptoms during the starvation and/or the refeeding phases include slowed gastric emptying, delayed bowel transit time, and a postulated decrease in inducible bowel enzymes responsible for metabolism of fats and milk products. The process of self-starvation and refeeding may each produce peripheral edema. In BN, discontinuation of laxative abuse, in addition, may result in substantial peripheral edema formation until intravascular and extravascular fluid spaces equilibrate and the state of hydration becomes normal.

In one sense, all these secondary medical mechanisms exert their effects on inhibiting normal feeding behavior by an operant behavioral feedback mechanism that promotes the return to self-starvation which then alleviates these medical symptoms. The difference here between this inhibition of eating and self-starvation for reasons of voluntary dieting is that the physiological changes that produce discomfort from normal eating are involuntary responses of the body.

Social mechanisms. In ways less well understood than the operant behavioral mechanism that underlies the initial development of clinical AN or BN, illness behavior may lead secondarily to the development of a social role dependent on the continuation of the illness behavior. This "sick role" leads to alterations in social functioning which would not be acceptable to society if the individual were not ill. The extra personal attention, the decreased amount of responsibility demanded by society, and the special privileges received by a person perceived by society to be ill all depend on maintaining the illness role which may be hard to give up for the seemingly abstract and potentially fearful goal of becoming well.

Existential mechanisms. As noted previously, the individual may not only be granted social privileges based on the illness behavior, but also becomes so identified with the illness that his personal sense of identity requires the continued presence of symptoms. He cannot imagine continuing life without the illness. We find it helpful to ask patients whether they "have" an illness or "are" their illness. Patients with severe identity problems from long experience with symptoms of eating disorders usually respond quickly to this question by stating that they *are* anorectic or *are* bulimic, not that they merely *have* AN or BN. Less chronically ill patients with better premorbid features and more normal development will usually choose the phrase "I *have* an eating disorder."

7. *Mood disorder is frequently associated with eating disorders because low mood is a commonly occurring antecedent condition whose severity is attenuated by abnormal eating behavior, partially by food restriction*

behavior, but more substantially by binge behavior. Past explanations of why there is an increased incidence of mood disorder in patients with eating disorders have varied from the one extreme, which views depression in a ED patient as being a consequence of weight loss or binge behavior (Johnson-Sabine, Wood, & Wakeling 1984), to the other extreme, of considering the eating disorder to be a *forme fruste* of depressive illness (Hudson et al., 1983.)

Neither of these polarized views explains satisfactorily the reason for the high coexistence of mood disorders and eating disorders. In families in which there are many generations of depressive illness, eating disorders have tended to occur only in the more recent generations. If eating disorders were truly a form of mood disorder, it is doubtful that their incidence would increase as generations passed, in contrast to the stereotyped expression and fairly predictable frequency of the affective illness through multiple generations.

We feel that the high incidence of mood disorders in patients with eating disorders may be explained more satisfactorily by understanding the operant conditioning effect of a behavior—dieting—now more frequently practiced in our society than in the past, on a primarily genetically based mood disorder, specifically depressive illness. A state of antecedent depression, operantly modified by bingeing may occur as well, in non-genetically predisposed persons, who are depressed for a variety of other non-genetic reasons, including learned irrational thoughts, psychodynamically understandable conflicts, and lifelong features of personality. To some extent, the behavior of dieting, but to a greater extent binge-eating, through its consequence of ameliorating the antecedent depressive state, thereby increases the frequency of the dieting or the binge behavior.

It appears that binge behavior more than self-starvation has the capacity to effectively alter, albeit temporarily and partially, the existence of depressive mood state as well as anxiety, anger, feeling stuck or bored, and other painful mood states. Being "stuck" or bored is probably not a primary mood state, but these terms are so frequently reported by patients as an antecedent to binge behavior that they need to be mentioned. These predisposing states appear to be a complex mixture of abnormal mood as well of self-defeating thinking.

8. *The antecedent conditions that are operantly affected by the eating disorders are variable in kind and often multiple in number. These antecedent conditions may be combined into a general mathematical equation that attempts to predict the probability that a specific individual will develop an ED.* Any given individual may have present in varying degree and number any of the typical predisposing antecedent conditions. This integrative explanation of how these multiple, diverse, potentially confusing, antecedent conditions all predispose to an ED because they all may be

ameliorated or stabilized by dieting behavior or by binge behavior helps unify into one conceptual whole the apparent multiplicity of these varied predisposing conditions and suggests that a single mathematically quantifiable statement can be formulated to concisely specify the combined vulnerability. There may be theoretical as well as practical value in attempting to describe an equation that would predict in a particular individual the probability that an eating disorder would develop.

The probability of a given individual (P_i) developing anorexia nervosa may be described in the form of a single general equation as being proportional to the product of the probability of the predisposing (dieting) behavior occurring in the general population for a person of that age and sex (p_g) multiplied by the risk conferred by the weighted sum total of the various individual vulnerability factors that have been empirically shown to correlate with increased probability of an eating disorder, expressed as a function of a, b, c,. . . . , z. This equation may be represented as follows, with k_1 being an empirically derivable constant:

$$P_i = k_1 \times p_g \times f\,(a, b, c, \ldots, z)$$

For example, if "a" represents the factor that a young woman (the study has not yet been done for men) belongs to a strenuous ballet school, then, all other factors being equal, p_i, that individual's risk for developing AN will be increased about 7-fold compared to a girl with identical characteristics who does not undergo ballet training. This particular risk factor is based on data collected by Garner and Garfinkel (1980) on girls attending ballet training. High school and college age male wrestlers appear to have an increased risk of developing abnormal eating patterns, but data are not yet available in quantitative forms.

ATTEMPTED REFUTATION OF HYPOTHESIS

Using Popper's idea that scientific statements are statements which are potentially falsifiable by experimentation, the above hypothesis suggesting that a behavioral mechanism underlies the development and progression of eating disorders may potentially be refuted in a variety of ways. If it is successfully refuted, an alteration in the operant paradigm would be required. The following discussion reflects some attempts at refutation that could be suggested based on data in the scientific literature, as well as on responses supporting the operant hypothesis, based on empirical and clinical data.

Low Incidence in Males

It has been suggested both for theoretical reasons and on the basis of some empirical studies that males are less frequently prone to dieting because they differ from females in some fundamental biochemical parameter, such as the obvious differences in sex hormones or to less well understood differences in neurochemical functioning, for example, lack of change in plasma prolactin after intravenous administration of L-tryptophan (Goodwin, Fairburn, & Cowen, 1987). There is no evidence to support the hypothesis that these differences in neurochemistry between the sexes have any causal significance for the differential frequency of dieting behavior between the sexes or for the increased likelihood of development of an ED in females more than in males.

There is evidence in favor of other, socially learned factors in the gender-related differential frequently of development of an ED. Studies done by Andersen and DiDomenico (submitted for publication) suggest that the decreased probability of males in our society having eating disorders is directly related to the differential frequency of social reinforcements for dieting behavior directed to males compared with females. In their study, they examined periodicals that had predominantly either male or female reader-ship, based on circulation data from publishers. The pre-study hypothesis was that there would be a 10:1 ratio in favor of female magazines regarding the number of times dieting was mentioned or the amount of space given to dieting. These periodicals were then read by "blind" raters who quantitated the number of articles, advertisements, and comments relating to weight loss and alteration of body shape in each periodical.

The study found that magazines read predominantly by women do indeed have 11 times as frequent mention of diets or methods of dieting compared to magazines read primarily by men. In contrast, and in accord with the studies by Drewnowski and Yee (1987), these magazines did make about equal mention of change in body shape. Drewnowski and Yee found that about the same percentage of males wish to change in body shape as women (85% of each category), but almost equal numbers of men wanted to gain weight or to lose weight, while virtually all the females wanted to lose weight. The high incidence of eating abnormalities found in male jockeys shows that when the appropriate behavioral reinforcements for abnormal eating in men are present, then men are just as likely to develop an eating disorder as are women (King & Mezey, 1987).

Early Secondary Amenorrhea in Seventy Percent of Anorectic Female Patients Prior to Loss of Weight

This observation has been quoted fairly frequently in the medical literature (Fries, 1977) as a sign of classical anorexia nervosa. Assuming that the datum is correct, does this finding suggest that a hormonal factor predisposes some individuals to developing anorexia nervosa? This is doubtful because another more integrative view can be advanced to explain early amenorrhea in AN patients which is more consistent with the operant behavioral hypothesis of mechanism. The critical weight necessary for menstruation is distributed in a curve (Frisch & McArthur, 1974) similar to the curvilinear distribution of height, intelligence, etc. This fact of statistical distribution leads directly to the deduction that a certain number of people require a weight in the upper part of a normal weight distribution curve to have normal menstrual functioning, just as some individuals will occupy positions one or more standard deviations above the mean in regard to intelligence and height.

Those individuals who require the higher part of the weight curve to maintain normal menses will be the most quickly affected by weight loss because they will fall below the critical body weight necessary for them to maintain regular periods soon after dieting has began. Because they are heavier than the average, in addition, they will feel fatter than their overweight peers and will be more likely to diet. In sum, early amenorrhea in some AN patients reflects their natural position on a normal distribution of critical body weight necessary for menstruation, as well as the fact that in this society their high weight predisposes them toward dieting behavior to a greater extent than lower weight peers.

Association with Mood Disorders

As noted above, an abnormal mood state may occur for a variety of reasons, including genetic predisposition, vulnerabilities of temperament, learned views of the self as being ineffective, difficulties in relationships, or problems in personal development. This abnormal mood, for whatever reason it occurs, is an antecedent condition which may be partially decreased in its severity by dieting behavior, but is even more responsive to binge behavior. Dieting behavior and binge behavior may well alter mood by different methods, but it appear that both are operantly mediated. Dieting, for example, produces weight loss that leads to favorable social recognition and praise, perhaps mediated by changes in biochemical parameters. Binge behavior, in addition to decreasing the antecedent emotional distress, provides a strong autonomic arousal, and may well provoke other subsidiary mechanisms altering mood such as the effect of nutrient intake on neurotransmitter levels, or the effect of binges on endorphin levels. As a consequence of these alterations toward decreased dysphoria resulting from abnormal eating behaviors, the frequency of the abnormal eating behavior will operantly increase.

Time and time again, in the weekly consultations at the Johns Hopkins

Eating and Weight Disorders Clinic, we meet individuals with dysphoric moods who have discovered that predictable, although temporary and partial, relief will occur as a result of their self-starvation or binge behavior. The relief of dysphoria by binge eating is short-lived, however. In addition, this behavior adds its own secondary worsening of mood because of the subsequent guilt and the feeling of loss of control, all of these leading to a "vicious circle" of increased binge behavior. Nonetheless, it appears for many people that some immediate relief of emotional distress is more urgent than any future, longer-term, adverse consequences.

Incidentally, because the binge episodes are only partially effective, and occur at somewhat random intervals, they may more strongly reinforce repeated episodes than if the consequences were absolutely regular. In this context, it may be appropriate to see the binge eating behavior as similar to a drug "fix" taken to improve an abnormal mood. While there are reasons not to apply uncritically the addiction model of drug abuse to bulimic behavior, there are also important similarities to be recognized and utilized.

The increased association between eating disorders and mood disorders is better explained, in summary, by an operant conditioning mechanism associating these two disorders rather than by redefining eating disorders as mood disorders. It is possible that the mechanism of "kindling" described by Post and Kopanda (1976) and others in explaining the increased sensitivity of animals to repeated doses of cocaine may be one additional biochemical mechanism associated with further strengthening the association between successive binge eating and subsequent relief of dysphoria.

Persisting Abnormalities of Biochemistry After Weight Is Restored

This method of analysis and reasoning utilizes a retrospective approach, and attempts to equate biochemical abnormalities existing after weight restoration with pre-existing, causal abnormalities. It is not nearly as convincing in methodology as a prospective approach which before onset of illness would identify biochemical parameters that would be causally related to a future eating disorder. One major critique of these retrospective studies that leads to further weakening of the suggestion that there are persisting causal biochemical abnormalities after weight restoration is that, first of all, these patients have often not been truly restored to their healthy pre-illness weight. Restoration to a mean population weight is actually an underweight condition for the majority of eating disorder patients. Prior to illness, we have found that female patients were generally 10 to 15% above the average weight of a normal population, while males, on the average, were 20 to 50% above normal. Restoring individuals to 100% of "ideal" or normal body weight may actually leave them below the truly healthy weight required for normal biological functioning in these individuals, some of whom are medically only "normal" at one or more standard deviations above the population mean of weight.

Secondly, these patients have not been followed long enough to see if these are enduring changes. Starvation and binge behavior produce profound alterations in biochemical functioning. It is not known how long a period of time is required for these changes to become truly normal. Studies of severely underweight patients suggest that at least 3-4 months may be necessary after simple weight restoration for an individual at this weight to have a return of normal physiological functioning of many body organs. Fichter, Pirke and Holsboer (1986), in contrast to these retrospective studies, have duplicated in a prospective manner the characteristic biochemical and hormonal abnormalities of AN in volunteers who underwent weight loss, further refuting the suggestion that there are predisposing casually related biochemical abnormalities related to the development of AN or BN. Their volunteers were normal prior to weight loss, developed typical hormonal and biochemical features of AN on weight loss, and returned to normal with weight restoration.

Animal Ablation and Stimulation Experiments

A number of alterations in brain functioning, especially ablation of the lateral or ventromedial hypothalamic nuclei, or interruption of crucial pathways coursing through or between these nuclei may lead, respectively, to decreased feeding behavior or to increased weight (McHugh et al., 1975). The essential and uniquely human characteristic of the eating disorders is not any change in the neurology or neurochemistry governing the eating behavior (which has never been shown to be present), but the specific psychopathology that promotes this behavioral change, namely, a morbid fear of fatness and a correlated pursuit of thinness.

In the medical literature, one occasionally find scientific papers which bear titles such as: "Hypothalamic Tumor Presenting as AN" (Heron & Johnston, 1976). These papers will, on careful inspection, usually reveal that no one had ever elicited the morbid fear of fatness as being present in these patients. To diagnose an eating disorder by a simple change in eating behavior and/or weight without finding an associated psychopathology leads to erroneous diagnosis. On the other hand, clear identification of a morbid fear of fatness has never led, in our experience with large numbers of patients, to any diagnostic errors in attributing the weight loss to an eating disorder. Stricker and Andersen (1980) have examined animal models for eating disorders and have concluded that no animal model can be satisfactory for AN because AN requires the presence of a particular psychopathology related to norms that occur only in human society.

High Incidence of Eating Disorders in Twins

Monozygotic twins share genetic endowment and frequently are exposed to similar environmental influences. It is not surprising that there would be a high concordance (about 50%) in the occurrence of eating disorders in MZ twins (Holland et al., 1984). Sharing the same genetic predisposition and very similar environmental influences would be expected to produce in twins very similar antecedent conditions which would be ameliorated or stabilized by alteration in the frequency of either food restriction behavior or binge behavior. The difference in incidence of AN between monozygotic twins and dizygotic twins (9/16 vs. 1/14) strongly suggests some genetic contribution to the condition, probably through the endowment of similar predisposing antecedent conditions. The nonconcordant twin for an ED, we have found, usually is larger at birth, spared a neurological injury or illness where one only has suffered, or has been otherwise more favored by circumstances, including a more extraverted personality. The genetic endowment may be expressed only in response to interaction with environmental factors.

IMPLICATIONS FOR UNDERSTANDING AND TREATMENT OF THE EATING DISORDERS RESULTING FROM THE OPERANT HYPOTHESIS

1. *The abnormal eating behavior, whether it is self-starvation or binge-purge activity, needs to be promptly interrupted and a normal eating behavior substituted early in treatment without waiting for prior development of "insight."* The older practice of first gaining insight into the cause of the disorder through extensive psychotherapy, assuming that insight would lead to change in the eating behavior, has not been demonstrated to be effective. Comprehensive inpatient treatment programs (Andersen, 1985) and outpatient programs (Fairburn, 1985; Mitchell et al., 1985) all begin treatment with early interruption of the abnormal eating behavior. Since the abnormal behavior often has a "life of its own" once it has been present for any significant length of time, direct efforts at altering the behavior come prior to or along with efforts at insight.

2. The prospective studies by Fichter, Pirke, and Holsboer (1986) as well as the operant hypothesis all suggest that *extensive, detailed studies searching for a preceding biochemical or neurophysiological abnormality as the*

cause of AN or BN have a low probability of success. There is often a great-disconcordance of degree of effort and methodological sophistication between the biochemical research and the psychopathological component in studies of the eating disorders. The biochemical efforts and methods are an order of magnitude more energetic and more refined that the psychological methods because these biochemical research methods are highly developed using reductionistic techniques. The psychological aspects of these studies often are rudimentary.

3. *The antecedent variables operantly modified by the abnormal eating behavior need to be identified specifically in each patient and each predisposing factor treated according to appropriate methods.* These antecedent variables are often multiple, and each variable (such as mood) may itself have several causes. For example, if a young person is engaged in ballet training, comes from an upper middle class family emphasizing slimness, has a perfectionistic personality, is surrounded by more extroverted siblings, and has a family history of mood and alcohol disorders, then each of these multiple antecedent variables additionally predisposes the individual to an eating disorder and each requires separate understanding and treatment.

4. *All primary motivated behavioral disorders*—that is, disorders of behavior that are not clearly due to some preceding causally determining abnormality of brain or body chemistry—*became disorders by being gradually shaped and generalized through practice and repetition from initial normal, volun- tary behaviors.* This implies that change can take place in the direction of improvement and normality just it did as toward disorder and abnormality. In addition to clearly implying a potential for bidirectional change, it also means that change toward normality takes time, repetitive practice, reinforcement of the normal behavior, and treatment of the predisposing antecedents.

5. *While treatment must begin by changing the abnormal eating behavior, strictly behavioral approaches are never in themselves completely adequate for comprehensive treatment of the eating disorder.* Medications may play an important and necessary role even if that role is adjunctive, for example, by treatment of a predisposing antecedent condition of low mood with antidepressants. Similarly, if the antecedent variable is a dynamically understandable condition, such as a phobic avoidance of normal development, then neither behavioral methods nor pharmacological methods are adequate, but a dynamic psychotherapy is essential. Andersen (1987) recently compared and contrasted the strengths of the behavioral method, the cognitive method, and the psychodynamic method in a comprehensive treatment program of eating disorders.

6. As noted previously, *the addiction model of treatment has strengths and weaknesses but cannot be entirely and uncritically applied to the treatment of eating disorders.* Bulimic behavior has more in common with addictive drug abuse then self-starvation. In the general sense that these are both maladaptive behaviors which generalize to treat a variety of painful mood states, there are factors in common between EDs and drug or alcohol dependence. A binge in many ways resembles a drug "fix." One of the implications of the addiction model, however, is that abstinence from the problem substance, for example, alcohol, remains a cornerstone of treatment. Abstention from food is not possible.

The approach of Overeaters Anonymous tends to divide the world into "safe" and "dangerous" foods. Some addiction models teach that certain foods are intrinsically dangerous, such as concentrated sweets, chocolate, etc. These teachings are not based on empirical research. Individuals with eating disorders need to come to terms with eating a variety of foods and with maintaining a healthy body weight. Abstinence is not possible, nor is abstention from certain "dangerous" foods necessarily helpful. An approach toward treatment which prescribes foods in a balanced, moderate way that includes occasionally, where socially appropriate, foods with some of the calories in the form of concentrated sweets and fats, appears to us to be a sounder approach for most people then the abstinence model.

7. *Eating disorders are not simply affective disorders in disguise.* They are separate disorders of behavior, whose probability of onset may, however, be closely related to the presence of an affective disorder. Books such as *New Hope for Binge Eaters* (Pope & Hudson, 1984) overstate the case for antidepressant treatment of bulimia. Each individual should be assessed for the presence or absence of a mood disorder. When in doubt about an individual case, assessment of his family history of mood disorder can help lead to an appropriate choice of treatment. Strober and Katz (1988) noted that mood disorder in patients with AN was associated with families having a 3.5 fold increase in mood disorders.

8. *Staging of each patient's illness will be helpful in planning treatment and giving some indication of prognosis.* An individual who has features of both Stage 3A (autonomous abnormal behavior which is completely out of control) and Stage 3B (a sense of personal identity which requires the continuance of the illness) will probably need a longer time for treatment, will need a variety of methods of treatment, and will have a less good prognosis then a patient with early Stage 2 bulimia nervosa, for example. Staging always involves some arbitrary boundary setting between the different stages, but in other areas of medicine, such as heart disease, cancer, etc., staging has proven to be useful in both treatment and prognosis.

9. *Anorexia nervosa and bulimia nervosa represent, respectively, the polar extremes of overcontrol and undercontrol. Most behavioral disorders include subgroups of excessive control and lack of control.* Research by Edwin, Andersen, and Rosell (1988) noted that anorectic patients of the restricting subgroup tended to do well on follow-up when they showed some impulsivity on MMPI. This impulsivity moderated the excessive overcontrol of food intake they usually demonstrated. Those with bulimic subtype of AN, on the other hand, who tend in their illness behavior toward being out of control, did better on follow-up when they showed more tendency toward increased control on MMPI. An overall guideline to treatment would be to encourage the growth of and practice of balance and moderation, two qualities that are not characteristic of the lives of the most patients with eating disorders, in place of the excessive or deficient control that characterizes AN and BN.

10. *Issues of identity and values are always involved in the treatment of the eating disorders.* A reductionist approach to understanding the origin and mechanism of these disorders or a narrow approach to treatment involving entirely behavioral or pharmacological methods is seldom by itself adequate because neither deals with issues of identity and values. The search for thinness takes place only in human beings who value thinness. The specific reasons for valuing thinness will vary from culture to culture, but valuing thinness is essential to the development of the generic state of anorexia nervosa with its twin motifs of the phobic fear of fatness and the pursuit of thinness. Search for thinness almost always is the first step in development of bulimia nervosa. Russell's early use of the term bulimia *nervosa* (1979) instead of bulimia alone, as used by DSM-III, recognized the intrinsic links between these disorders.

Psychiatry passed through the stage of being an arbiter of social values and an architect of social change from the mid 1960s to the late 1970s. It now has, at least in some academic centers, entered an almost opposite value-free phase, with a predominant emphasis on scientific psychiatry, claiming it has no role in matters of value. Respect for and clarification of the patient's individual values does not require the imposition of the therapist's values on the patient. These issues, however, do need to be addressed as part of a comprehensive treatment program.

While the pursuit of thinness may be termed "an overvalued idea" and perceptual distortion may be considered simply a kind of "dysmorphophobia," the complex approach-avoidance patterns of AN and BN patients do not always fall within the neat conceptual boundaries of these logical nosological phrases. The concept that search for thinness is an overvalued idea suggests that this quest is not strictly a delusion, nor is it, on the other hand, simply a commonly held cultural norm. Diagnostically it is somewhere in between—remaining a belief that does not seem to be appropriate but one that is not fixed and false. In fact, the pursuit of thinness has overlapping aspects of overvalued ideas, cultural norms, obsessionality, and at times seemingly fixed beliefs. The psychopathology of a patient with an eating disorder is more pleomorphic within a given individual and especially throughout the individual's course of an eating disorder than some of the psychiatric literature would suggest. Admixed with all the formal psychopathology is the problem of excessively *valuing* thinness, a condition that is uniquely human.

In addition to involving issues of value, identity struggles are a central feature in any patient who has had an eating disorder for any length of time. Not only must an individual value thinness to begin the path to anorexia nervosa or bulimic behavior, but a preexisting confusion in one's sense of identity is also usually involved. When an individual has a firm, confident, socially appropriate identity, then an eating disorder seldom is found to be present or even possible. Dissatisfaction with self as being fat, overweight, or of undesirable shape is almost a requisite for development of AN or BN. It is usually during the time of identity formation and role definition that eating disorders begin. This may occur during the chronological time of adolescence or later in life when a state of psychological adolescence persists. When AN or BN begins later on, it does so because adolescent issues have been revived or have never been resolved despite the biological aging of the patient. A lack of a secure, confident, and appropriate identity is a major predisposing factor for development of an eating disorder.

Individuals who have an "external locus of control" seem to be especially vulnerable to developing EDs. These are individuals who take on the characteristics of the society around them and respond to the wishes of those around them, not having an established sense of who they are on the inside. Resolution of the eating disorder, in addition to its many complex aspects of behavior and pharmacology, often is aided greatly by the development of a sense of identity. Relief of the symptoms of AN or BN by themselves without development of a more age-appropriate healthy identity leaves a kind of psychological "vaccum" in which other abnormalities of behavior may appear.

11. Another implication resulting from the operant hypothesis would be that *AN and BN are simply two of many possible forms of generic eating disorders*—defined as acquired abnormal patterns of eating that are voluntarily initiated, often reflecting exaggerations of psychosocial norms, and which may lead to drastic but stable alterations in weight as well as in eating behaviors. There is nothing completely specific about anorexia nervosa in regard to either its psychopathology or its pathophysiology. The same abnormal behavioral eating pattern that characterizes AN may spring from other

systems of belief that value thinness beside the ideal of slimness now prevalent in Western culture. Any abnormality of eating behavior which grows out of an interaction between voluntary food restriction and a variety of antecedent conditions that leads to operantly mediated changes in the frequency of the abnormal eating may be seen as a generic form of eating disorder.

The specific psychopathological motif leading to fear of fatness and pursuit of slimness need not be narrowly defined, but may derive from a variety of culturally sanctioned beliefs and norms. For example, if plumpness is believed to be a sign of spiritual laxness in a particular society, then this belief will almost certainly lead to dieting as a means of attaining holiness in predisposed individuals. The condition of generic AN may develop in such an individual once the behavior of dieting is no longer under personal control, and causes significant social, psychological, and biological consequences. The following are some examples of normal adaptive dieting behavior vs. examples of generic forms of AN or generic fear of thinness and pursuit of fatness.

Slimming to get a job (normal weight-losing behavior.) A man voluntarily decreases body weight in order to secure a position as a television announcer because he has heard that the camera will "put weight on" him. This condition does not constitute a disorder if the weight loss is not severe enough to cause serious alteration of biological, psychological, or social functioning and if the behavior does not escape from personal control. If the behavior is under individual control and used to advance the individual's life, then this slimming behavior may be seen simply as a "situational" or "adaptive" eating behavior. The differentiation in this case as to whether this adaptive slimming behavior is voluntary or a behavioral disorder can be made on the basis of whether it remains under personal control or has serious adverse consequences. If this individual, for example, were to decrease his weight down to 75% of his predieting weight, becoming emaciated and unable to eat normally, then the condition would be classical AN. Models who slim for vocational reasons generally fall into either the adaptive (voluntary weight loss) or the clinical AN categories according to the presence or absence of a morbid fear of fatness and a determined pursuit of thinness.

Holy anorexia (generic AN). The provocative book, *Holy Anorexia* (Bell, 1985) examines the lives and behavior of fasting Italian female saints during the medieval period, and suggests that this state is analogous to modern AN. Initially it seemed to us that the author was describing a condition quite different from modern AN. But as these accounts were examined closely, it became apparent that these saintly women developed the same morbid fear of fatness as modern women with AN have, although the desire for thinness and fear of fatness were prompted by a different kind of belief occurring within their own society, different in content from those norms that motivate most contemporary slimming.

The Italian saints felt guilty if they ate normal amounts of food, and believed that slimming produced control over unholy forces within the body and also promoted the growth of sanctity. For some of these women, the anorectic state allowed them to develop a sense of personal and social power, as well as a sense of personal identity and effectiveness which they did not possess while at normal weight. There now appears to be no reason why these women should not be considered to have had a generic form of AN, responding to a different socially sanctioned motive for weight loss—the quest for holiness—but producing an identical end state. The German term for AN *(pubertätsmagersucht*—pubertal search for thinness) would appear to be well suited to these individuals instead of the term anorexia nervosa.

Sumi wrestlers (adaptive or out of control weight increase). The concept that the operant consequences of eating behavior on antecedent states can alter the frequency of future eating behavior can just as logically be applied to gaining weight as to losing weight. Sumi wrestlers may have significant medical consequences from their increased weight. Despite an intellectual awareness of this possibility, there is a consistent behavioral change in them toward seeking increased weight because of understandable, positive vocational consequences of heaviness. Increased weight in these individuals leads to increased self-esteem, increased feelings of effectiveness, and to the experience of being literally more in control of their wrestling situation. Depending on whether the eating behavior remains under personal control or not, this form of initially adaptive overeating may remain voluntary or become a behavioral disorder. Because the medical consequences of severe weight loss may be present long before the adverse consequences of weight gain, it may be that most forms of operantly based weight gain are not as easily recognized as disorders of weight loss. We see this not infrequently in clinic patients with fear of thinness and pursuit of fatness.

In summary, many cultures predispose vulnerable individuals to drastic alterations in eating and weight that may lead to stable syndromes of abnormal eating and consequent alternations in weight that escape from personal control. The specific culturally sanctioned reason for weight loss or weight gain varies from culture to culture, and these norms and beliefs may predispose to weight gain just as well as to weight loss. In some third world nations, for example, increasing social class leads to increased weight, rather than to lower weight as occurs in Western society.

12. A final implication of this hypothesis for the eating disorders concerns the use of language. *The words used in English for severe self-induced*

starvation (anorexia nervosa) and for binge eating associated with morbid fear of fatness (bulimia nervosa) are linguistically imprecise terms, somewhat misleading in their implied concepts of origin, and potentially misleading for treatment strategies. The term anorexia nervosa means loss of appetite of nervous origin. The German term for AN, "pubertal search for thinness" (*pubertätsmagersucht*), together with the British phrase "weight phobia" better capture in complementary language the two essential psychological motifs characteristic of these eating disorders. An English term that would combine phobic fear of fatness and the operantly understandable pursuit of thinness would be very helpful, but is not presently available.

Some additional information further confuses the situation by suggesting the term AN may sometimes be accurate. In studies done at Johns Hopkins Hospital by three different methods, it appears that patients with clinical anorexia nervosa may indeed have some degree of medical anorexia purely on the basis of their weight loss, but usually only when the weight loss is severe. The change in appetite associated with weight change is probably curvilinear in nature, with an initial increase in appetite being present as weight is first decreased, and then as weight is severely lowered, a true decrease in appetite occurs. Misleading terminology may be of clinical importance to the treatment of patients with eating disorders. Some individuals with AN continue to be treated with medications that stimulate appetite based on the belief that the term anorexia nervosa means true medical loss of appetite. This approach is, of course, seldom helpful.

BRIEF APPLICATION OF THE OPERANT HYPOTHESIS TO OTHER DISORDERS OF MOTIVATED BEHAVIORS

Disorders of Sexual Behavior

Normal sexual functioning involves an interaction between arousal states (orgasmic or preorgasmic) and a variety of antecedent conditions. Sexual behavior may be decreased in frequency when there are beliefs that sexual behavior is unacceptable or where there is lack of availability of sexual partners. Sexual behaviors may be increased where there is more partner availability, where there are beliefs that sanction sexual behavior, and especially where sexual behavior has an operant effect on a variety of antecedent conditions. As with eating behavior and drinking behavior, sexual behavior is a widely practiced normal voluntary behavior. When sexual behavior stabilizes or ameliorates an uncomfortable antecedent condition and/or brings a sense of pleasure, effectiveness, or control, then there occurs as a consequence an increase in the frequency of the sexual behavior, modified more or less in different individuals according to internal beliefs of conscience or external sociocultural norms as well as individual differences in "drive."

As with eating disorders and alcoholism, the net frequency of the behavior, in this case sexual, may be understood as the integral outcome of those competing or collaborating antecedent factors which increase and decrease the frequency. Sexually deviant behavior such as self-exposure, pedophilia, etc., are initially voluntary behaviors, either impulsive or planned in nature. Impulsivity, incidentally, does not mean involuntary. The probability that the particular sexual behavior, whether "normal" or "deviant" in nature, will be increased or decreased, depends on the operant effect of the behavior on the multiple antecedent conditions which may be as diverse as the internal hormonal milieu, the demands of or the absence of conscience, the competing demands of other motivated behaviors, and the availability of sexual outlets. In the clinical condition where an individual has a personality disorder characterized by lack of social bonding, emotional coldness, and callousness, combined with a sense of pleasure or a decrease in anxiety resulting from deviant sexual behavior, then there is a large probability that the deviant behavior will be increased in frequency by an operant mechanism.

As with the eating disorders, sexual disorders may exist in the twin, polar extremes of inhibited or overcontrolled sexual behavior, as well as excessive, unmodulated sexual behavior. The goal-seeking phase of sexual behavior is more clearly under operant voluntary control than the stereotyped orgasmic response. The most common reasons currently for patients seeking consultation regarding sexual performance have to do with inhibited sexual desire, anorgasmia, or expressions of sexual life, whereas excessive, inappropriate sexuality less often leads to voluntary consultation.

Abuse of Alcohol

Much of the discussion concerning the nature of alcoholism leads to a state of falsely dichotomized opinions, alternating between the idea that alcoholism is a disease and the belief that alcoholism is a voluntary moral choice. Recently, in settling an issue of medical reimbursement for alcoholism, the courts have ruled in the direction of alcoholism being a voluntary choice. Alcoholism has aspects of the disease process as well as aspects of being a moral issue, but neither of these views is completely satisfactory. Alcoholism is, in fact, first and foremost an operantly conditioned behavior. As in the scenario of a man getting into a canoe going over Niagara Falls, alcohol consumption is initially a voluntary event, but in about 5% of the population drinking soon escapes from personal control. While the first drink by an individual with subsequent alcoholism is almost always voluntary, future drinks may not be. The frequency of subsequent alcohol consumption may be instrumentally conditioned as the result of an operant behavioral mechanism.

A requirement for considering alcoholism to be a behavioral disorder, as noted previously, is that it begin with a normal behavior. Clinicians usually do not see disorders of behavior when the behavior in question is rare in that society. There is a higher likelihood of having a disorder of a particular behavior when the behavior in question is a widely practiced one in a given society, as is alcohol consumption. Alcohol is used to some extent by almost half of our society.

Alcohol abuse also passes through a series of stages much like AN or BN, an observation that has been captured in humorous art work from a century or more ago. The initial stage of what later becomes abnormal drinking behavior usually occurs in a normal manner by social drinking. The future frequency of drinking alcohol will be determined by its operant consequences on a variety of antecedents. For example, decreased frequency of drinking alcohol occurs when the alcohol use leads to a toxic reaction such as flushing and systemic discomfort or when its use produces a condition such as migraine in a predisposed individual. Individuals in some Asian countries, for example, appear to be less tolerant of alcohol intake than Caucasians.

Alcohol taking behavior may be increased in frequency, in contrast, when it gives an individual an increased sense of self-confidence, when a depressed or anxious mood is improved, when one is praised for drinking, and when there are relatively few uncomfortable physical effects after the alcohol ingestion. Alcoholism progresses by steps to the next stage of generalization, at which time drinking behavior now responds to a wide variety of environmental, social, and emotional triggers.

Finally, alcohol ingestion increases, in some people, to the point of being completely out of personal control and having serious medical, psychological, and social consequences. Alcoholism may be considered an abnormality of motivated behavior whose progression through stages is governed by an operant behavioral mechanism. Chronic abnormal drinking behavior is governed by the general operant hypothesis and fulfills the general conditions for all disorders of motivated behaviors.

Just as with eating disorders, supplemental mechanisms may later come into play in alcoholism. These other mechanisms have often been the exclusive focus of research on alcoholism out of all proportion to their role in the onset of illness. In medical schools, the secondary biochemical and pathological consequences of alcohol abuse are usually taught with much greater intensity than the behavioral regulation of alcoholism, largely because of the reductionistic emphasis in medical research that can relatively easily examine the effects of alcohol on the brain or the liver.

The secondary consequences of alcohol abuse and dependence do not in themselves help us to understand the growing dependence on alcohol by a particular individual, which is much more understandable as a disorder of drinking behavior modifying antecedent conditions, including prevention of withdrawal effects. As with the eating disorders, there may be multiple and variable antecedent conditions that are affected by drinking behavior. These antecedent conditions may differ considerably in number and kind in different individuals. While excess alcohol intake is abnormal, there is no clinical state associated with too little alcohol intake since this is not an inborn motivated behavior.

OTHER APPLICATIONS

Application of the operant hypothesis to other disorders of behavior, such as "compulsive" gambling, "impulsive" spending, etc., may or may not be warranted. In their general form, these disorders do follow the operant hypothesis of beginning as normal behaviors in our society. They escape from personal control in a progressive, stage-like manner. Their treatment involves change in the behavior, as well as identification and treatment of the associated antecedents stabilized by the behavior. As with alcohol abuse, these are syndromes of excess, but not of deficiency. The issues of symptom choice are complex, and not yet resolved, concerning why general vulnerabilities should lead to one specific abnormality of behavior rather then another. These abnormal behaviors, like the motivated behaviors, can be studied in an empirical manner, but do need an overarching conceptualization guiding the testable hypotheses.

SUMMARY

The operant hypothesis suggests that the fundamental mechanism underlying anorexia nervosa and bulimia nervosa is the operant (voluntary, instrumental, Type II) behavioral conditioning described by Skinner. Common to all abnormalities of motivated behavior are the following: they begin with voluntary normal behaviors that progress in stages in predisposed individuals to become disorders when they meet conditions of not being under personal control and/or causing substantial adverse medical, social, and psychological consequences. The process of transition from behavior to disorder ischaracterized, additionally, by stimulus generalization. Eventually, these disorders become essentially autonomous and confer a sense of existential identity on the individual.

While a behavioral mechanism may be fundamental to the development and progression of disorders of motivated behavior, behavioral treatments are rarely adequate for comprehensive treatment. These behavioral disorders often stabilize a wide variety of antecedent conditions deriving from various sources, including mood, self-esteem, developmental conflicts, family dynamics, and traumatic experiences. While our methods of biochemical and neurophysiological research are well developed, they are usually not directly applicable to determining origin and mechanism of behavioral disorders, which appear to involve a separate level of integration not analyzable by references to these methods of analysis.

Anorexia nervosa and bulimia nervosa do not fall neatly into other nosological categories, such as affective disorder, although they may be related closely to them in development. The operant hypothesis suggests that individual treatment is best accomplished by identification of a variety of antecedent states contributing to the development of the eating disorder in that individual and treating each of them according to established methods. Interruption of abnormal behavior constitutes an early part of treatment and cannot be deferred until insight has been achieved.

The operant hypothesis appears to unite in one explanatory mechanism empirical findings from a variety of studies, and is not currently refuted by available data. A mathematical expression of the probability that an individual will develop an eating disorder may be useful in quantitative analysis of individual risk.

REFERENCES

Andersen, A. E. (1985). *Practical Comprehensive Treatment of Anorexia Nervosa and Bulimia.* Baltimore: Johns Hopkins University Press.

Andersen, A. E. (1987). Contrast and comparison of behavioral, cognitive-behavioral, and comprehensive treatment methods for anorexia nervosa and bulimia nervosa. *Behavior Modification, 11*(4), 522–543.

Andersen, A. E. (1988). Anorexia nervosa and bulimia nervosa in males. In D.M. Garner, & P.E. Garfinkel (Eds.), *Diagnostic Issues in Anorexia Nervosa and Bulimia Nervosa.* New York: Brunner/Mazel.

Andersen, A. E. & DiDomencio, L. (Submitted for publication). Sex differences in anorexia nervosa and bulimia nervosa: Role of differential sociocultural reinforcement in magazine articles.

Bachrach, A. J. (1975). Learning theory. In A. M. Freedman, H. I. Kaplan, and B. J. Sadock (Eds.), *Comprehensive Textbook of Psychiatry/II* (pp. 285–296). Baltimore: The Williams and Wilkens Co.

Bell, R. W. (1985). *Holy Anorexia*. Chicago: University of Chicago Press.

Deutsch, H. (1981). Anorexia nervosa. *Bulletin of the Menninger Clinic, 45*(6), 502–511.

Drewnowski, A. & Yee, D. K. (1987). Men and body image: Are males satisfied with their body weight? *Psychosomatic Medicine, 49,* 626–634.

Edwin, D., Andersen, A. E., & Rosell, F. (1988). Outcome prediction by MMPI in subtypes of anorexia nervosa. *Psychosomatics, 29,* 273–282.

Fairburn, C. G. (1985). Cognitive-behavioral treatment for bulimia. In D. M. Garner and P. E. Garfinkel (Eds.), *Handbook of Psychotherapy for Anorexia and Bulimia* (pp. 160–192). New York: The Guilford Press.

Fichter, M. M., Pirke, K. M., & Holsboer, F. (1986). Weight loss causes neuroendocrine disturbances: Experimental study in healthy starving subjects. *Psychiatry Research, 17,* 61–72.

Fries, H. (1977). Studies on secondary amenorrhea, anorectic behavior, and body-image perception: Importance for the early recognition of anorexia nervosa. In R. A. Vigersky (Ed.), *Anorexia Nervosa* (pp. 163–176). New York: Raven Press.

Frisch, R. E. & McArthur, J. W. (1974). Menstrual cycles: Fatness as a determinant of minimum weight for height necessary for their maintenance or onset. *Science, 185,* 949–951.

Garfinkel, P. E., Moldofsky, H., & Garner, D. M. (1980). The heterogeneity of anorexia nervosa. *Archives of General Psychiatry, 37,* 1036–1040.

Garner, D. M. & Garfinkel, P. E. (1980). Socio-cultural factors in the development of anorexia nervosa. *Psychological Medicine, 10,* 647–656.

Gold, P. W., Gwirtsman, H., Avgerinos, P. C., Nieman, L. K., Gallucci, W. T., Kaye, W., Jimerson, D., Ebert, M., Rittmaster, R., Loriaux, L., & Ghrousos, G. P. (1986). Abnormal hypothalamic-pituitary adrenal function in anorexia nervosa. *New England Journal of Medicine, 314*(14), 1335–1342.

Goodsitt, A. (1985). Self psychology and the treatment of anorexia nervosa. In D. M. Garner & P. E. Garfinkel (Eds.), *Handbook, of Psychotherapy for Anorexia Nervosa and Bulimia* (pp. 55–82). New York: Guilford Press.

Goodwin, G. M., Fairburn, C. G., & Cowen, P. J. (1987). Dieting changes serotonergic function in women, not men: Implications for the aetiology of anorexia nervosa? *Psychological Medicine, 17,* 839–842.

Heron, G. B. & Johnston, D. A. (1976). Hypothalamic tumor presenting as anorexia nervosa. *American Journal of Psychiatry, 133*(5), 580–582.

Holland, A. J., Hall, A., Murray, R., Russell, G. F. M., & Crisp A. (1984). Anorexia nervosa: A study of 34 twin pairs and one set of triplets. *British Journal of Psychiatry, 145,* 414–419.

Hudson, J. I., Pope, H. G., Jonas, J. M., & Yurgelun-Todd, D. (1983). Phenomenologic relationship of eating disorders to major affective disorder. *Psychiatry Research, 9,* 345–354.

Johnson-Sabine, E. C., Wood, K. H., & Wakeling, A. (1984). Mood changes in bulimia nervosa. *British Journal of Psychiatry, 145,* 512–516.

King, M. B. & Mezey, G. (1987). Eating behaviour of male racing jockeys. *Psychological Medicine, 17,* 249–253.

Kuhn, T. S. (1962). *The Structure of Scientific Revolutions.* Chicago: The University of Chicago Press.

Leibowitz, S. F. (1983). Hypothalamic catecholamine systems controlling eating behavior: A potential model for anorexia nervosa. In P. L. Darby, P. E. Garfinkel, D.M. Garner, & D. V. Coscina (Eds.), *Anorexia Nervosa: Recent Developments in Research* (pp. 221–229). New York: Alan R. Liss, Inc.

McHugh, P. R., Gibbs, J., Falasco, J. D., Moran, T., & Smith, G. P. (1975). Inhibitions on feeding examined in rhesus monkeys with hypothalamic disconnexions. *Brain, 98*(3), 441–454.

Mitchell, J. E., Hatsukami, D., Goff, G., Pyle, R. L., Eckert, E. D., & Davis, L. E., (1985). Intensive outpatient group treatment for bulimia. In D. M. Garner & P. E. Garfinkel (Eds.), *Handbook of Psychotherapy for Anorexia Nervosa and Bulimia* (pp. 240–253). New York: The Guilford Press.

Morton, R. (1694). *Phthisiologica: Or a Treatise of Consumptions.* London: Smith & Walford.

Nylander, I. (1971). The feeling of being fat and dieting in a school population. *Acta Socio-Medica Scandinavica, 1,* 17–26.

Orbach S. (1985). Accepting the symptom: A feminist psychoanalytic treatment of anorexia nervosa. In D. M. Garner and P. E. Garfinkel (Eds.), *Handbook of Psychotherapy for Anorexia Nervosa and Bulimia* (pp. 83–104). New York: Guilford Press.

Piran, N., Lerner, P., Garfinkel, P. E., Kennedy, S. H. Brouilette, C. (1988). Personality disorder in anorexic patients. *International Journal of Eating Disorders, 7*(3) 589-599.

Pope, H. G., Jr., & Hudson, J. I. (1984). *New Hope for Binge Eaters.* New York: Harper & Row, Publishers.

Popper, K. R. (1959). *The Logic of Scientific Discovery.* New York: Basic Books.

Post, R. M. Kopanda, R. T. (1976). Cocaine, kindling and psychosis. *American Journal of Psychiatry, 133*(6), 627–634.

Root, M. P. P., Fallon P., & Friedrich, W. N. (1986). *Bulimia. A Systems Approach to Treatment.* New York: W. W. Norton & Company

Rosman, B. L., Minuchin, S., Baker, L., & Liebman, R. (1977). A family approach to anorexia nervosa: Study, treatment, and outcome. In R. A. Vigersky (Ed)., *Anorexia Nervosa (pp. 341–348).* New York: Raven Press.

Russell, G. (1979). Bulimia nervosa: An ominous variant of anorexia nervosa. *Psychological Medicine, 9,* 429–448.

Simpson, S. G., DePaulo, J. R., & Andersen, A. E. (1988). Bipolar II Affective Disorder and eating disorders. Presented at *Society of Biological Psychiatry,* 43rd Annual Meeting, Montreal, Canada, May 4–8.

Skinner, B. F. (1953). *Science and Human Behavior.* New York: MacMillan.

Sours, J. A. (1980). *Starving to Death in a Sea of Objects.* New York: Jason Aronson, Inc.

Stricker, E. M., & Andersen, A. E. (1980). The lateral hypothalamic syndrome of anorexia nervosa. *Life Sciences 26*(23), 1927–1934.

Strober, M. & Katz, J. L. (1988). Depression in the eating disorders: A review and analysis of descriptive, family, and biological findings. In D. M. Garner & P. E. Garfinkel, (Eds.), *Diagnostic Issues in Anorexia Nervosa and Bulimia Nervosa* (pp. 80–111). New York: Brunner/Mazel.

Szrynski, V. (1973). Anorexia nervosa and psychotherapy. *American Journal of Psychotherapy, 26*(4), 492–505.

Woodall, C. & Andersen, A. E. (Submitted for publication). Anorexia nervosa and bulimia nervosa as professional identities.

Subject Index

Name Index